Gambling
and War

Gambling and War

Risk, Reward, and Chance in International Conflict

Justin Conrad

NAVAL INSTITUTE PRESS
Annapolis, Maryland

This book was brought to publication with the generous assistance of Marguerite and Jerry Lenfest.

Naval Institute Press
291 Wood Road
Annapolis, MD 21402

Library of Congress Cataloging-in-Publication Data is available.
ISBN: 978-1-68247-219-4 (hardcover)
ISBN: 978-1-68247-220-0 (eBook)

♾ Print editions meet the requirements of ANSI/NISO z39.48-1992 (Permanence of Paper).
Printed in the United States of America.

25 24 23 22 21 20 19 18 17   9 8 7 6 5 4 3 2 1
First printing

For Alanna,
who took the biggest gamble on me.

Contents

Illustrations

Acknowledgments

I want to thank the staff and editorial team at the U.S. Naval Institute Press for their enthusiasm about what is, admittedly, an unsual concept for a book. From the beginning of the process, they have been encouraging and helpful in preparing the manuscript for publication. In particular, I would like to thank my editor, Laura Davulis, for her valuable insight and guidance and for her support at every step of the process. As a scholar and a practitioner I have long valued the books and resources that the Press makes available. I am honored to now make my own contributions to this prestigious organization's catalog.

I also want to thank the University of North Carolina at Charlotte, the College of Liberal Arts and Sciences, and my department, the Deparment of Political Science and Public Administration. They provided me with much needed time off to complete the manuscript, as well as financial resources that greatly expedited the process. Without this generous support, the book likely would have remained unfinished. I am grateful to work at an institution that trusts, values, and supports the scholarly pursuits of their faculty.

Finally, I want to thank my advisor and friend, Mark Souva. Much of my thinking about international conflict and cooperation has been shaped by Mark's expert instruction and mentoring. He taught me how to think rigorously about the subjects that interest me most, and he taught me to value different methodological perspectives. I sincerely appreciate his guidance and support throughout my career.

Gambling
and War

Introduction

On August 1, 1914, as the German military mobilized all its strength in preparation for what would be the most destructive conflict in world history to that point, German chancellor Theobald von Bethmann-Hollweg addressed the country's legislators. After securing their unanimous approval for the conflict, he said, "If the iron dice must roll, then God help us."[1] The chancellor's implication was clear: Germany had done everything in its power to prevent a war, including trying to restrain its ally, the Austro-Hungarian empire. But after failing to reach a negotiated settlement regarding the question of Serbian independence, war had become inevitable. Many of the key participants in World War I, including German military chief of staff Helmuth von Moltke, would later echo this popular view that war had become unavoidable.[2] But Bethmann-Hollweg's famous quote implied something else as well. By "rolling the iron dice," he had suggested that the outcome on the battlefield would be determined by chance alone. In the absence of a diplomatic solution, the military solution to Europe's problems would resemble a random process. No state seemed to hold a clear advantage, so it was left to chance (or perhaps fate or divine will) to select the winners and losers. It is somewhat disturbing to know that a leading architect of World War I compared the war to a game—and a random one at that! But much of the analysis of the war since that time has also

1

depicted it as beyond the control of those involved, with the outcome resembling a coin toss or a roll of the dice.[3] This characterization has become so widespread that the war itself is sometimes referred to as "the War of the Iron Dice."

The characterization of war as an uncontrollable, unpredictable event, however, is not limited to depictions of World War I. In 2013, an article in *Foreign Policy* examined whether North Korean leader Kim Jong Un was likely to initiate a war against South Korea and whether he would use nuclear weapons in the event of such a war. The article pointedly asked if Kim would be willing to "roll the iron dice."[4] The implication was again clear: if North Korea decided to launch a war against its southern neighbor, all diplomacy and bargaining would come to an end, and the outcome would be decided by chance—again, not a comforting thought.

Juxtaposed with the common analogy of war as a coin toss or roll of the dice is the popular image of international relations as a game of chess. For centuries, military leaders and heads of state have fancied themselves as playing a real-life version of the game. This depiction suggests that relations between states and even war itself, far from being random, can be deliberately managed and controlled. Achieving one's goals in international relations is a matter of anticipating the moves of one's adversaries, developing effective countermeasures, and implementing carefully prepared strategies to secure victory.[5] Unlike a dice game, the only thing outside of a chess player's control is the actions of the opponent. But more sophisticated and experienced players should be able to predict their opponents' decisions and respond accordingly. Theoretically, there is no role for chance or randomness in the game of chess. Victory is a matter of skill and strategy. War is often depicted in just such a way: once diplomacy and bargaining between states have failed, the victorious party is the one that can outthink and outmaneuver its enemy on the battlefield. Not coincidentally, the classic image of war as an oversized chess game often invokes the nineteenth-century-style "setpiece" battles between large armies. Contemporary scholars have frequently portrayed the American Civil War, for instance, as a "sort of chess game—neat, orderly, quiet, and rational."[6] Napoleon

Bonaparte's skill in battle has also been compared to that of a chess player, as he focused primarily on identifying the weaknesses of his opponents' armies and then directed all of his efforts and capabilities to attacking those weaknesses.[7] Napoleon's shocking success during the early years of the Napoleonic Wars is often attributed to strategic superiority and his ability to see the conflict in the same way a player sees the pieces on a chess board. Such comparisons were fueled by the man himself, who was an avid chess player and frequently compared his command of the *Grande Armée* to the game. Ironically (or perhaps tellingly), however, Napoleon was a poor chess player![8] And his disastrous attempt to invade Russia in 1812 suggested that winning wars might be more complicated than just outthinking or outmaneuvering one's opponents. Distilling international conflict down to purely strategic or random considerations, then, misses some of the most crucial information about why wars begin, how they are fought, and how they end. And this is perhaps why Bethmann-Hollweg and Napoleon are now considered two of history's biggest losers.

STRATEGY, CHANCE, AND HUMAN ERROR

In reality, the business of negotiating with adversaries, fighting wars, and ending wars is far more complicated than a quiet game of chess, during which each player can see all the pieces on the board and knows the possible paths that can be taken. Even a casual observer of history can see that the business of war is more chaotic and unpredictable. And yet international bargaining and international conflict is not a dice game in which human beings have no control over the outcome. Human beings make deliberate decisions that lead states to war, and they make decisions in the midst of war that have dramatic consequences. To suggest that European leaders in 1914 had no control over the subsequent course of events is incorrect and irresponsible. An honest assessment of international bargaining and conflict over the centuries reveals that there are always elements of both types of games. War and diplomacy involve a wholly strategic element that, like the game of chess, requires the anticipation of opponents' actions and the development of effective counteractions. But war also involves significant elements of chance and human error that influence the outcomes we see at the bargaining table as well as on the field of battle. Stripping war down to a single element understates the complexity—and danger—of the subject. A comprehensive analysis of why wars occur and how they are fought must take into account a variety of factors, including strategy, pure chance, and human error.

Perhaps no game in human history better captures these elements than the game of poker. Carl von Clausewitz remarked that "war most closely resembles a game of cards."[9] While noting throughout his work *On War* that there is an important probabilistic element to warfare, he also devoted significant attention to its strategic component. All games of chance can offer lessons and analogies for conflict situations, but poker might offer the most useful and obvious comparisons. Unlike chess or a simple dice game, poker involves *both* strategy and pure chance. Poker players must confront two distinct opponents: the intimidating, sunglass-wearing, cigar-chomping opponent who sits across the table, and the opponent known as probability (in other words, the random distribution of cards in the deck). It is not enough to anticipate the actions of other players and try to outsmart them. A successful player must also have an understanding of, and a healthy appreciation for, the role of randomness. By the same token, "a knowledge of mathematical probabilities will not make a good poker player, but a total disregard for them will make a bad one."[10] In addition to lacking an element of chance, chess is a game of "perfect information," as players can see all of the pieces on the board and know the range of possible moves that their adversary can make. Poker, like international negotiations and war, is a game of "imperfect information," where players cannot see their adversary's capabilities. Each player holds a set of cards visible only to them (known as pocket cards), significantly complicating their opponent's job. And the ability to win at poker is complicated further by the random distribution of cards. As one author observes, "In chess, there is only one right move. In poker, there is a probability distribution of right moves."[11]

The relationship and the tension between strategy and chance in the game of poker have been studied and debated for centuries, even in courts of law. In 2012, a federal judge in Brooklyn, New York, overturned the indictment of a man in Staten Island who illegally ran poker games out of his house. The judge argued that poker is a game of skill rather than chance and therefore could not be regulated under federal law.[12] The ongoing debate over certain types of online betting, such as fantasy football, also centers on whether such games are games of skill or games of chance. Most would agree, however, that the most popular forms of poker involve significant elements of both strategy and luck. A player may have a keen understanding of their adversary and may effectively anticipate their actions. But the sophistication of their strategy may be completely undone if the player ends up with an unlucky draw of the cards (or if their opponent ends up with a particularly lucky draw). Conversely, short of drawing a royal flush (an unbeatable hand), lucky draws are often undone by poor strategy and implementation.

Poker offers another aspect that helps us understand the real-life choices that international political and military leaders face. In addition to anticipating an opponent's behavior, players must also consider the possibility that their opponent might not conform to expected patterns of behavior. Human beings regularly make errors in judgment and thus wind up choosing options that do not provide them with the greatest expected benefit. In other words, sometimes we just play stupidly. Not only do poker players confront this reality with respect to their opponent (which makes prediction of the opponent's behavior particularly challenging), but they must also deal with their own susceptibility to biases and cognitive errors. Because success often hinges on such psychological considerations, a common axiom in poker is to "play the player, not the cards." This is also why poker remains one of the most popular games in human history—"playing the player" naturally results in aggressive play, bluffing, and other types of behavior that heighten the entertainment value for players and spectators.

The game of poker, like the much higher-stakes game of international conflict, requires a deep understanding of strategy, probability, and psychology. The main purpose of this book is to illustrate how all three of these factors influence why wars start, how they are fought, and why they end. Poker offers the most readily accessible analogy, but we will also glean important insights from other games of chance. By focusing on these central elements of international conflict and presenting them in what is hopefully an entertaining way, the goal is to offer a holistic appreciation for the challenges inherent in conflict situations. This book argues that the role of chance and cognitive error, in particular, has been underappreciated in studies of diplomacy and war. Most studies have also failed to recognize the combined influence of strategy, cognition, and chance on the outcomes we have observed. While it is foolish to think that we can always predict and manage conflict, it is equally foolish to think that we can learn nothing by studying the conflicts of the past.

Studies of diplomacy and war should ultimately strive to identify the most important causal patterns—those that span regions and time. But they should also respect the roles of randomness and cognition—in other words, the simple fact that sometimes it is the "luck of the draw" or human error that best explains warfare. Because of these additional challenges, war may ultimately be "an equation that is unsolvable and unpredictable."[13] By focusing on common themes in the outbreak and prosecution of international conflict, we may also be able to learn something that helps us to understand and manage future conflicts before they occur. As Bruce Bueno de Mesquita argues, "The instant of initiation, the specific event triggering the eruption of violence, may be a surprise or even an accident, but it occurs in a context of prior planning and preparation that can leave no doubt that the inauguration of a conflict serious enough to become a war has been carefully calculated."[14] The truth lies somewhere between the extremes. Driven by strategic considerations, human psychology, and pure randomness, international conflict resembles the largest and most devastating poker game ever played. And it's a game that no one wants to lose.

The focus of this book is on all of these elements and how they ultimately influence the choices that states, organizations, and leaders make. Many of the concepts and ideas discussed here are not new. In the twentieth century, mathematicians John von Neumann and Oskar Morgenstern developed a formal way of examining and predicting choices that takes into account both strategy and probability.[15] Known as game theory, this approach was quickly applied to the natural sciences and has subsequently been employed in other fields, including economics and political science. Game theory offers a particularly important tool for fields that focus on human decisionmaking because it explains how choices are made in both competitive and cooperative situations.[16] In particular, the insights provided by game theory have been useful in understanding international conflict—why it occurs, how it unfolds, and how it ends.[17] Game theory has been used to explain everything from arms races to international trade to terrorist attacks because it focuses on how actors make competitive and cooperative choices under situations of risk.[18] At its core, this book is an exploration of international bargaining and conflict using many of the insights from the mathematical theory of games formalized by von Neumann, Morgenstern, and others. But although this book examines a number of insights formalized by game theory, it is merely an interpretation of these insights. By analogizing decisionmaking in international conflict to games of chance, the interpretation of game theory is presented in a more accessible fashion and does not presuppose any baseline of mathematical knowledge. Just about anyone can learn the simple rules of poker or blackjack and can play competently without advanced mathematical skills. In other words, the goal is to emphasize the key concepts of strategy and chance that are central to game theoretic analysis and how these influence human decisionmaking in the realm of international bargaining and conflict.

DRAW POKER

Throughout the book we consider poker situations as particularly suitable analogies to real-world situations in international conflict. Unlike many other games of chance, poker offers useful lessons because it involves a balance between strategy, chance, and psychology. Players must take all three into consideration if they hope to win the game.[19] In fact, von Neumann's ideas about game theory are said to have been largely developed from playing poker. As he played the game more, he realized that it was in many ways analogous to social situations.[20] Just as in many social situations, including international bargaining and conflict, the poker player must deal with multiple challenges simultaneously. First, the player "must be willing and able to recognize and come to terms with the conflicting desires and actions of others."[21] This is the strategic element of the game, and it involves identifying the likely course of action for the other players at the table and developing plans to counteract them. By contrast, games such as craps and solitaire have no strategic element because the player does not play against others; a basic knowledge and understanding of probabilities is enough to be victorious. Second, in poker, the player also faces "the random distribution according to the luck of the draw."[22] Simply put, the player has to confront the reality that their best laid plans mean nothing if the next draw of the cards doesn't turn out in their favor.

Poker is therefore a game of strategic decisions made under conditions of risk. Risk means that the players know the possible range of outcomes and the probabilities of those outcomes occurring. But they cannot perfectly predict the outcomes because of the role of chance. Further, imperfect information about the opponent's strategy (or lack of strategy) means they cannot perfectly anticipate the opponent's decisions. Either chance or a lack of knowledge about an opponent's decisionmaking process (or an opponent's faulty decisionmaking process) can pose a significant challenge for a player on their own. All of these issues create risk, but combined, they form the constructs of a nuanced and complicated game that requires the player to process a great deal of information to make the optimal choice in any given situation. And yes, that means poker is deceptively difficult to master.

While all versions of poker involve some level of chance and strategy, variations on the game largely differ by the relative balance of each element. Just about any variation of poker, in fact, can be grouped into one of two categories: draw or stud. In draw poker, the player "draws" additional cards after being dealt their initial hand, usually after placing a wager. In most forms of stud poker, the player must play whatever they were initially dealt. The purpose of stud poker, therefore, is to remove as much strategy as possible from the outcome and distill the game down to the element of chance. The "luck of the draw" is the key determinant of many games of stud. By contrast, draw poker is designed to maintain the element of chance while increasing the role of strategic decisionmaking. Players can improve their own hand as the game develops, but so can their opponents. Because of this dual focus in draw poker, the examples in this book come from the most popular form of the game, Texas Hold 'Em. One professional poker player sums up its attractiveness as follows: "Texas Hold 'Em is so popular because it manages to accurately hit the mark between 'enough information to devise a consistently winning strategy' and 'not enough information to do much more than guess.'"[23]

The premise of Texas Hold 'Em is fairly simple, although its execution can be quite complicated. Appendix B includes detailed rules for the game, but the basics are as follows: Each player, beginning with the player to the immediate left of the dealer, places an initial bet. These forced bets, known as blinds, are another reason Texas Hold 'Em offers a good analogy for many social situations, because it ensures that some players have already made an investment before the game is even played. Such "sunk costs" are common in many issues of international relations.[24] Each player is then dealt two face-down pocket cards. The game proceeds, alternating between betting rounds and additional turns of the card. In each betting round, players can either call (that is, match) the current bet on the table, raise the current bet, or fold (exit the game, forfeiting whatever money the player has already wagered). After the first betting round, three cards are dealt face up in the middle of the table. Players can use these cards, known as the flop, in combination with their pocket cards to build their hands. After another betting round, a fourth card is dealt face up—the turn card. A fifth card known as the river is revealed following another bet. After a final round of betting occurs, players are required to show their pocket cards for the final showdown.

HOW TO WIN AT POKER

No matter which variation of poker is played, the basic concepts and strategies, including bluffing, are common to all of them. Players become successful not by mastering the intricacies of a specific variation of the game, but "only by understanding and applying the underlying concepts of poker" as a whole.[25] Playing the game of poker successfully can be boiled down to a few essential questions to which players must know the answers and act appropriately. Professional poker player Marcel Vonk breaks down the game into the following questions:[26]

1. What cards do I have?
2. What range of cards do I think my opponent has?
3. Given question 2, what is the probability I will win after all the cards have been dealt?
4. Given question 3, will I make money in the long run?

Examining each question, we see that the first is an analysis of the strategic situation (the capabilities of each player at the beginning of the game based on the cards they have drawn), followed by an analysis of probability (what are the odds that I will outdraw my opponent). This information can be further boiled down into a single question, known as the "strict calculation maxim": Are my odds of winning the pot better than the odds I am getting from the pot?[27] In other words, the player compares their expected return on a bet (in dollars) to their chances of actually winning. If the anticipated return on a bet is higher than the odds of winning the bet, the strict calculation matrix suggests that the player should make the bet. For instance, if the return on a bet after winning would be 5:1, but the odds of actually winning are 7:1, the strict calculation matrix says the player should not place a bet. But if the odds of winning are 3:1 instead of 7:1, the pot odds are higher than the odds of winning, and it is considered a sensible bet. This is a simplified view of a complex game, but sophisticated players use very simple calculations like this to determine if betting is in their best interest. Like decisionmaking in many social situations, including international relations, the choice is reduced to an expected cost-benefit analysis. But in situations of imperfect information, such as at the poker table or the negotiating table, often the best one can do is "make a very broad guess."[28]

While the role of probability in the game of poker is straightforward, the most critical barrier to success is a lack of information. David

Sklansky's famous "Fundamental Theorem of Poker," in fact, focuses specifically on the role of incomplete information as the key to success (and failure) in poker. The theorem suggests that if a player plays their hand differently from the way they would play *if they could see their opponent's cards,* they will likely lose. Conversely, if they play their hand in the same way they would play if they could see the opponent's cards, they will win more often than not. The opponent will win and lose according to the same logic. This implies that even with a weak hand, a player might still be able to win; some of the most dramatic hands in poker history have involved players with weak hands upsetting their much more powerful opponents by playing as if they could see the opponent's cards. Not coincidentally, some of the most enduring examples of international conflict are the ones in which the weak army bests the far superior (and often overconfident) army.

ONE ADDITIONAL CHALLENGE

Simplified to these core elements, poker should be easy to master, right? Of course not! Referring to the Fundamental Theorem of Poker, Sklansky notes that "the whole theorem is obvious, which is its beauty; yet its applications are often not so obvious."[29] A player might have a sophisticated understanding of their adversary and an extensive knowledge of probability, but the successful application of the theorem is often disrupted by basic human limitations. Even with a limited number of possible outcomes, the game is often too complicated for human beings to decide the optimal course of action under all circumstances. This is particularly true when there are many players in the game, and each player must consider the strategic dynamics of playing several adversaries simultaneously. In short, even when provided with extensive information, human beings often make cognitive errors, take mental shortcuts, and choose options that are suboptimal given the circumstances.

The probability of making such errors—for instance, miscalculating one's advantage or underestimating an opponent's advantage—is even higher in international bargaining and conflict situations. In fact, although choices made in these situations are typically thought of as decisions made under conditions of risk, they are more accurately considered decisions made under conditions of *uncertainty*. Under conditions of risk, the possible outcomes and probabilities of those outcomes occurring are known to the decisionmakers. In poker, for example, given the cards in your hand and the cards showing on the table, there are limited combinations of cards that the other player could be holding, and we can even assign probabilities to those outcomes. Under conditions of uncertainty, on the other hand, the possible outcomes and probabilities of outcomes are not completely known.[30] Such conditions better capture those present in the high-stakes world of international relations; when states negotiate with one another, or fight wars against each other, they don't know all of the possible outcomes that could occur. And unlike a game of chance, it is certainly not an exact science to assign probabilities to outcomes in the real world.

Even in poker, as Sklansky observes, the task of winning is often not as simple as it appears. In addition to probability and strategic concerns, a host of "other, more subtle factors" influence outcomes, including "the pot, your position, the opponent or opponents you are facing, the way they have been playing, the amount of money they have and you have, the flow of the game."[31] Even the best players cannot hope to process all this information, and thus they become susceptible to mental errors and biases. In the latter part of this book, we explore how these cognitive mistakes ultimately influence decisions that are made, and how this complicates our ability to predict or anticipate the behavior of others.

The sheer complexity of the human world, then, creates a situation of great uncertainty for international relations. But in an effort to gain some understanding of why wars occur and how they manifest themselves, we follow the bulk of scholarly work on conflict and assume that international actors make decisions under conditions of risk. In other words, throughout this book, we assume that actors have a basic understanding of the possible outcomes and their probability of occurring. Even with this basic assumption, however, we will see that strategic challenges, human error, and probability itself can conspire to prevent peaceful outcomes.

A NOTE ABOUT THE PLAYERS

One final question must be addressed: who are the "players" in this story? Everything discussed in this book focuses on human decision-making, whether individually or in groups. Poker and other games of chance involve decisionmaking at the individual level. It is therefore relatively straightforward to study a poker game by studying the decisions that individual gamblers make. But the study of international relations has largely focused on the *aggregate* decisions made by *groups* of individuals. Sometimes, this can be a traditional group, such as a rebel organization, a political party, or other nonstate actors. But in the field of international relations, scholars usually focus on states as the unit of analysis. That is, we examine the decisions made by a state's government, and those decisions are considered to be the aggregation of individual preferences of some subset of the population within a given country. The way these individual preferences are aggregated and how final foreign policy decisions are made varies from state to state depending on the political institutions, cultures, and other factors unique to each country. But to study many problems in international relations, we treat states as *unitary actors*. Most of this book therefore focuses on states as the unitary actor of interest, but we also extend the discussion to include nonstate actors such as terrorist and rebel organizations.

Whether examining states or nonstate organizations, this focus on aggregations of individuals is an abstraction from reality that is necessary to identify some of the broader trends and processes in international conflict. In the later chapters, though, we shift our focus to the decisionmaking of individuals, particularly those who have final decisionmaking authority in matters of war and peace, such as presidents, prime ministers, and generals. These are the types of individuals, after all, that history often portrays as skillful gamblers or complete suckers. Because of this multilevel focus, the study of international relations has been compared to the layers of an onion.[32] We begin our discussion by looking at the outermost layers (states and nonstate organizations), and we focus on their strategic interactions. We eventually work our way down to individual decisionmakers to consider both strategy and cognitive limitations. But even though we discuss states, organizations, and individuals at various points, this book follows a popular approach in international relations known as the "strategic-choice" approach, which treats the strategic interaction at any level as the unit of analysis. This approach "presumes that strategic interactions at one level aggregate into interactions at other levels in an orderly manner."[33] Games of chance like poker are also examined by considering the strategic interaction of players. Ultimately, then, we consider the decisionmaking calculus of all actors—from the gambler at the poker table to the Russian government to transnational terrorist organizations—as following the same logic outlined in the pages of this book.

The term "actor" is used as a catch-all term at any level of analysis, which serves to emphasize the universality of many of the concepts described in this book.[34] One of the key goals of this book, in fact, is to illustrate how the concepts of strategic decisionmaking under conditions of risk are applicable at all levels and across all variations of human decisionmaking. One final note about nomenclature: throughout the book, I frequently use such terms as "opponent," "adversary," and "enemy." In gambling, these terms are self-explanatory. In international relations, though, they do not necessarily indicate that other states or groups or individuals are *enemies* in the colloquial sense of the word. The terms simply indicate that the actor wants something different than the main actor we are considering. If the United States and Canada disagree on a trade issue, they may be considered "opponents" or "adversaries" from a strategic perspective. Obviously, this does not necessarily mean they hate each other or that armed conflict between them is particularly likely.

OVERVIEW OF CHAPTERS

This book has two central goals. First, through the use of gambling analogies, the book introduces basic concepts and theories of international relations in a way that is intended to be accessible to a wide audience. By focusing on examples from games of chance, especially poker, the hope is that the reader will consider this an entertaining exploration of what are otherwise very serious matters. Second, the book seeks to emphasize the many challenges that decisionmakers face in international conflict situations: strategic challenges, cognitive limitations, and pure chance. International decisionmakers are at the mercy of all these challenges, and successful outcomes hinge on understanding and appreciating them. The book is loosely divided into two sections, the first of which covers strategic considerations, while the second focuses on cognitive limitations and the role of randomness.

In the first part of the book, we focus primarily on strategic interactions between states. We analyze how states make decisions and how they model the decisionmaking of their opponents. We also examine a range of strategies that states can use to get what they want. Chapter one explores why the decision to go to war is always a gamble (often in spite of assurances by governments that the outcome is nearly certain), and why states still choose this option despite the considerable amount of risk involved. Specifically, we examine the role of two strategic problems that complicate negotiations between states and frequently lead them to choose war over peace: information problems and credible commitment problems. We also examine the related strategy of bluffing, which influences the credibility of states and often has the perverse effect of raising the probability of conflict. Finally, chapter one explores how states use costly signaling to establish credibility and concludes with a brief discussion of how costly signals and bluffing behavior allow states to build crude models of their opponents' decisionmaking process in an effort to anticipate their behavior.

Chapter two examines why weak actors challenge strong actors and why they sometimes win. This chapter focuses on how power asymmetries (when one actor is vastly superior in capabilities to their opponent) influence the strategies and tactics of weaker actors. We first examine how asymmetric power relationships between states have been portrayed in the scholarly literature. We then extend the discussion to focus on civil conflicts, including terrorist campaigns—which are, by definition, asymmetric conflicts. Next, we consider why bluffing may be a particularly optimal strategy for nonstate actors in such cases and how it influences their long-term reputation. Finally, we consider randomization as a specific strategy and look at how it can bolster the credibility of a weak actor and increase the effectiveness of their bluffs.

Whereas chapters one and two focus on why wars occur, in chapter three, we consider how bargaining between states continues over time, *in the midst* of conflict and in successive bargaining scenarios. We examine how the bargaining process evolves during repeated interactions and during actual conflict, as information about players' capabilities and credibility changes over time and as actors develop reputations based on their past behavior. We first consider how reputations are actually developed and how their development is inextricably linked to an actor's credibility. We then consider some of the more interesting types of reputations that international actors can develop, such as for being unpredictable and for being unusually aggressive. Next, we examine how reputation and information about one's adversaries change on the battlefield and how these changes influence the likelihood of conflict termination. As such, we explore for the first time how the bargaining process continues and evolves during actual combat. Finally, we examine a tactical and strategic issue that influences both war onset and termination: the role of offensive and defensive advantages.

All of the discussions featured in the first part of the book assume that states and nonstate groups are rational actors. That is, in the first three chapters, we assume that "actors make purposive choices, that they survey their environment and, to the best of their ability, choose the strategy that best meets their subjectively defined goals."[35] This is a rather significant and limiting assumption that we relax in the second part of the book. In chapter four, we specifically consider the cognitive limitations that might prevent actors from choosing the best strategies (that is, prevent them from making the perfectly rational choice in every situation). We consider the implications of a theoretical approach known as prospect theory, which offers an alternative to the standard assumption of perfect economic rationality used in many studies of international relations.[36] This theoretical framework allows us to look more closely at the often puzzling decisions made by policymakers, particularly in circumstances where the stakes are high, such as in international negotiations and situations of armed conflict.

Finally, chapter five focuses on the uncomfortable reality of randomness in international relations. In all human interactions, including international bargaining and conflict, there is an ever-present element of chance that threatens even the most sophisticated and strategic-minded actors. The size and the variance of this random element, in turn, can have dramatic effects on the outcomes that we observe. Chapter five also considers whether this undermines our ability to predict with any great accuracy where conflict will occur, how it will play out, or how it will end. If so, international bargaining and conflict may more closely resemble a spin of the roulette wheel than a game of poker.

While the direct application of gambling to international conflict scenarios admittedly has its limits, we can nonetheless learn much from watching gamblers at work. As one poker expert puts it, "The battle in poker resembles real battles and wars in general."[37] It also resembles the negotiations and bargaining that occur prior to, during, and following conflicts. Ultimately, we can think of a game of chance as a laboratory experiment that reveals important information about the real world. The game of poker is one such experiment, though by no means can it explain everything about international bargaining and conflict.[38] Real-world bargaining and conflict are simply too complex to ever fully explain or predict. As a Soviet military theorist once argued, "Not even a genius has the power to foresee how a war will actually turn out."[39]

The Bet to End All Bets

*Show me a gambler and I'll show you a loser,
show me a hero and I'll show you a corpse.*
—Mario Puzo

Most of us are amateur gamblers at best. So why do we happily pay thousands of dollars to travel to Las Vegas, only to throw more money away? The central puzzle in the study of international relations involves a similar question. Specifically, why do states go to war *if war is so costly?*[1] Even modern "limited" wars take massive economic and human tolls, so why do states still choose to fight instead of reaching some mutually beneficial agreement? At some point, states deliberately make the decision to engage in armed conflict against one another. The decision to do so is a high-stakes gamble. States, like gamblers, estimate their own probabilities of victory over their opponents while simultaneously factoring in their anticipated costs. These estimates influence how they behave in negotiations and whether they choose the path of conflict over peace. And, like poker players, their success can be distilled into two important factors: the amount of information they have access to (for example, about their opponents' capabilities) and their own credibility.

Former U.S. secretary of defense Donald Rumsfeld once famously made a distinction between "known unknowns" and "unknown unknowns." The decision to go to war, in light of the costs, is a "known unknown." In the lead-up to every war, there is a large volume of unknown information, including the true capabilities of the adversary, the tactics the adversary will deploy in conflict, the willingness and resolve of citizens to support the war effort, and so forth. Yet despite this long list of unknowns (which no leader or government can ever fully know), states frequently make the decision to engage in armed combat. In other words, states knowingly accept the certainty of war costs, as well as the risk of defeat, in order to achieve their goals through warfare. Even the most casual observer of history knows that war is not only costly, but it also is a hugely risky endeavor. From the Japanese destruction of the Russian navy at Tsushima to the surprising Israeli victory in the Six-Day War, history is replete with outcomes that defy the conventional wisdom.[2]

One important clue that suggests states may not fully understand the consequences of their decisions is that, in almost every conflict, there is quite a bit of optimism prior to the outbreak of fighting.[3] Governments, leaders, and citizens are frequently upbeat about their chances of victory, as well as their relative costs of fighting. Just months after making the statement about "known unknowns," Secretary Rumsfeld gave his prognostication of a future U.S. invasion of Iraq: "Five days or five weeks or five months, but it certainly isn't going to last any longer than that."[4] While their predictions may not always be so specific, states nonetheless have a common tendency to be more optimistic about conflict than the circumstances usually warrant. This makes intuitive sense: states would not go to war if they expected to lose or to achieve only a Pyrrhic victory. Despite arguments that there is evidence of pessimism in the days prior to World War I, Geoffrey Blainey notes that this pessimism only seemed to be about the potential destructiveness of new technological advances; most of the states involved still expected a relatively short war, and they all assumed that they would be victorious and their opponents would be defeated.[5] Optimism, therefore, is a common theme in the outbreak of war.[6,7] It is also a common theme among inebriated tourists in Las Vegas.

It is pervasive optimism that links so many conflicts throughout human history, and it is this optimism that suggests that war is ultimately a gamble on a very large scale. Just as in a simple game of cards, the players are perpetually, and unrealistically, optimistic about their chances for victory. Certainly no one bets their own money during a game of cards under the assumption that they are likely to lose. They may recognize and understand the *possibility* that they will lose, but this possibility is often divorced from the actual *probability* of losing. Rarely do gamblers accurately assess the relative risks, benefits, and costs of their bets. If players assumed that there was a high probability that they would lose their money (as is the case in a casino game like Keno, where the house edge averages around 25 percent), why do they even play the game?[8] Gamblers, like states, make conscious decisions to risk a great deal on the chance that they will be better off in the future. States in particular take enormous risks when seeking better long-term arrangements vis-à-vis their adversaries. Unrealistic optimism, then, is a hallmark of both international conflict and gambling.

This chapter explores why the decision to go to war is always a gamble despite assurances from governments to the contrary, and why states still choose this option despite the staggering amount of risk involved. Specifically, we examine two problems that lead states to choose war over peace: information problems and credible commitment problems. We also examine the related issue of bluffing, which influences credibility and often has the perverse effect of raising the probability of conflict. Finally, this chapter explores how states use costly signaling to establish credibility and concludes with a brief discussion of how costly signals and bluffing behavior allow states to build preliminary models of their opponents in an effort to anticipate their behavior.

GETTING TO THE GAMBLE

Before we consider how the decision to go to war resembles a classic gamble, we must examine why states find themselves in such a position. Most states, especially in today's increasingly globalized world, are explicitly or implicity dealing with each other at all times. Through formal diplomatic relations, commerce, the movement of populations, and other interactions, states have ongoing contact with other states. And in the midst of this ongoing contact, issues necessarily arise over which states disagree. At any given time, therefore, two states have divergent preferences over some issues. Such issues may be obvious, such as a disputed piece of territory, or they may be more intangible, such as general disagreement over the status quo of the international system.[9] Thus, states are constantly negotiating or "bargaining" over issues, even though they may not be engaged in formal, direct negotiations. As Carl von Clausewitz argues, war is simply a continuation of such political bargaining "by other means."[10] The decision to go to war represents an effort to resolve divergent preferences with the ultimate goal of coercing one's opponent through the use of force.[11]

Surprisingly, though, war is used relatively rarely as a foreign policy tool.[12] Information on the frequency of interstate conflict in the international system indicates that there were only 95 conflicts considered to be full interstate wars between 1816 and 2007.[13] (The full list of wars is available in appendix A.) Considering all the possible combinations of states and their disputes over the past 2 centuries, however, the fact that there were only 95 interstate wars is a striking feature. Further, only 2 of these have occurred since the year 2000, apparently indicating that interstate war is only becoming more rare.[14] Even if we relax the definition of interstate conflict to include any militarized dispute between states, such events are still relatively rare.[15] Roughly 2,500 of these less serious incidents occurred over a period of nearly 200 years. While this may not accord with popular intuition about the frequency of interstate conflict, the data nevertheless suggest that most states resolve their issues short of armed conflict and well short of full-scale wars. So while war may indeed be "politics by other means," it is seldom employed by states. The infrequency with which it is used emphasizes the fact that interstate conflict is a far riskier proposition than any other foreign policy tool in terms of the potential for human and material losses. The riskiness of the "war option" therefore implies that an issue has escalated dramatically before the first shot has even been fired.

BETTING ON WAR

When states are unable to find amicable ways of resolving their issues, the use of force becomes an increasingly likely option. In the next section, we will examine why states fail to reach amicable solutions, but for now, we look at the structure of the resulting "bet." In such a scenario, where military force is considered to be a serious option, states must essentially place bets on the probability that they will be victorious in a given conflict with their opponent. Such an insight is by no means new in international relations, but it has benefited from more formal thinking in the past fifty years of research, most notably by Thomas Schelling, Geoffrey Blainey, and James D. Fearon.[16] This approach to understanding international conflict is frequently referred to as the bargaining approach or the bargaining theory of war. Bargaining between states resembles a classic game of chance in which players bet something of value with the hope of increasing their current level of wealth, while simultaneously facing the prospect of losing more than they gain.

The basic setup of the game is as follows. Assume for the moment that two states are bargaining over a given piece of land, which both claim is part of their own historic sovereign territory.[17] An extreme example would be the long-running dispute over ownership of the city of Jerusalem, but of course, territorial disputes across the globe have been, and still are, deeply divisive and controversial. Figures 1-1, 1-2, and 1-3 display various ways for two states to divide an imaginary piece of territory. Note that we are assuming here that every piece of the territory is equally valuable to the two parties. In the game, the states can divide the territory at any point by drawing a line from north to south, giving State A everything to the left (west) of the line, and State B everything to the right (east) of the line. Figures 1-1 and 1-2 show the ideal (preferred) divisions for each state. For State A, the ideal agreement would involve State B voluntarily recognizing the entire territory as the sovereign possession of State A. For State B, the reverse is the most preferred outcome. Obviously, neither of these is a likely scenario given a real-world disagreement over something as valuable as disputed territory.[18] An alternative option might involve the two states peacefully agreeing to divide the territory 50/50, with State A taking the western half of the territory and State B taking the eastern half (figure 1-3). While such an agreement is more likely than total voluntary capitulation by either side, in most cases it is unlikely that states would agree to such an equal settlement.

We can think of a similar process occurring if the states negotiated over *any* issue or good. For instance, the two sides might be negotiating over something more simple, like $1,000. They could then pick a "point" to divide the sum (for instance, if they divided the money at the $600 point, the division would be 60/40 in favor of State A). With such a contentious issue as territory, though, States A and B may consider the use of force as a viable option to compel their adversary to accept their ideal resolution (the all-or-nothing settlements in figures 1-1 and 1-2).[19] At this point, the two states have finally entered the part of the scenario that most resembles a betting game. If one of the states does not agree to a proposed split, or if no mutual agreement can be reached, both states have the option of choosing war as a way to compel their adversary. State A would fight with the intention of wresting the entire territory from State B, and vice versa. Few military conflicts, however, have resulted in such clear and total victory,[20] so some lesser division of the territory is likely in any given conflict between states.

In figure 1-4, we assume that the likely division of the territory in the event of State A and B fighting is exactly 50/50. The probable division of the territory, in turn, reflects the relative capabilities of each side. In other words, if the most likely outcome is an even division of the territory, the implication is that both sides are evenly matched in terms of their military capabilities. Such an assumption is most strikingly illustrated in how the Korean War played out. When the South Korean military faced the overwhelming invasion of North Korean forces between June and September of 1950, the disputed territory (the Korean Peninsula) fell almost entirely into the North's hands. South Korean and United Nations (UN) coalition forces were pushed into the most extreme southeastern corner of the peninsula, located near the port city of Pusan. In September, however, the United States spearheaded the UN effort to retake and reunify the Korean nation under a democratic regime. The arriving U.S. forces subsequently shifted the balance of military

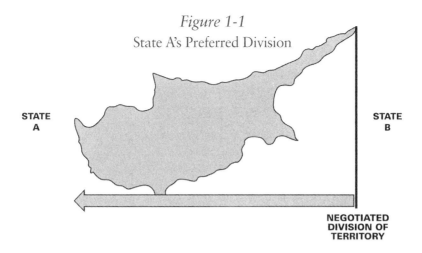

Figure 1-1
State A's Preferred Division

STATE
A

STATE
B

**NEGOTIATED
DIVISION OF
TERRITORY**

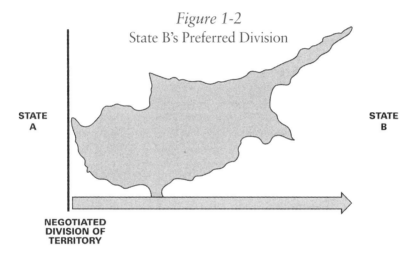

Figure 1-2
State B's Preferred Division

STATE
A

STATE
B

**NEGOTIATED
DIVISION OF
TERRITORY**

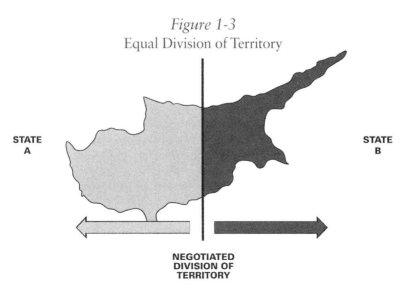

Figure 1-3
Equal Division of Territory

STATE
A

STATE
B

**NEGOTIATED
DIVISION OF
TERRITORY**

capabilities in favor of the coalition forces. By October, UN forces had recaptured nearly the entire peninsula, eventually reaching the Yalu River on the border with China. But China's entrance into the war once again shifted the balance of power (to something resembling a 50/50 split), this time undermining the UN forces' advantage, and the result was a final stalemate and armistice agreement in 1953 that divided Korea into two roughly equal territories. The final outcome, therefore, was a direct function of the distribution of capabilities between the two sides. A key assumption of the bargaining approach, then, is the correlation between a state's relative capabilities and the likely outcome of any armed conflict.

Of course, when states decide to go to war, they don't simply calculate their expected probability of victory and then deploy their forces. That would be like placing a bet while only thinking about the amount of money you could win and ignoring the potential losses. States must also factor in the likely costs they will incur, including human and economic costs. Nazi Germany was arguably superior to the Soviet Union in terms of military capabilities when it launched Operation Barbarossa in the winter of 1941. Yet the costs of opening an eastern front eventually robbed Germany of anything resembling a victory. The eastern front, according to Christian Hartmann, "was not decided, as in the final phase of a game of chess, by a few brilliant moves."[21] The German army, which had reasonably expected victory based on its numerical

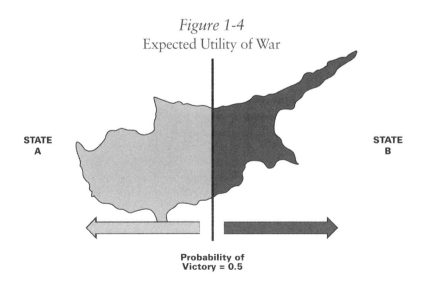

Figure 1-4
Expected Utility of War

STATE
A

STATE
B

Probability of
Victory = 0.5

and tactical superiority at the outset of the war, had not anticipated the eventual costs of securing such a victory. It was "only when almost all of Germany, right down to the Command Headquarter, had been occupied and Hitler himself had finally abdicated responsibility by means of suicide (30 April 1945), only then did the shooting stop."[22] While the probability of victory is directly related to the military capabilities of either side, the expected costs and the willingness to endure them (that is, resolve) also influence the outcome.

Factoring in both the probability of victory and the expected costs of war, figure 1-5 shows the expected utility for State A in fighting over the territory. If State A's chance of victory is 50 percent and its expected costs are equivalent to 30 percent of the territory, its total expected utility for fighting State B is 20 percent of the territory—that is, $(0.5 \times 1) + (0.5 \times 0) - 0.3 = 0.2$.[23] In other words, even if it wins half the territory, it will have paid such significant costs that its "net profit" is really only equivalent to 20 percent of the territory. Assuming that State B expects the same probability of victory and costs of warfare, it too has a total expected utility of 20 percent of the territory if it chooses to go to war (figure 1-5). The arrows now represent the amount of territory for each state that would be *worse than what they could expect if they went to war*. In other words, if State A or State B is offered less than 20 percent of the territory, that is less than they could expect to get from war. War, in this case, would actually be the preferred option!

Figure 1-5
Expected Utility Including Costs of War

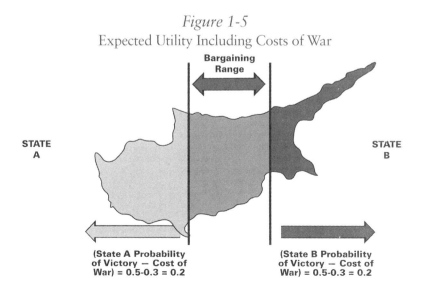

Bargaining Range

STATE A

STATE B

(State A Probability of Victory — Cost of War) = 0.5-0.3 = 0.2

(State B Probability of Victory — Cost of War) = 0.5-0.3 = 0.2

While a state might be willing to go to war for even 20 percent of a highly coveted piece of land, combining the expected utilities of State A and State B offers another important observation. It should be evident by looking at figure 1-5 that a wide range of possible divisions of the territory would offer each side more than it would expect to get if it went to war. For instance, if State A were offered 30 percent and State B took 70 percent, even State A would be better off than the scenario where the two states fight each other. This, in fact, is the key insight of the bargaining approach to understanding international conflict: there always exists some range of negotiated settlements that both sides should prefer to war.[24] Why war still occurs despite such a perpetual bargaining range will be discussed in depth, but the bottom line is that states often miscalculate important information about their relative capabilities and resolve, causing them to fundamentally misunderstand this bargaining range.[25]

THE PREFLOP

In poker, every game starts with a struggle over the antes. Indeed, if there were no antes, there would be no reason to play the game at all (unless you just like drawing cards and seeing which combinations you can make).[26] The ante, a required bet before any cards are dealt, resembles the issue at stake in negotiations between states. Once two states have dismissed the possibility of an amicable settlement over the antes and have instead begun to place wagers on their probability of victory, their interaction starts to resemble the "preflop" bet in a game of Texas Hold 'Em. The cards have been dealt to each player and the antes have been established, but none of the cards on the board have flopped (that is, none of the community cards on the table have been revealed). Each player therefore has some private information about the two pocket cards they are dealt, but beyond this information, they know little to nothing about their probability of victory. Once a player makes a preflop bet, other players must then make a decision of whether to call or raise that bet or to stay out of the hand altogether by folding. Like states, players must make an initial assessment of relative capabilities, based primarily on the likely strength of their own pocket cards and the anticipated strength of their opponents' cards.

In many ways, the preflop bet is the riskiest bet that a player will make because it is made with the least amount of information. Yet players are often most optimistic at this point in the game, much like the football fan who notes that his team is "undefcated" before the season even begins. In the introduction, we discussed how decisionmaking in poker is influenced by a number of factors, which include information about one's opponent, how the opponent has played in the past, and the "flow of the game."[27] But if this is the first hand played against an opponent, a player has no information whatsoever on these factors. Even without information about the opponent's cards or how the opponent is likely to play under a given set of circumstances, players must still estimate their opponent's likely strength relative to their own. Further, a player must assess the opponent's *resolve,* or their willingness to endure costs in order to secure a victory. This resolve is frequently judged by looking at the size of the opponent's initial bet and by whether they raise or reraise that initial bet prior to the flop.

A common goal of the preflop betting round, as with many bets, is to convince other players to fold rather than to call or raise the initial stakes. In general, the larger the size of the ante (that is, the larger the issue at stake), the more likely players are to try and "steal" the ante.[28] "Stealing the ante" describes large preflop betting that is intended to convince other players to fold before the flop occurs. When players drop out of the game, it serves two important functions. First, it may preclude the necessity to risk larger portions of one's holdings in later betting rounds. And second, it is cognitively easier to make effective decisions when there are fewer players in the game.[29] Ultimately, "even when your hand is the best hand, you generally prefer your opponent to fold rather than call when the pot is large."[30] In some cases, however, the purpose of raising the prefold pot is to encourage others to put *more* into the pot (something we discuss more below). But in international relations, the pot is usually sufficiently large (that is, the stakes are sufficiently high) that the most desirable scenario is for your opponent to voluntarily cede the issue to you.

By analyzing preflop betting strategies, it should be evident that the most important function of military force is not its actual use but the strategic *threat* of its use to coerce other states into capitulation. The opponent's threat of military force serves the same purpose. Further, it is not necessary to have the stronger hand, but rather to project the *image* that you have the stronger hand. The ability to create this false image is much easier to accomplish in the earliest betting rounds like the preflop. Successfully bluffing one's position becomes much more difficult as additional betting rounds are completed and additional cards are drawn. Bargaining is inherent in all interstate relations (because we assume some basic level of preference divergence), and so the threat of the use of force is also a constant, even if it is not explicit. This means that in bargaining over most issues, neither side wants to bet on the outcome of war because the issue is not salient enough (that is, the pot is too small) or because they concede that they have a weak hand that they would rather not risk in a head-on fight against their opponent.

INFORMATION AND CREDIBLE COMMITMENT PROBLEMS

Ultimately, in games of chance and war, there is only one particular outcome that will occur given each side's capabilities and willingness to endure costs. If both sides knew this outcome at the outset of their interactions, at least one side would not risk their "skin in the game" in the first place. So how do two states reach the point at which both are confident of their own capabilities and resolve relative to their opponent's and are willing to risk significant capital to prove it? Why do states resort to war even when they know it is a costly endeavor and the outcome is far from certain given the limited information that they have? A prime culprit is overconfidence or optimism by one or more sides. Bueno de Mesquita analyzes the outbreak of conflict and determines that positive expected utilities (that is, when states expect a net benefit by going to war) are key predictors of conflict.[31] Examining the evidence from nearly 250 conflicts, he notes that "almost all initiators of international conflicts appear to have had a reasonable expectation of success in their conflict."[32] And Blainey argues that "recurring optimism is a vital prelude to war. Anything which increases that optimism is a cause of war. Anything which dampens that optimism is a cause of peace."[33] Many of the states that have optimistically initiated wars, of course, have suffered some of the more infamous and ignoble defeats. This phenomenon has been referred to colloquially as the "Victory Disease."[34] International relations theorists have concluded that there are two important sources of the Victory Disease: incomplete information about an opponent's capabilities and resolve and the inability of actors to credibly commit to future courses of action.[35]

We will discuss the implications of both incomplete information and credible commitment problems in turn. But first, it is important to note that divergent preferences alone do not lead to armed conflict. We have already discussed that a basic assumption in understanding why war occurs is that two states have divergent preferences, which represents a necessary but insufficient cause of war. The idea that states go to war because they simply can't agree implies that there are some issues that are too hotly contested to be solved peacefully. As the bargaining model indicates, however, there should always be some bargaining range or negotiated settlement that states prefer to fighting—assuming that they had complete information about the outcome of such fighting. Further, states always have divergent preferences; Canada and the United States had some divisive and acrimonious trade disputes during the 1930s yet never resorted to full-scale war. By contrast, France and Prussia fought one of the bloodiest wars of the nineteenth century over seemingly inconsequential issues of succession in the Spanish monarchy.[36] Divergent preferences alone, therefore, do not explain why states fail to reach negotiated settlements and instead gamble on the outcome of war.

We cannot discard the importance of preferences altogether, however.[37] Preferences play an important part in determining the likely onset of conflict, because resolve (or willingness to endure costs) is tied to the salience or importance that each side places on the issue. If a matter is particularly important to one side, its resolve will be higher, it will be willing to endure greater costs, and the acceptable bargaining range for both states will be smaller, raising the probability of conflict. Existential issues are particularly likely to generate the highest level of resolve, a point we return to in chapter four.

Although preferences are important in determining the size of the bargaining range, the ultimate decision to initiate the gamble of war arises because states miscalculate either the importance of these preferences to their adversary (that is, their adversary's resolve) or their basic military capabilities. States are always trying to estimate the capabilities and resolve of their adversaries, and many of their efforts are aimed at actively gathering such data. States will never have perfect information about their opponents, but even if they did, they might still go to war.[38] Even accurately knowing its opponent's capabilities and resolve, for instance, one state may still decide to fight because it is concerned that its opponent could grow even stronger and might subsequently judge a fight today to be less costly than a fight in the future.[39]

INCOMPLETE INFORMATION ABOUT CAPABILITIES AND RESOLVE

Incomplete information about an opponent's military capabilities can lead to conflict, usually because states overestimate their own capabilities relative to those of the opponent. If a state miscalculates its opponent's military capabilities, it directly miscalculates its own probability of victory. One important area of research in international relations has focused on the role of power distributions—how powerful states are relative to each other—in the outbreak of armed conflict. A range of literature has concluded that the distribution of power (both military and nonmilitary) between states significantly influences the probability of conflict because it affects each state's perception of its probability of victory.[40]

Arguments about power, then, are often arguments about problems of incomplete information. Some have argued that in cases of a wide power disparity between two sides (something we return to in detail in the next chapter), the stronger state should be more likely to initiate a conflict.[41] The implication is that since the power disparity is so wide, one state will feel overwhelmingly confident and should therefore be willing to accept fewer negotiated settlements, raising the probability of war. The logic here is similar to that outlined by David Lake regarding war hawks. According to Lake, individuals who advocate aggressive foreign policy positions do not cause war on their own. Instead, some peaceful negotiated settlements may be eliminated from consideration if these individuals play a significant role in the development of foreign policy. With fewer acceptable settlements, the overall probability of conflict will be higher.[42] Similarly, a state that is highly optimistic about its chances of victory is likely to disregard a certain range of negotiated settlements. Such a state will likely demand more and concede less in negotiations, raising the probability of conflict.

Clausewitz and Blainey suggest quite the opposite, however—that clear power distributions *deter* conflict because one state "knows its place," and it therefore will be easier for the stronger state to extract concessions without a fight.[43] The implication is that with a wider power disparity, while the states may not perfectly know each other's capabilities, the weaker party is unlikely to expect it could beat its adversary simply through its military capabilities.[44] By contrast, when states approach parity, a weaker state is far more likely to overestimate its probability of victory because the capabilities of each side are more comparable. The bulk of empirical research has supported this argument: rather than reducing conflict, power parity is often associated with increased levels of conflict between states.[45] Relatively equal capabilities, therefore, produce higher probabilities of conflict between states because weaker actors are more likely to *perceive* that they have sufficient capabilities to overtake their rivals in a military contest, whether or not that is factually the case.

The logic is similar to a poker game in which a player judges the chances of winning to be 50/50 before the last betting round. The player must make a decision and either fold or call the opponent's final bet. The optimal decision in this case is to call, even though there is a 50/50 chance that the player is making a mistake. If the player folds when they actually have the winning hand, they lose the whole pot. If the player calls, however, there is a 50 percent chance they will win the whole pot and a 50 percent chance they will lose the pot plus a presumably marginal bet (but they would lose the whole pot anyway if they folded).[46] In this way, parity in the player's hands leads to more aggressive betting behavior and a greater willingness to accept risk.

States also lack information about the resolve of their adversaries. They may underestimate just how far their opponents are willing to go to win a conflict. When placing bets in a game of poker, even if one player has a fairly accurate idea of the cards their opponent is holding, the other player may raise and reraise the bet until the player with the stronger hand is no longer willing to incur those costs. In this way, high resolve can actually compensate for deficiencies in capabilities, and some of the weakest actors in history have pulled off the most stunning victories precisely because their resolve was higher than that of their much stronger opponents. Either through assessments of military capabilities or resolve, therefore, the lead-up to war is frequently marked by miscalculations and overconfidence on the part of at least one state.[47]

Unlike military capabilities, however, resolve is an intangible concept. And while a state is likely to miscalculate both the capabilities and resolve of their opponent, they may also lack accurate information about *their own* resolve. Both capabilities and resolve may change during the course of a war (a matter we will discuss in chapter three), but one's own resolve is difficult to predict in the long run. And if it is difficult to predict one's own resolve, then it is nearly impossible to estimate the resolve of another state. It is reasonable to believe that Adolf Hitler would have never ordered the Nazi invasion of the Soviet Union if he had accurately understood that nation's true resolve. Despite overwhelming military superiority, evidenced by a far lower body count than that of the Soviets, Nazi Germany's invasion was turned back at Stalingrad. Hitler could not have predicted that the Soviet Union would lose millions of soldiers and civilians—as many as 26 million people by some estimates—and would continue to fight.[48] So while Hitler may have made a fairly accurate assessment of the two states' relative capabilities in 1941, he could predict neither the costs that Nazi Germany would incur nor the price that the Soviets were willing to pay.

U.S. calculations during the escalation of the Vietnam War also underestimated the opponent's resolve. While the military capabilities of the U.S. forces were clearly superior to those of the North Vietnamese (NVA), U.S. policymakers dramatically underestimated the willingness of the NVA as well as the civilian population to endure the costs of war. In fact, following early stalemates in the conflict and a realization that it was not going to win through traditional strategies (that is, by seizing and controlling territory), the United States shifted to a strategy of "body counts." More NVA casualties were seen as a sign of progress, implying that a breaking point existed at which the enemy would theoretically suffer so many casualties that it would sue for peace. That breaking point may have existed, but U.S. military leaders and policymakers severely underestimated where it lay for the North Vietnamese.

BLUFFING: TAKING ADVANTAGE OF INCOMPLETE INFORMATION

Incomplete information about capabilities and resolve, in turn, generates incentives for actors to "bluff" or misrepresent this information. In poker, bluffing is "a bet or a raise with a hand which you do not think is the best hand."[49] In war, bluffing is lying, and all states are liars. States go to great lengths to either hide or misrepresent their capabilities in an effort to maintain the tactical advantage of surprise or to strategically deter others at a lower cost. Iraq under Saddam Hussein actively deceived the world about its weapons capabilities with the intention of deterring other states, including the United States and Israel but primarily its regional rival, Iran.[50] And Nikita Khrushchev successfully misrepresented the extent of Soviet nuclear capabilities throughout the 1950s. This misrepresentation, in fact, was central to his strategic negotiations with the John F. Kennedy administration during the Cuban Missile Crisis.[51]

In high-stakes international relations, as in high-stakes poker, these misrepresentations or bluffs can mean the difference between winning and losing. In the lead-up to the finals of the 2003 World Series of Poker, two of the world's most skilled and most famous players squared off against each other. Humberto Brenes seemed to be in an advantageous position, with an ace of spades and a ten of clubs, great pocket cards regardless of whatever later appeared on the table. On the other hand, Scotty Nguyen, winner of the 1998 World Series of Poker, held a three of spades and an eight of clubs. In an effort to force Brenes to fold, Nguyen made perhaps one of the biggest bluffs of all time. He bet $100,000, challenging Brenes to call his bluff. The announcers covering the game on television, aware of the cards that Nguyen held, remarked that he had just bet $100,000 on "cards the Salvation Army would reject." Given the distribution of their cards, Brenes' estimated chance of winning the hand was nearly 70 percent, among the best chances possible in a game of No Limit. As if the bet itself was not enough of a bluff, though, Nguyen continued to play the part of a gambler confident that he held the winning hand. As Brenes considered calling his bet, Nguyen taunted him by saying, "You can't call $100,000. That's too much for you." The bluff turned out to be very convincing, as Brenes folded and Nguyen revealed that he had been holding nearly worthless cards.

Bluffing is a strategy that relies not on the use of actual capabilities, but on the creation of misperceptions regarding those capabilities. If an opponent's capabilities are *perceived* to be far greater than they actually are, other actors will be less likely to challenge them, regardless of the actual power distribution. Bluffing, or misrepresentation of capabilities, can be used to *coerce* others; in poker, players may pretend to have weaker cards than they actually do so they can trick their opponents into giving up more of their money. Bluffing may also be used, as Scotty Nguyen demonstrated, to *deter* others; players may pretend that their cards are stronger than they actually are in order to encourage others to fold. Misrepresentation can therefore be used to indicate either strength (as in the case of the Soviet Union during the Cold War) or weakness (as in the case of Japan in the Russo-Japanese War).

The most common use of bluffing strategies, however, involves the projection of strength. Among those actors who bluff to indicate a greater level of strength, there are two distinct types who benefit the most from such behavior. First, there are actors like Saddam Hussein during the 1990s who recognize their relative weakness. For such actors, bluffing may be the only viable strategy to achieve their goals vis-à-vis their stronger opponents (we return to the role of bluffing as a strategy for the weak in the next chapter). The second type of actor that benefits from overselling its capabilities is one that may actually have a strong level of military power but has low resolve. In other words, the state may have the capabilities, but not the *willingness*, to fight. For such actors, bluffing can help them achieve their foreign policy goals without actually engaging in fighting, which they may have no desire to do in the first place.

Incentives to bluff in international relations, in turn, significantly affect the information environment. As we have already discussed, it is difficult to assess the true military capabilities of another state. Even absent a strategic incentive to bluff, the collection of completely accurate information on all military capabilities is cost- and time-prohibitive, if not impossible altogether. But the most important reason why states have difficulty forming an accurate picture of their adversary's military capabilities is because the adversary has an incentive to keep this information private. Governments are therefore actively and constantly engaged in the business of keeping their military capabilities (and intentions) as secret as possible. Information asymmetries are near-constants in international relations, but as Kenneth Schultz argues, "Informational asymmetries are compounded by a strategic environment that encourages concealment, deception, and bluff."[52]

Japan during the late nineteenth century is one of the best examples of a state deliberately concealing its capabilities for strategic purposes. After the restoration of the emperor in 1868, Japan embarked on an ambitious program of technological advancements in an effort to "catch up" with Western nations. Central to this progress was a complete reformation of the state's military. But this reformation was largely kept secret, and the lead-up to the Russo-Japanese War reveals why. Russia, and indeed much of the West, continued to base its assessment of Japan on its pre-1868 profile: a backward, largely feudal nation. As Japan's foreign policy goals became more ambitious and it began to assert itself in Korea and Manchuria, it necessarily came into conflict with Russia. Russia remained unconcerned, however, regarding the capabilities of the Japanese military. As Japan became increasingly belligerent, Russian officials seem to have concluded that Japan was indeed engaging in bluffing behavior.[53] Ironically, though, Japan was not bluffing greater capabilities, but by continuing to keep its military developments secret, it was nurturing the perception that it was weaker than it really was.[54] Japanese leaders thought that their advancements in East Asia benefited from uncertainty on the part of Russia: as long as there was debate about Japan's true capabilities and intentions, Russia might willingly concede. Russia, for its part, was incredulous that Japan would actually risk war against a clearly greater power, a judgment that, according to Ian Nish, was based on "misinformation, misjudgment, and wishful thinking."[55] In addition to its strategic importance, Japan's misrepresentation of its capabilities also offered a major tactical advantage that was perfectly illustrated at the naval battle of Tsushima, in which the Russian fleet was surprised and almost entirely decimated by the upstart Japanese military. Japan's deliberate campaign of misinformation and Russia's subsequent overconfidence resulted in one of the most important and devastating armed conflicts of the twentieth century. Yet it probably could have been avoided if Russia had a more accurate assessment of Japan's capabilities and willingness to endure war costs.

Japan's behavior in prewar negotiations was ultimately designed to reduce the risks of war and achieve its foreign policy goals. Likewise, the Soviet Union sought to reduce the risks of war by misrepresenting its capabilities during the first part of the Cold War. As historian John Lewis Gaddis notes, the early years of the Khrushchev regime were marked by a deliberate effort to deceive the United States into thinking it suffered from a "bomber gap" and later a "missile gap," and that it lagged behind the Soviets in the quantity of nuclear weapons it possessed.[56] Khrushchev intentionally kept up this ruse because he assumed "that even a seeming strategic superiority could be decisive."[57] The reality was far from the image that Khrushchev projected. The United States did not suffer from a gap; the reverse was in fact true.[58] The significance of such bluffing behavior played out in real time during the Cuban Missile Crisis, as President Kennedy had unprecedented access to reconnaissance photos and, for the first time, called Khrushchev's bluff. As a result, U.S.-Soviet relations entered a transition phase as the Soviet Union "lost the kind of atomic leverage [it] had been employing for . . . years, but the Americans . . . gained it."[59] Bluffing, then, can provide significant benefits, but it can also result in spectacular failures.

WHY BLUFFING IS A RISKY STRATEGY

In poker, as in international negotiations, bluffing is a dangerous strategy because it involves accepting a great deal of risk. Bluffing ironically increases the risk of war *in an effort to avoid war*. Japan risked war in an attempt to avoid it but ultimately failed to secure its desired outcomes and fought a costly conflict with Russia (which, however, suffered far greater costs). Likewise, to successfully bluff in poker, players must voluntarily place more of their own money into the pot. They must risk a significant portion of their own wealth in order to gain even more. As we have seen, this can be particularly effective in the preflop stage of the game, where players may raise significant amounts of money in an effort to "steal" the ante before anyone at the table has seen any of the community cards. But such a strategy runs the risk of escalation, and a player may be raised and reraised to the point that they cannot feasibly remain in the game. This is especially the case if the effort to steal the ante is actually a bluff.[60] Likewise, in international relations, bluffing is dangerous because it usually involves escalation of a dispute. States bluff successfully by bringing themselves and their adversaries closer to armed conflict. Something of great value must be risked to secure the possibility of greater returns.

Bluffing about nuclear weapons offers the most dramatic illustration of the dangers inherent in bluffing or misrepresenting one's true intentions and capabilities. The logic of such voluntary risk-taking is captured in the theory of mutually assured destruction (MAD), to which many of the leading policymakers and scholars of the Cold War subscribed. The theory concluded that neither the United States nor the Soviet Union would voluntarily use nuclear weapons because it would result in their own destruction if their adversary counterattacked. The logic is similar to the popular maxim among poker players that "in order to live, you must be willing to die." The phrase captures the idea that to survive in a game of poker, players must accept and even embrace the risk of defeat. The presence of nuclear weapons, although raising the risk of conflict because of the fear they engendered, were nevertheless seen as a stabilizing force. The U.S.-Soviet strategic dynamic shifted because not only had the fictitious Soviet missile advantage been exposed, but also the United States was newly confident in its second-strike capability: the ability to launch a devastating retaliatory nuclear attack on the Soviet Union even if the Soviets attacked first. Such a capability made any bluffing behavior a moot point. Ironically, even the idea of a second-strike capability may itself be a bluff (because those who maintain such an advantage may not ultimately use it, even in the face of a nuclear attack). Nuclear weapons, therefore, are the ultimate bluff in international relations. Perhaps because they are often viewed as a bluff, states do not seem to heed them, and for the most part, nuclear states seem to have no additional diplomatic leverage over nonnuclear states.[61] All of the so-called arms races, in fact, can be viewed as bluffs. Blainey, for instance, points out that most of the armaments and other war matériel developed during the late nineteenth-century arms race between Germany and other European states were never used.[62] But despite the inherent blustering in arms races, including nuclear arms races, even the implicit use of such threats may, on average, raise the probability of war.[63]

CREDIBLE COMMITMENT PROBLEMS

Information problems are a key source of conflict. But even with perfect information today, states might still go to war because they are uncertain about the future. The inability of states to credibly commit to a course of action represents the second important source of conflict. The strategic dynamics between the United States and the Soviet Union are widely thought to have changed following the revelation that the United States had not fallen behind in the nuclear arms race and was in fact leading it.[64] The new information shifted the dynamics of the Cold War so dramatically because it placed the Soviet Union at a severe disadvantage. Its credibility had been irreparably harmed; Moscow could no longer rely as heavily on its bluffing strategy to extract concessions from Washington because the United States had a diminished view of the credibility of the Soviet threat. Like the movie character who fires a gun only to reveal the chamber is empty, tables can quickly turn. The Soviet Union's rapid advancement and competition with the United States during the 1950s and early 1960s, then, largely hinged on its ability to bluff. But having established a reputation for noncredible threats, the Soviet Union could no longer benefit from employing the same strategy. Over the remainder of the 1960s, the growing convergence between the perception and the reality of the Soviet Union's capabilities likely contributed to the decision to remove Khrushchev as premier.[65]

The inability to make credible commitments is the second fundamental source of bargaining breakdowns leading to war. Like the problem of incomplete information and the related incentives to misrepresent that information, states' inability to convince other states of their capabilities or their intentions is a key predictor of conflict.[66] Some level of credibility was of course necessary for the Soviet Union to engage in the kind of bluffing behavior that occurred during the 1950s. While the United States and the Soviet Union may not have fully trusted each other, they nonetheless seemed to believe each other's threats as well as their stated capabilities. Credibility is therefore central to the ability to bluff, which is a key strategy for many states. But credibility is also crucial when making honest statements. For instance, a state may wish to *honestly* reveal its intentions and capabilities in an effort to deter or coerce another. But it cannot do so if its statements and diplomatic commitments are seen as noncredible.

If credibility is critical for achieving goals in international relations, and if it is such an important contributor to international conflict, how do states actually generate credibility? In other words, how does a state get another state to believe its threats, capabilities, and/or intentions, regardless of whether it is trying to accurately represent, or actively misrepresent, such information? Credible commitment relies on the development of a long-term reputation for such behavior, and in chapter three we will explore how states and other actors establish reputations as credible (or noncredible) through repeated interactions with one another. But for now, we continue to assume that two states are interacting for the first time. How does one state get the other to believe its statements, promises, and/or threats? How does a state convince another that it means what it says and that its threats to use military force (or its pledges to *not* use force) are genuine?

MAKING BLUFFS (AND NONBLUFFS) BELIEVABLE

Interactions within the international system are typically marked by "cheap talk." States have no reason to believe each other based on their word alone. In an anarchical system, there is no greater body that enforces "contractual" obligations and negotiated promises between states.[67] Because of this lack of central enforcement, states are unlikely to believe each other based on simple verbal declarations alone (especially if states understand that their counterparts have incentives to bluff). This is why belligerent talk from the world's tinpot dictators is often met with laughter. Even deliberate actions can sometimes be "cheap" if they do not allow observers to distinguish the type of actor based on their behavior alone. For example, James Morrow argues that even if Nazi Germany was only seeking moderate political changes in Europe in the 1930s (in other words, if Germany would have been satisfied with only annexing Austria and Czechoslovakia), its actions would look identical to what really happened: Hitler pledged that he would expand Germany's borders no farther and was content with unifying the German-speaking peoples of Central Europe.[68] In other words, Hitler's agreements with Britain and France to that effect did not allow the British and the French to distinguish a moderate Nazi Germany from an imperial, dominant Nazi Germany.

In this particular case, it benefited Hitler to stick with cheap talk, but in many cases, states wish to honestly reveal their intentions. To lend credibility to their declarations and threats, states must back up their cheap talk with *costly signals*—actions that create for the sender "some cost that [it] would be disinclined to incur or create if [it] were in fact *not* willing to carry out the threat."[69] A state must take some tangible, observable action that demonstrates it means what it says and is willing to invest significant resources or risk war to do so. For this reason, costly signals in the form of political accommodations are considered central to resolving civil wars.[70]

For insight into how a state can credibly signal such information, the concepts of raising and reraising in poker are perhaps most useful. In the earlier example, why did Nguyen choose to risk $100,000 on such a weak hand? Because such a large sum was the only way to get Brenes to consider his bluff credible! After all, who would bet so much money on a hand that is sure to end in defeat? Importantly, Nguyen could not simply "declare" to Brenes that he held the winning hand; such cheap talk would understandably be dismissed by Brenes. Brenes might have believed it based on Nguyen's reputation for being a good player, and even perhaps a conservative player, but making such a statement does not *persuade* others that the hand is a winning one. Players must *back up* their claims that they have a competitive hand with something tangible. In other words, risking greater sums, an action that is visible to the adversary (while the cards being held are not visible), tells the adversary that the player is committed enough to run the risk of great losses. Such behavior, even in a single hand of poker, has the effect of generating immediate credibility for a player who otherwise has no reputation to fall back on.

Importantly, in poker, large raises are not the only way to demonstrate credibility. A player does not have to make outrageous bets like Nguyen did in order for others to view their bets and/or bluffs as credible. The simple act of "reraising" another player—raising their bet after they have already raised (known as "three-betting" or "four-betting")—can also convince others that the player's hand is likely to be a competitive one.[71] This type of behavior in poker games is a useful way to demonstrate credibility without necessarily investing large sums of money.[72] Even a small three-bet or four-bet indicates to other players that the player is willing to continue increasing the size of the pot (and therefore willing to accept more risk) because they believe in the value of their hand. The goal of any of these tactics is to *decrease the perception of holding a weak hand*. The aim is to provoke other players into asking, "If my adversary's hand was truly weak, why would they bet so much (or so often)?"

On the other hand, a player may wish to credibly give off the impression that they have a weaker hand than they actually do. The goal here is to entice other players to risk more, increasing the size of the pot, until the time when the player reveals the winning hand.[73] The reverse of the previous logic applies here: a player would likely refrain from betting too much, or refrain from three-betting and four-betting in order to entice other players to risk more of their own money. When a player implies a lack of confidence in their own hand, they may be able to coax their adversary into risking more money, even if the adversary is also not confident in their hand. No matter whether a player wishes to bluff a weaker hand or a stronger hand, though, the common theme is that one cannot successfully do so without first generating credibility, which can only be earned through costly signals (by publicly taking greater risks).

In international relations, states can raise and reraise each other's threats to signal their own commitment to an issue. In other words, states can "escalate" an issue in an effort to achieve their desired outcome. Escalation, then, can be seen as a series of costly signals that involve ever-increasing amounts of risk.[74] Often, the only way to make a threat credible is to visibly demonstrate a willingness to incur great costs to achieve one's goals.

It is important to note that a state does not have to have lofty goals (those requiring "absolute war," according to Clausewitz) to benefit from such behavior.[75] On the contrary, a state may have relatively limited goals that it is not willing to fight over. However, it may choose to engage in escalatory behavior to gain concessions from its adversaries. In other words, it may choose to run the very real risk of war in order to avoid war and achieve its desired outcome. Eventually, though, "entire resources of nations are wagered" in an effort to coerce or deter the opponent.[76]

The specific mechanisms by which states are able to convince others to believe their threats can be broken down into two non–mutually exclusive categories: sunk costs and tying hands.[77] The concept of sunk costs is perhaps most analogous to a betting game in that it involves taking some action that is inherently costly so that the costs cannot be recovered if the state backs down from its threat. Military mobilization is the classic example of how states can sink costs; while a state may not ultimately use its military in armed combat, the deployment of troops and equipment, mobilization of reserves, and other types of actions nonetheless involve great costs, which indicate a greater willingness by the state to follow through on its threat(s). Interestingly, in a formal model involving bargaining between two states, Fearon demonstrates that states that use costly signals have reduced incentives to bluff.[78]

The second mechanism by which states can generate credibility is by "tying" their own hands. Tying hands also involves creating costs for backing down from a challenge, but unlike sunk costs, there are no costs incurred in the absence of a challenge. By stationing hundreds of thousands of troops in Europe during the Cold War, the United States was essentially tying its hands. If the Soviet Union did not make a military push into Europe, the United States would incur no additional costs.[79] But if the Soviet Union decided to attack western or central Europe, the United States could not renege on its agreement to protect Europe, as the troops stationed there literally acted as a "trip wire" that would instigate full-scale armed conflict.[80]

Tying hands is also common in domestic politics. That is, a leader can make an international threat or promise more credible by invoking some level of domestic political costs in the event of failure. Such costs, known as *audience costs*, are inherently more prevalent in democracies, where leaders are more easily replaced and punished for failures.[81] President Richard Nixon's visit to China in 1972, for instance, was a tying of hands that generated greater credibility for U.S. commitments to China thanks to the president's audience costs. Nixon, a staunch anticommunist, would likely have suffered much greater audience costs (particularly with his core supporters) by cooperation with China than would his political opponents. If such a move resulted in failure, Nixon would undoubtedly be held accountable, which in turn made his administration's pledges to cooperate with China that much more credible.[82]

Since governments know that such threats or promises made by democratic leaders are inherently more credible, the calculus of potential challengers is affected. States may be more likely to challenge non-democracies, which are assumed to engage in bluffing behavior more frequently than their democratic counterparts.[83] Greater credibility generated through domestic political institutions, therefore, can ensure that threats made by democratic governments are believable.

STRATEGY AND MODELING THE OPPONENT

A single round of play with an opponent (the kind of interaction addressed in this chapter) limits strategic decisionmaking because actors have no information about their opponent's previous actions. With more information about an opponent's past behavior, states have more evidence from which to judge their credibility. States may then be able to form rudimentary models of their opponent's likely behavior under given circumstances, which can in turn help them in their own strategic decisionmaking. This is the true essence of strategy: making decisions while simultaneously anticipating the adversary's decisions (who is engaging in the same process). A situation is therefore strategic "if an actor's ability to further its ends depends on the actions others take."[84]

Strategic Interaction: The Prisoner's Dilemma

The classic example of strategic interaction in international relations is captured in the Prisoner's Dilemma game, which demonstrates how actors make decisions when there is no enforcement of their behavior and when they have limited information about their opponent. The now-famous premise of the game is that two people have committed a crime and are subsequently captured and isolated from each other by the police. The police then tell each of the prisoners separately that they are going to spend a long time in jail *unless they rat out their partner*. If they do so, they will be set free. If both prisoners decide to cooperate with each other and keep their mouths shut, they will be held for a brief time and then released. Figure 1-6 shows the setup of the game and the payoffs. In the rows, Player 1 has a choice between cooperating with their partner (C) or defecting (D). In other words, Player 1 can cooperate and say nothing to the police or defect and "snitch" on the partner. Player 2 has the same choices as Player 1. The cells in the table list the payoffs to each player for a given set of actions—the first number in parentheses is Player 1's payoff, and the second number is Player 2's payoff. Higher numbers represent higher payoffs (that is, more preferred outcomes for the player). As we can see, the greatest single payoff for either player is the scenario in which they defect and rat out their partner, while the partner cooperates and says nothing to the police (one gets a payoff of 1 while the other gets a payoff of 4). Clearly, though, the best scenario that ensures the highest payoff for *both* players simultaneously is the one where they cooperate with each other, say nothing to the police, and are released quickly (both players receive a payoff of 3).[85]

The key insight of the Prisoner's Dilemma game, and the reason it has become foundational in the study of international relations, is that the players in such a scenario tend to make "suboptimal" choices. For instance, no matter which action Player 2 chooses, the best response in either case for Player 1 is to defect. In other words, despite both players understanding that the best joint outcome for them would be to cooperate and say nothing, anticipation and fear that the other player will defect drive them *both* to defect and rat out each other (the bottom right cell). Despite understanding that the optimal choice is to cooperate, the structure of the game and the credibility (or lack thereof) of the players cause them to make unwise choices.

Like the Prisoner's Dilemma, in the international system there is no central power to enforce agreements among actors, which complicates their ability to cooperate. So why do we still see states cooperating with one another? If they are worried that others are likely to defect, why do they ultimately choose cooperation? While the Prisoner's Dilemma and other simple games have provided important insights into the study of international relations, they are nonetheless quite limited in their applicability to real-world issues.[86] In reality, states typically have more than just two strategy choices, a fact that allows for the possibility of peaceful solutions.[87] But perhaps the most important limitation of the basic Prisoner's Dilemma game is that it does not take into account the possibility of iterated play.[88]

Figure 1-6
Prisoner's Dilemma

PLAYER 2

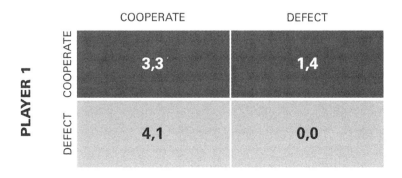

Imagine the potential reward you might reap by cheating an opponent. Now think about the implications if you had to play them again and again! Often, the best way to ensure cooperation is through iterated play. The utility of cheating others can change dramatically if you know that you will deal with them again in the future. The possibility of retaliation or reciprocity in the future is often a key means of deterring defection in the current round of play.[89] Reciprocal actions, in turn, are often selected based on the past behavior of players.

Iteration and the development of reputations over time in international bargaining are therefore key to understanding many of the decisions that states make. And it is through reputation, and the "mapping" or modeling of another state's previous behavior, that states are better able to select optimal foreign policies. Iterated play allows states to develop better models of their opponents and thus may reduce the probability of conflict. But as we have seen with bluffing and mutually assured destruction, it may also provide states with a means of manipulating outcomes in their favor (often by raising the probability of conflict).

Modeling Opponent Behavior

By studying opponents over time, states can develop expectations about what their adversary will do given a specific set of circumstances, much like players in games of chance. Assume, for example, we wanted to determine if an opponent's threats are sincere or if they are simply bluffing—in the parlance of Old West gambling rooms, whether the opponent is a "straight shooter" or a "flannel-mouthed liar." The most sophisticated and experienced poker players model their opponents over the course of several hands in an effort to predict their future behavior and select the right strategy to defeat them. A simple example of a series of hands in a game of poker illustrates how a player might glean useful information about the likelihood that their opponent is bluffing.[90] For each hand that is dealt, we assume that the adversary has only four real choices, observable to other players at the table. First, if they draw a hand that is unlikely to put them in a position to win, they can fold (denoted as *F* in the sequence below). Second, they may draw a hand that is somewhat competitive but not necessarily a winning hand, so they may make the decision to call others' bets but not to raise them (call, or C). Third, they may draw a worthless hand, but instead of folding they may decide to bluff and create the impression that they have a strong hand by raising the stakes (bluff, or B). And finally, they may draw an objectively strong hand, which would also result in the same observed outcome—they will raise the stakes. This last scenario is referred to in poker as "valuebetting" (V). Over the course of ten hands, a player observes their opponent's behavior and notes the following sequence, with each letter indicating the observed outcome of a single hand of play:

$$C \rightarrow V \rightarrow B \rightarrow F \rightarrow F \rightarrow C \rightarrow V \rightarrow B \rightarrow F \rightarrow F$$

One initial conclusion that a savvy player might draw after observing these ten hands is that their opponent can reasonably be considered a high-stakes player. That is, the hands in which the player raised (that is, bluffed or valuebet) represent 40 percent of all hands dealt. This is important information in itself, because it gives the player a reputation for frequently being aggressive in their betting behavior, regardless of the actual value of the hands drawn. We also note that in two of the cases, the player called but did not raise, indicating a lack of faith in the competitiveness of those hands. In poker, hands where the player calls usually follow a systematic pattern.[91] That is, there is usually a range of hands where the typical player will call but will not raise. Like states that predictably "protest" an issue and make a lot of noise (that is, cheap talk), they may nevertheless be unwilling to fight over said issue. Ultimately, then, the decision to call represents a "nondecision" that doesn't give us any additional information about a player's likely bluffing behavior.

We might also consider valuebetting a nondecision, since players don't really "choose" to valuebet; if you have a strong hand, you valuebet no matter what. In other words, it is highly unlikely that someone who draws a royal flush (the best possible hand) would choose any of the other options. Instead, they will always raise and reraise their opponents. The certainty of valuebetting diminishes, of course, as we move down the line into less competitive hands, but there is some subset of hands that removes the burden of choice from the player, who will always bet aggressively when drawing one of these hands. But as Haseeb Qureshi points out, we must understand the circumstances under which they valuebet, because until each player's final hands are revealed, valuebetting looks identical to bluffing.[92] Recall the earlier point about an aggressive Nazi Germany being indistinguishable from a moderate Nazi Germany: the key distinction in international relations and poker is appropriately judging when the adversary is bluffing and when they mean what they say. By removing the calls from the above sequence and focusing only on those situations in which the player bets aggressively (valuebetting or bluffing) or folds outright, we now have the following information:

$$V \rightarrow B \rightarrow F \rightarrow F \rightarrow V \rightarrow B \rightarrow F \rightarrow F$$

In just a few hands, then, we might be able to detect some patterns. It appears, for instance, that in a sequence of three poor hands, this opponent likes to bluff initially but then backs off and folds for a couple of hands thereafter. While not perfectly predictive of future behavior (a point we will examine in depth later), this is still the kind of information that a player can use to anticipate an opponent's strategy, thereby making their own strategy choices more effective.

While this process is much simpler in a game of Texas Hold 'Em, states essentially do the same thing every day. Governments observe the ongoing behavior of their counterparts and build crude models of how they are likely to act under specific circumstances with respect to specific issues. One of the most important foundations of a state's foreign policy apparatus is understanding the interests and intentions of other states. And to build a complete model, states must be able to distinguish between genuine interests and intentions and bluffs. Much of the United States' foreign policy resources, for instance, are devoted to making such distinctions with regard to North Korea. Its nuclear weapons program, particularly under Kim Jong Il, has frequently been used as a bluff. North Korea has repeatedly promised to dismantle its weapons programs in return for economic concessions from the United States and other countries, only to subsequently intensify those programs. Identifying the precise circumstances under which North Korea was likely to bluff, as well as identifying the circumstances under which it might genuinely cooperate, has been crucial to the U.S. strategic decisionmaking process.[93]

Understanding and modeling opponent behavior also allows states to categorize other states by their past actions, sometimes eliminating and sometimes adding strategic actions to their range. In other words, not all players are going to play the same way, but we might have a handful of "profiles" of poker players, just as we might develop a few standard "profiles" of state behavior. For instance, if we are able to identify the circumstances under which an actor is likely to bluff, then we may be able to successfully implement strategies such as "bluffcatching" to counteract their choices. Such a strategy relies on the premise that in order to beat a bluff, a player does not necessarily need a hand that is strong on its own. On the contrary, the player only needs a hand that is just good enough to beat the bluffing player's actual hand (which is almost always an objectively weak hand). Employing such a bluffcatching strategy gives poker players and international actors the potential to reap benefits they might not have otherwise enjoyed. President Kennedy's "hand" during the Cuban Missile Crisis was not necessarily strong; he acknowledged the U.S. understanding of the Soviet Union's nuclear arms bluff, but the consequences were not as clear (Would the embargo continue? Would the United States launch an attack in Cuba?). But the weak options available to the United States managed to be just enough to call the Soviet Union's bluff. The United States received far more concessions in return for the Soviets backing down, and the strategic dynamic of their relationship subsequently changed in favor of Washington. The United States therefore earned more from the episode than it would have in the absence of such a crisis because it had caught Khrushchev's bluff.

But bluffcatching is a completely useless strategy if you are playing against someone *who never bluffs*. While rare, such players do exist, and never bluffing might even be part of a concerted strategy for a sophisticated player. In relations among states, similarly, some states bluff more than others due to the nature of their political institutions. Kenneth Schultz finds that states rarely escalate disputes against democracies, because democracies are understood to rarely bluff.[94] Because their audience costs generate greater accountability, external observers (including adversaries) know that democratic leaders often mean what they say, because they are likely to be held accountable by their constituents. On the other hand, regimes such as North Korea, which clearly rely heavily on bluffing behavior, make bluffcatching a potentially attractive strategy. A whole generation of foreign policy professionals would probably love to bluffcatch Kim Jong Un.

CONCLUSION

One of the most puzzling features of humanity is the persistence of war. If war is so costly and so risky, why do states continue to choose this option, rather than finding some peaceful agreement that both sides would prefer? Admittedly, states rarely "want" war. They frequently use the threat of force as a means to coerce or deter other states. But ultimately, as a result of incomplete information (and related incentives to bluff) as well as problems of credible commitment, states miscalculate their own probabilities of victory or determine the risk of war today to be more desirable than the near certainty of defeat in the future. Even under circumstances of perfect information (say, if you knew your opponent's hand in poker, or if a state knew everything about its adversary's capabilities), no one can predict what will happen in the future, which has repercussions for how the game is played today.[95]

Because states understand the roles that information and credibility play, they have become adept in exploiting these issues for their own gain. Like a sophisticated poker player, skilled governments may use costly signals such as military mobilization or economic concessions to successfully deter or coerce others. Over time, states may develop "models" of other states, helping them to anticipate how their adversaries will behave under certain circumstances.

The central theme of this chapter and, indeed, this entire book is that neither war nor peace is ever certain. There is always some level of risk involved, and outcomes are truly unpredictable. While there are a limited number of anecdotes in which states seem to have benefited from war, even these rare "successes" involve considerable costs. The unification and establishment of a dominant German state following the Franco-Prussian War, for instance, came at the expense of nearly 30,000 German lives and almost 90,000 wounded. Despite the sense that war can be managed, controlled, and strategically executed, risk can never be fully avoided. Just as high-stakes poker players may have enough experience and knowledge to manage the situations they encounter during a game, they nonetheless face considerable risk in every betting round and turn of the cards.

The outbreak of war has been attributed to a number of a causes, including divergent preferences, ambitious leadership, and miscommunication. But whenever negotiations break down and states make the decisions to settle their differences on the battlefield, they have faced at least one of the problems discussed in this chapter: incomplete information and/or credible commitment problems. As we shall see in the next chapter, these problems take on entirely new dynamics when one player is dramatically weaker than their opponent, as in civil wars and terrorist campaigns.

How Weak Players Overcome Stronger Adversaries

The guerrilla wins if he does not lose.
The conventional army loses if it does not win.
—Henry Kissinger

In the poker movie *Rounders,* one of the characters remarks, "If you can't spot the sucker within the first half hour at the table, then you are the sucker." The character was observing that in many games, unskilled players frequently face off against far more sophisticated and experienced players. Also known in poker terms as "the fish," the unskilled or inexperienced player represents a seemingly valuable opportunity for stronger players. Just about every player has, at one time or another, faced the uncomfortable reality that they are playing a more skilled opponent. And as a game progresses and this disparity becomes clearer, stronger players often attempt to exploit their adversary's weaknesses. But why do weaker players knowingly continue to challenge stronger opponents? Why do weak armies voluntarily confront stronger ones, knowing full well that they are outmatched? The answer is not stupidity, although there is frequently a healthy dose of that at any poker table or battlefield. One reason poker is such an attractive game to players of all skill and experience levels is because it offers opportunities for weak players to turn the tables on stronger players.[1] When there is a wide disparity in the cards that players hold, for instance, a player with a weak hand still has a number of tools and strategies at their disposal that may allow them to win.

In conflict situations, weak actors also use a variety of strategies to overcome superior forces. While a state with greater capabilities would seem to represent an insurmountable challenge for a much weaker state, actors in such a position have effectively employed strategies to use their opponents' strength against them. David Lake refers to such mechanisms as "political jiu jitsu," and such strategies are often the only means by which weak actors can obtain concessions from stronger adversaries.[2,3] Weak actors may also reduce a stronger actor's willingness to fight by changing *perceptions* of their relative capabilities, giving the impression that they are stronger than they actually are. Bluffing is therefore one of the most important strategies for weak actors, who otherwise might not be able to compete with their adversaries.[4] By creating an impression of strength where little to none exists, actors may be able to convince their stronger opponents to offer concessions. Indeed, the Athenians inflicted enough costs on the superior Persian forces at the Battle of Marathon to convince the Persians to stay away from Greece for some time.[5] And in 1941, recognizing its military inferiority in the Pacific, Japan struck at Pearl Harbor with the intention of both appearing stronger than it really was and stalling for time while it increased its military capabilities. Even as the war dragged on, the Japanese continued to look for a singular victory (like that at Tsushima) that would give the impression of great strength and thus convince the United States to reduce its war aims.[6]

Although weaker states frequently rely on bluffing strategies to level the playing field, bluffing is a matter of survival for nonstate actors such as rebel organizations and terrorist groups. These actors, by default, are facing opponents with superior capabilities. Since one side (the government) has a monopoly on force and usually controls most of the military capabilities within a given theater, insurgent groups, rebel groups, terrorist groups, and other nonstate actors begin their challenge to the state at a serious disadvantage in terms of capabilities.[7] In 2013, the

Somali terrorist organization Al-Shabaab launched a spectacular assault on a public shopping mall in the Kenyan capital of Nairobi. Most observers agreed that Al-Shabaab was at a low point in terms of capability when it attacked the mall.[8] But the dramatic nature of the attack gave the impression that the organization was more capable than it actually was, leading to a particularly harsh backlash from the African Union Mission in Somalia as well as the United States.[9] This was likely the desired outcome for Al-Shabaab, which hoped to divide the civilian population and turn it against the American and Kenyan governments.[10] Al-Shabaab, then, clearly understood the value of employing nonconventional means to address the power disparity between it and its opponents.

This chapter focuses on how power asymmetries influence the strategies and tactics of weaker actors. First, we examine how asymmetric power relationships have been portrayed in past literature. We then extend our discussion to focus on civil conflicts (including terrorist campaigns, which are by definition marked by asymmetric power distributions). Next, we consider why bluffing may be the optimal strategy for nonstate actors in such cases and how it influences their reputation. Finally, we consider randomization as a specific strategy and explore how it can bolster the credibility of a weak actor and increase the effectiveness of its bluffs.

POWER DISTRIBUTIONS AND STATES

A common focus for scholars who study conflict has been power, and in particular, relative power. Some of the most prominent theories of conflict variously argue that the abundance of power, the relative lack of power, the fear of losing power, the fear of opponents' growing power, and other issues are at the heart of why conflict occurs.[11] Balance of power theory, for instance, argues that the most powerful states cause anxiety among other states, which in turn determines their behavior.[12] Even in the bargaining approach we examined in chapter one, power is a fundamental part of the equation. Incomplete information and credible commitment problems are at the root of bargaining breakdowns (as the bargaining approach argues), but it is incomplete information about power and commitment issues related to its use that ultimately prevents states from reaching peaceful settlements.

When considering state-level interactions, the empirical evidence points to a strong relationship between power parity and conflict.[13] That is, two states are more likely to fight each other when they have roughly equal capabilities.[14] The corollary of this empirical observation is that power preponderance is more likely to deter conflict. The logic is that when there is a particularly wide gulf in capabilities, both states should essentially "know their place." The weaker state knows that it is almost impossible to defeat its adversary in a head-on fight. And since this is mutually understood, any military threats it makes are inherently noncredible. In other words, "War is a kind of experiment, a test that generally would not be made if the opposing forces could measure accurately one another's strength. Unless there is a great disparity in the sides, the possibility of such measuring seems like daydreaming."[15]

A sophisticated poker player may recognize that their opponent cannot be holding pocket cards better than a pair of eights. If the opponent then bets large sums of money in an attempt to bluff, the more sophisticated player knows that such "threats" are noncredible. In international relations, wide power disparities are even more readily apparent. In such a scenario, the stronger state knows that it has a significant military advantage and uses it to achieve what it wants. The stronger state's implicit or explicit threat of force should coerce or deter the weaker state into submission, averting the need to resort to actual armed conflict. In such situations, the stronger state's threats are inherently credible (unlike threats made by the weaker opponent). Recall that when you have a strong hand, you always valuebet; there is no reason to bluff when you hold a relatively strong hand.[16] Similarly, states that are overwhelmingly more powerful than their adversaries should have fewer incentives to bluff.

On a related point, Blainey argues that "decisive" victories in warfare dramatically reduce the probability that conflict will recur between two states because such victories clarify the power distribution (which is unclear at the outbreak of a conflict).[17] According to Blainey, it is not the power distribution per se but rather a lack of information about the distribution that leads to conflict. And once that information problem is solved (when one side resoundingly defeats the other), there is no longer any ambiguity about capabilities.

If it is true that power preponderance deters conflict because one side assumes a dominant position while the other side is forced to submit, then why do we still see weak actors getting their way? Why do the Davids still defeat the Goliaths? Frequently, weak actors are able to extract concessions from their stronger adversaries by using one or more types of bluffing strategies. While bluffing is one of many tools that a state may use in its relations with other states, it may be the *only* means for a much weaker state to achieve its goals. Iraq, during the lead-up to the 2003 war, consistently engaged in bluffing behavior because Saddam Hussein knew that it was the only realistic way at that point to deter the United States from attacking.[18] Ultimately, Saddam's gamble failed, but given the circumstances, he was probably choosing the right strategy to play against his vastly stronger opponent. Likewise, a player holding incredibly weak cards only has two options: to fold or to bluff their way through additional betting rounds, encouraging others to fold.[19]

The case of Iraq is also illustrative of a relatively new trend in international relations: bluffing with weapons of mass destruction (WMDs). Many policy papers and academic studies have defined "rogue states" as those that pursue the development of WMD programs in opposition to international nonproliferation treaties.[20] The serious concern over proliferation of WMDs goes beyond just the ability of these states to harness significant destructive power; the acquisition of such weapons provides a relatively quick and easy way for otherwise weak states to even the power distribution. A weak state might be ignored, but a weak state with its "finger on the button" is suddenly of interest to everyone. In other words, while a state may not be able to compete with its stronger adversary in conventional terms, WMDs may give the state a new advantage that levels the playing field. Fear of some states acquiring such capabilities, therefore, is ultimately a fear of the coercive power they might obtain in bargaining scenarios.

Threats to use nuclear capabilities may be inherently viewed as bluffs, because it is considered unlikely that many states would actually use them. But much debate has centered around whether the new crop of rogue states may be more willing to use them as well as other WMDs.[21] Would Iran, for instance, be more willing to use a nuclear weapon than the United States and Russia have been? Nobody wants to find out! The interesting implication here is that since both a weaker state and a stronger state know that the weaker party can never compete in conventional armed conflict, the simple *pursuit* of weapons (and rhetoric indicating a willingness to use them) may offer a bluffing advantage to the weaker state. In other words, a weaker state does not necessarily need to *acquire* the actual technology, but rather make it appear that it intends to do so. Saddam Hussein's pursuit of nuclear technology, for instance, was at times more of a bluff than a serious endeavor, but it was used for the strategic purposes of deterring other states like the United States and Iran while simultaneously giving Iraq greater bargaining leverage with these countries.[22] Power preponderance, then, while generally deterring conflict, may perversely affect the incentives of weaker states, causing them to rely more heavily on bluffing strategies. Similarly, a "fish" may sense the sophistication of a poker player and not wish to risk their money playing such a strong adversary. But occasionally, a weaker player can topple even the most seasoned player through successful bluffing.

One final issue is worth noting that takes us further from the classic bargaining scenario in which states have only two choices: peace (in the form of a negotiated settlement) or war. There are other nonconventional foreign policy tools available to states. Weapons of mass destruction offer one such tool. And research suggests that states that cannot compete with their much stronger adversaries directly may be more likely to turn to state-sponsored terrorism to achieve their goals.[23] States that lack the military capabilities for a head-on fight against their adversary are far more likely to consider furtive sponsorship of terrorism as an alternative to achieve their political goals. Muammar Gaddafi's dissatisfaction with the international and regional status quo in the 1980s, combined with his recognition that Libya could not compete militarily with its perceived adversaries (the United States, United Kingdom, and Israel), led Gaddafi to consider alternative ways to apply pressure on his opponents. Libya became one of the foremost sponsors of terror during this time, along with Iran, which found itself at a similar power disadvantage.[24]

TACTICS AND STRATEGIES OF NONSTATE ACTORS

If weak states frequently resort to nonconventional means to obtain concessions from other states, then nonstate actors live and die by such means. In civil conflicts, nonstate actors are almost always dramatically weaker than the governments that they are fighting. Data compiled by David Cunningham, Kristian Skrede Gleditsch, and Idean Salehyan capture the strength of rebel groups relative to the governments they fight.[25] Analyzing 575 civil conflicts, they determined that in 87 percent of those conflicts, the government was "significantly" stronger than the rebels. Only in 13 percent of the cases did they judge the rebel group to be at least an equal match for the government forces. Civil conflicts, unlike interstate conflicts, are in fact defined as a conflict between actors, one of whom maintains a "legitimate monopoly on force."[26] Following the Peace of Westphalia in 1648, the accepted sovereign boundaries became state borders, and governments became the legitimate rulers of their own sovereign territory. Anyone else using violence to achieve political purposes—insurgents, rebels, terrorists, and so forth—is considered illegitimate according to these international norms. So not only do these nonstate actors face problems of legitimacy, they are also vastly weaker than the governments they target. While power disparities may prevent some conflict among states, a power disparity between a state and a nonstate actor is often the very root of the conflict. It is the raison d'être of most nonstate actors, and it is also their greatest challenge.

IMPLIED ODDS

This is why bluffing strategies are an inherent part of such conflicts, and why rebel groups, terrorist groups, and other nonstate actors rely so heavily on misdirection. Nonstate actors frequently use bluffing strategies to prolong their campaign until they are in a stronger position vis-à-vis their opponent. The key to understanding how such strategies work is best illustrated by the concept of "implied odds" in poker. As one guide to poker states, "There are times when the existence of future bets is the very reason you play the hand."[27] Successful blackjack players also frequently rely on implied odds. Novice blackjack players are often afraid to hit when they are holding weak cards (cards totaling twelve through sixteen) and the dealer is showing a strong card (seven, eight, nine, ten, or ace). But the correct play is to hit, "giving yourself a chance of making a better total."[28] In other words, some may place a bet when they are at an obvious disadvantage because their chances of succeeding in the future are higher. Insurgents or terrorists may not be able to win a showdown today against the state, but their immediate strategies can improve their ability to win a showdown in the future. Not coincidentally, much of the Islamic State of Iraq and the Levant's (ISIL's) propaganda stresses the need to prepare today for the "final" showdown against the West.[29]

Whether a player should bet in poker is determined by comparing two things: the "pot odds" and the "true odds."[30] If you were to place a bet on a single flip of a coin, for instance, the true odds of you correctly calling heads or tail would be 1:1. You can expect, on average, to make an incorrect call one time for every time you make the correct call. If you and an opponent each bet $1 on the flip, then your pot odds would also be 1:1 (you would expect to earn $1 for every $1 you lose in the long run). But what if your opponent foolishly bets $2 to your $1? Then you will be getting 2:1 pot odds (you would expect to earn $2 for every $1 you lose over time). Compared to the true odds of guessing correctly (1:1), you should take the bet because the pot odds are better than the true odds.

Now, assume the reverse is true. Assume that a player is playing a card game and is currently getting 2:1 true odds (the player can expect to lose twice as many times as they win) but only 1:1 pot odds. That player has a higher probability of losing any particular bet than winning. Logic would suggest that they should not place a bet, given such odds. But in a game like poker, where there are several consecutive betting rounds and the player's capabilities can change over time by drawing cards that put them in a better position, sometimes a player who is currently at a disadvantage may still wish to bet because the implied odds are high.

As an example, if a player is considering betting $10 on a pot that is currently at $20, and the chances of winning with their current cards are roughly 5:1, then the player would normally fold (2:1 pot odds are less than the 5:1 odds of winning). But if the player expects that on the next turn of the cards their hand may improve, placing a bet now can turn the odds ultimately in their favor. For instance, if an additional $40 is likely to be the bet in a future round, that would make the implied pot odds 7:1. In other words, the player's $10 investment now could ultimately lead to a $70 payoff in a future round. The 7:1 implied odds are greater than the 5:1 true odds (even though the current pot odds remain at 2:1).

And when the initial bet or investment is particularly low, implied odds become even more attractive. At one point, Las Vegas had a number of poker games that started with fifty-cent bets. The betting in later rounds would jump to $1, $2, or $3, making the implied odds particularly attractive. In such a structured game, with relatively low costs up front, it paid for players to always bet, no matter which cards they had drawn. When the cost of the initial investment is low, then, the implied odds can be "enormous."[31] Additionally, as the structured limits of a game escalate in later rounds, implied odds in earlier rounds become higher.

This is the exact logic of many terrorist campaigns and insurgencies. Facing short odds at the moment, these actors adopt strategies primarily with implied odds in mind. Terrorist organizations, for instance, frequently launch attacks under no illusion that the attacks will change the political situation today. Facing overwhelmingly strong adversaries, they cannot hope to win the fight immediately. Instead, they are betting that their actions today may change the odds of achieving their goals in the future.

The most successful insurgencies and terrorist campaigns have been those that have avoided direct fights with government forces. The Cuban revolution of the 1950s is considered a successful example of a relatively weak insurgency overcoming the superior capabilities of its adversary. In the initial stages of the insurgency, Fidel Castro's forces numbered in the hundreds. A direct assault on the government or the Cuban military was out of the question. A series of unsuccessful attacks on military installations—including one on the Moncada Barracks in Santiago de Cuba, an attack in which Castro lost many men, including his second in command—confirmed the futility of such a strategy. Castro subsequently shifted the tactics of the insurgency to a focus on hit-and-run guerrilla-style attacks, combined with a concerted propaganda campaign. As a result, Castro was able to create the perception of a credible threat to the government of Fulgencio Batista, who eventually fled after the revolutionaries seized the town of Santa Clara. While not able to compete directly against the Cuban military, the revolutionaries were nonetheless able to employ unconventional tactics in a way that won popular support and demoralized the government's forces, ultimately shifting the odds in their favor.

Governments and insurgents, then, understand the utility of such unconventional tactics. Even in cases of wide power disparities, where the government is vastly superior in capabilities to the rebel group, such tactics allow rebels to give the impression that they are a credible threat. Consequently, nonstate actors such as terrorist organizations and rebel groups that would otherwise have no leverage are able to effectively use coercion against the state.[32] While states use the threat of traditional military force to coerce nonstate actors, nonstate actors use the threat of unconventional tactics and shifting popular opinion to coerce the state into making concessions.

IMPROVING YOUR HAND WITH PUBLIC OPINION

The weaker the nonstate actor, the more important popular support becomes in constructing a credible threat. The key strategy of many insurgent groups, and particularly extremist terrorist organizations, is to shift public support away from the state and toward the group. The goal is to change people's opinions so that the government is seen as the "bad guy." Doing so can allow a particularly weak organization (one that might not even have the capabilities to mount a guerrilla-style challenge to the state) to effectively threaten the state. Terrorist organizations are often defined as "extremists" not because they are violent, but because the viewpoints they hold are extreme.[33] In other words, their views and goals are often at the extreme tail end of the distribution of public opinion.[34] Such organizations, with little popular support for their ideas, are also unlikely to have significant military capabilities. Their only true hope, and their only credible threat, lies in turning the tide of public opinion.

But how does such an organization turn public opinion in its favor? Let's return to our bargaining scenario from chapter one, but this time assume we have a state actor bargaining with a nonstate actor. As shown in figure 2-1, the balance of power is overwhelmingly in the state's favor. Not only does the organization have little to no military capabilities, the fact that it is extremist also means that it has very little public support. An unpopular organization with few capabilities cannot seriously challenge the state today, let alone coerce it into making concessions. The nonstate organization seemingly has no chance of mounting a credible threat to the state, so any negotiations or bargaining between the state and the group should be a nonstarter. The organization might as well negotiate with a brick wall. Such organizations, however, have successfully changed the relative power structure by launching violent attacks against noncombatants, in turn provoking a heavy-handed response from the state.[35] Many terrorist attacks, therefore, are not intended to pose an immediate military challenge to the state but rather are designed to instigate the state to respond in a way that alienates the broader population. The response itself, often resulting in civilian casualties, can convince moderates among the population—"fence-sitters"—that the state poses a greater threat than the terrorist organization. By shifting public opinion in this way, the organization subsequently has access to new recruits and resources and may win the support of a cooperative, sympathetic population. With all these additional advantages, the power distribution may shift, as seen in figure 2-2, where the state must now reconsider its willingness to try and reach a peaceful settlement with the organization.

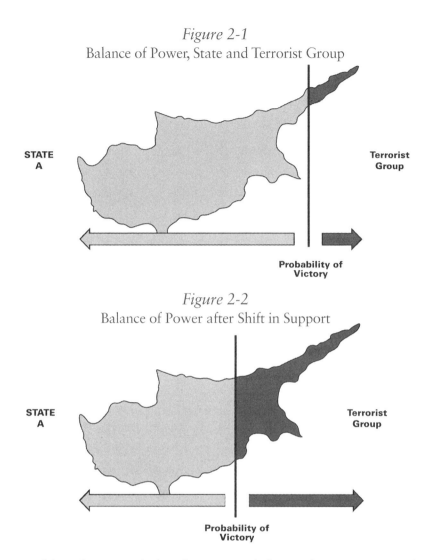

Figure 2-1
Balance of Power, State and Terrorist Group

Figure 2-2
Balance of Power after Shift in Support

Although some scholars have argued that such a strategy rarely works,[36] there are a handful of cases that were so incredibly successful for the nonstate actor that contemporary terrorists and rebel groups continue to look to them as models. The case of the Algerian fight for independence from France in the 1950s is one such model. The initial movement for independence, beginning in 1954, was not widely embraced by the Algerian population, nor did it seem important to those living in France.[37] By 1956, however, after the Front de Libération Nationale (FLN) consolidated its power and began launching terrorist attacks in Algiers, the support of the larger population began to shift in their favor. This support came as a result not of the terrorist attacks themselves, but of the repressive tactics used by the French, which included brutal forms of torture.[38] The broader Algerian population began to view the French government as the single greatest threat to their security, and even the population within France came to support the Algerian movement for independence.[39] Overwhelming support at home for an independent Algeria, in fact, convinced French president Charles de Gaulle to abandon the war effort and grant the country independence. The FLN and the various organizations that eventually joined it did not have the conventional means with which to fight the French military. The French, as they had experienced in the mid-nineteenth century when they first attempted to dominate Algeria, found that a superior military and advanced weapons were no match for an insurgency supported broadly by the population of the country.

In bargaining scenarios, then, a lack of military capabilities and resources may preclude nonstate actors from credibly threatening the state with the use of force. This, in turn, can undermine their bargaining position. But through the use of unconventional tactics like terrorist attacks (and the state's response to such attacks), some organizations may be able to gain enough public support to improve their bargaining position. As the FLN learned, newly acquired public support has the dual effect of providing sympathetic supporters while actively denying that support to the state. An organization that can pose such a credible threat today may be more likely to receive concessions in the future.

Despite being at a relative disadvantage in capabilities, rebel groups and terrorist organizations often benefit from the information environment in a civil conflict. Incomplete information can cause bargaining breakdowns that lead to war, but it can also offer actors an advantage in bargaining scenarios. In civil conflicts, while the power asymmetry typically favors the state, the information asymmetry often favors the nonstate actors. Most of these groups are clandestine, secretive organizations that actively limit information about their operations and intentions. Additionally, since most of these organizations only exist for a few years, it is more difficult for a government to learn about new organizations. The average lifespan of a terrorist organization is 3.33 years, while nearly 70 percent of them survive for less than a year.[40] Due to the clandestine and opaque nature of such threats, a critical barrier to effective counterterrorism and counterinsurgency policy is a lack of intelligence about the details of these organizations. During the height of the Iraq War, U.S. government sources frequently cited a lack of information about terrorist groups as a key reason for their persistence. As an example of the staggering dynamism and complexity of terrorist movements in that conflict, one journalist compiled a list of 103 groups claiming responsibility for attacks on Americans and Iraqis during a 6-month period in 2005.[41] And the number of groups operating during the Syrian civil war reportedly has numbered in the thousands.[42] Imagine trying to develop effective strategies when you don't even know who your opponent is! Ironically, one way in which governments try to compensate for a lack of information about such organizations is to use torture as an information-gathering technique.[43] If torture then generates a backlash against the government and strengthens the nonstate actor's bargaining position (as it did in Algeria), the state puts itself at an even greater disadvantage.

Incomplete information is a key source of bargaining failures and conflict between states. Since information problems can be even more acute in civil conflicts, we might reasonably conclude that it is more difficult to prevent conflict between states and nonstate actors. This seems to be the case, as nearly 75 percent of all conflicts since the end of World War II have been civil conflicts.[44] Once an active resistance forms within a state and demonstrates its willingness to use violence to achieve its purposes, it is particularly challenging to find a peaceful settlement.[45]

BLUFFING IN CIVIL CONFLICTS

The primary disadvantage of nonstate actors in civil conflicts is their lack of capabilities relative to the state. In this section, we explore further how bluffing can dramatically change this dynamic. Power asymmetries put the weaker actor in a position where it cannot reasonably expect to challenge the adversary in a head-on fight. As the power asymmetry grows, the prospect of such a direct fight becomes increasingly less realistic. Success for rebel groups and terrorists, therefore, often hinges on making the enemy (that is, the state) think they are more powerful than they actually are. Since states typically lack accurate information on the capabilities and resolve of such organizations, the groups have an incentive to misrepresent this information and exaggerate their capabilities, resolve, and intentions. Bluffing the state in this manner may encourage it to make concessions where it otherwise would not. Certain actions on the part of weak actors can affect the outcome of a conflict by influencing the stronger actor's *perception* of the probability of success. You don't have to actually win, you just have to make it *look like* you are winning. Bluffing behavior can also be useful in misrepresenting capabilities to the larger population, which might encourage some members to shift their support to the group. Not surprisingly, at least one study of poker strategy refers to the act of "bluff raising" (continuing to raise other players even though you have a weak hand) as "terror tactics."[46] By bluffing others into thinking that your hand is stronger than it is, you might cause them to commit foolish mistakes or take unreasonable risks. The goal, therefore, is not to directly challenge another player through the particular capabilities of your hand, but to "scare" them into conceding (folding) or betting an unreasonable amount on a hand of their own.

There are actually two different kinds of bluffs. The first, a pure bluff, occurs when a player bets on a hand that has almost no chance of winning in a showdown. The second, a semi-bluff, occurs when a player bets on a hand that is probably not the best at the moment but that has a reasonable chance of becoming the best hand after drawing additional cards (that is, when the implied odds are high). For instance, a player who currently holds a four-flush (four cards of the same suit) may raise their opponent even though a four-flush is worthless. Although the player would be hoping to convince their opponent to fold, the opponent might call. But the player has a reasonable chance of drawing a complete flush in future turns of the cards, so this strategy is considered a semi-bluff.

When weak actors such as terrorist organizations and rebel groups bluff about their capabilities and resolve, they are engaging in a form of semi-bluffing. Semi-bluffs can only occur when there are more cards to come; thus, semi-bluffing behavior by nonstate actors only occurs when they anticipate future interactions with their opponents. The goal, therefore, is to provoke the opponent into making unwise decisions today, or at least to postpone defeat until one's position can be improved. The use of terrorist attacks is specifically designed to spread fear among the population and the adversary that the terrorist organization is capable of far more than it actually is. Similarly, one tactic when bluffing in Texas Hold 'Em is to hope to draw a "scare card," which doesn't objectively change a player's hand but that causes the adversary to *perceive* that his or her position has been diminished.[47] For instance, if the board shows a jack and a queen, and the river comes up as a nine, this can "scare" other players into thinking that their opponent has a reasonable chance of making a straight or a flush. The reality may be nothing of the sort, but such a scenario may convince other players to fold pre-maturely, even if they objectively hold a good hand.

Many of the most stunning examples of successful rebellions and terrorist campaigns hinged on the ability of the weaker nonstate actor to bluff the stronger state actor into thinking they were more powerful than was actually the case. Such a strategy is as old as warfare itself. Clausewitz argued that a weaker actor might gain an advantage over a stronger adversary by taking control of some undefended territory.[48] While an undefended territory is unlikely to be strategically important (hence, the reason it is undefended), such a maneuver may nonetheless deal a psychological blow to the enemy. Capturing territory may change the stronger actor's willingness to make concessions if it raises that actor's perceived costs or lowers their perceived probability of victory.[49] ISIL wagered on such a strategy during the summer of 2014 when it took control of large stretches of territory in Syria and Iraq. By all accounts a relatively weak organization in terms of capability and public support, the group nonetheless raised its profile as a credible threat in the eyes of Iraq, Syria, and other countries when it made a spectacular show of capturing undefended territories and attacking unarmed civilians. Even the infamous capture of Mosul was carried out with limited capabilities thanks to the minimal resistance that the group encountered.[50] The move, however, raised the perceived costs of fighting ISIL and lowered its enemies' perceived probability of success, although objectively ISIL was not immediately stronger than it had been before capturing the city. ISIL's entire strategy, therefore, was a kind of bluff: taking un- or under-defended territory gave the impression that it would also be capable of taking well-defended territory, regardless of whether that is actually the case. If you've ever played the game of Risk, you've probably played with someone who captures several disparate, undefended territories. Although this isn't strategically the best way to achieve victory in the game, it sure is intimidating to see so many of the opponent's pieces on the board!

This kind of strategy also influences audiences outside of the government and the military. Changing the perception of the organization's viability among the larger population can serve the same purpose as terrorist attacks: it may convince moderates among the population, or those individuals who are uncertain about the effectiveness of the organization, that the group is in fact a credible threat. ISIL's rapid acquisition of territory in 2014 did not immediately increase its objective military capabilities in a meaningful way. But reports suggest its recruitment and public support increased dramatically within weeks of capturing Mosul.[51]

OPTIMIZING THE BLUFF

As with any decision made in games of chance or in bargaining scenarios, decisions to bluff are *strategic* because the outcomes are based on both the choice of the key actor and the course of action that their adversary chooses. Recall the Prisoner's Dilemma and how the outcome was based on both the player's decision and their anticipation of the other player's choice. Likewise, the potential benefit that a rebel group derives from engaging in bluffing depends in part on their adversary's response. With these strategic dynamics in mind, certain bluffing strategies may allow nonstate actors to optimize their returns while simultaneously increasing their risk of defeat. Similarly, in poker, certain bluffing strategies may offer extensive rewards to the weaker player but may also pose considerable, even existential, risks in the sense that a player may be eliminated from the game if the adversary successfully calls their bluff (or successfully engages in bluffcatching).

An example illustrates how a successful bluffing strategy relies on the decisions of both a player and their adversary. Consider a game of Texas Hold 'Em in which there are only two players, Player A and Player B.[52] Imagine that the players have already completed the river betting round and the river card is about to be revealed. Player A holds cards that put them in a good position to hit a flush or straight on the river. We will assume that a flush will give A the winning hand, while anything else will result in A's defeat. We will also assume that, of the remaining forty-six cards, there are nine that would give A the flush—a roughly 1 in 5 chance. A 20 percent chance of winning equates to an 80 percent chance of a busted flush. This suggests that Player A has an objectively weak hand, but if we assume that Player B has the exact opposite chances (20 percent chance of losing and 80 percent chance of winning), we can say that Player A is also weak relative to their opponent.

After the most recent betting round, the pot contains $120. Player A has a few options. If A makes the flush, then they will valuebet the entire amount of the pot. In other words, if Player A actually draws the winning hand, they will bet the full $120. The more likely scenario, however, is that A busts (does not draw the winning flush), and in this case, there are two distinct options: either check (decline to bet) or bluff (still bet the full $120 despite having a losing hand).

Now assume that this exact scenario is repeated many times. The key decision for Player A is *how often* to bluff. Again, A has a few options. First, A can decide to *never* bluff, so that every time they bust, they simply check instead of betting further (and valuebet whenever they draw the winning hand). The outcome of this decision, in turn, depends on the strategy of Player B. If we assume that Player B is risk averse and never calls Player A, then Player A will win every two hands out of ten (Player A draws the winning flush two out of ten hands). Player A therefore wins $120 twice out of ten hands, for an average of $24 per hand. If, however, Player B is a highly risk-acceptant player (or just belligerent) and calls Player A's bet every time, the outcome will be different. Out of the ten hands, Player A will still win twice, but in each case, Player B will have doubled the pot, so Player A wins a total of $480 for an average of $48 per hand. We might think of another scenario in which Player B calls Player A's bet exactly half the time. So if Player A never bluffs, then one time out of ten A will valuebet and B will fold, resulting in a $120 take for Player A. And one time out of ten A will valuebet, B will call, and A will take $240. Player A will therefore average $36 per hand in the scenario where B calls half the time.

A second strategy for A would be to *always* bluff. In two out of ten hands, A will have the winning hand and thus will actually be valuebetting in those cases. But in the other eight hands, A will continue to bet despite holding a losing hand. If B never calls, A simply wins the $120 pot every time. That amounts to $72 more per hand than the best-case scenario when Player A never bluffs! But this strategy can be extremely dangerous. In the situation where Player B always calls, Player A will win $240 twice out of ten hands. But the other eight hands, where Player A is simply bluffing with a bad hand, Player B calls the bluff, and Player A loses $120 per hand for a total loss of $960. Player A's total loss across the ten hands is $480 ($480 minus $960), or $48 per hand. This is a far cry from the $120 per hand profit that Player A was making when Player B never called.

Table 2-1 summarizes the expected gains and losses for Player A based on a number of potential strategy combinations for both players. As we can see, Player A's decision to always bluff has the highest potential payoff ($120 per hand), but it also entails the greatest risk (losing $48 per hand if Player B always calls). Similarly, rebel groups, terrorist organizations, and other relatively weak actors may derive maximal benefits from engaging in bluffing behavior. But if the state responds appropriately, calling the bluff in every case, this strategy can be devastating for the organization. This helps explain why some movements have bluffed their way into success (such as the FLN in Algeria) but why many others are ultimately unsuccessful.[53] The difference between the two scenarios, in turn, relies on whether the adversary is playing in a risky manner (an issue we will return to in chapter four).

Bluffing, however, may still be a useful strategy for a weak actor. As table 2-1 shows, Player A can choose a strategy that, while not maximizing potential payoffs, can nonetheless be an *optimal* strategy by "guaranteeing" a specific profit. The so-called basic strategy of blackjack offers the same advantage: it is mathematically optimal because it minimizes losses while also "guaranteeing" specific payoffs over time.[54] As the table reveals, if Player A engages in bluffing behavior at a ratio of 1:2 (one bluff for every two nonbluffs), A can expect an average profit of $36 per hand. Regardless of how many times Player B calls Player A's bet, B is unable to prevent A from earning the $36 average. The most successful terrorist organizations are those that adopt a similar *mix* of bluffing and nonbluffing behavior to establish a baseline of credibility. Bluffing, then, is a risky strategy, but some mixture of bluffing and actual credible threats is the key to success.

SUCCESSFUL BLUFFING BY WEAK ACTORS: CREDIBILITY AND RANDOMIZATION

Bluffing is an optimal strategy when used by actors who have established some level of credibility and who successfully mix their choices. The key to successful bluffing in conflict scenarios is both credibility and unpredictability. An opponent must believe that you are willing to use violence and capable of following through on threats to do so, but

Table 2-1
Optimal Bluffing Strategies

Player A Bluffs	Player B Calls		
	Never	50%	Always
Always	$120	$36	–$48
2:1	$72	$36	$0
1:1	$48	$36	$24
1:2	$36	$36	$36
Never	$24	$36	$48

the opponent should not be able to predict when you will do so. The "boy who cried wolf" is a tale of someone who bluffs repeatedly until he has lost all credibility and no one believes him anymore, even when he is objectively telling the truth.

We will return in the next chapter to a discussion of how credibility can be established and managed over time, but for actors to make credible coercive and/or deterrent threats, they must first establish a minimum level of credibility. This may be one reason North Korea has been successful in gaining concessions from its opponents. Although much of the government's behavior, first under Kim Jong Il and then under his son Kim Jong Un, may be classified as bluffing, many policymakers considered their empty threats to have been largely successful in gaining concessions.[55] By "rattling the sabre" and threatening attacks on South Korea, the United States, and others, North Korea has won a number of economic benefits. And although the state likely never intended to engage in direct armed conflict with these other states, its threats still maintain a level of credibility precisely because it has established a reputation for being willing to use aggression and force (the credibility also stems in part from the proximity of the two Koreas and the salience of their long-running disputes). The attempts by Kim Il Sung, the first premier of North Korea, to assassinate South Korean officials, as well as Kim Jong Un's and Kim Jong Il's intermittent low-intensity bombardment of Yeonpyeong Island and ballistic missile tests, have established a baseline of credibility that permits the regime to successfully bluff its way into achieving its goals.

A lack of credibility, on the other hand, can have the reverse effect. For Saddam Hussein, a lack of credibility and his subsequent inability to bluff directly contributed to his downfall and that of his regime.[56] After intentionally bluffing throughout the 1990s about the existence of weapons of mass destruction and repeatedly kicking weapons inspectors out of Iraq, he established a reputation for being highly noncredible. When it became clear that the United States was going to launch an invasion in early 2003, his last-ditch attempts to reveal the truth about the weapons programs were no longer believable. Although we now know that Saddam was apparently being genuine in offering to finally cooperate with weapons inspectors, U.S. secretary of state Colin Powell stated that "we are where we are today with Iraq because Saddam Hussein and his regime have repeatedly violated the trust of the United Nations, his people and his neighbors."[57] So a basic lack of credibility meant that Saddam was able to neither successfully bluff nor make a credible commitment about the (non)existence of the weapons. In the cases of North Korea and Iraq, bluffing was a central strategy for both governments, even though they differed in their outcomes.

How do power asymmetries influence the role of credibility? Because they are lacking in capabilities, weak actors are at a disadvantage when it comes to their ability to make credible threats and commitments. As a result, these actors may be driven to commit violent acts simply to establish some baseline of credibility. Only after doing so are other actors likely to fall for their bluffs. And since civil conflicts are defined by asymmetric power distributions, they pose the greatest challenges in terms of credibility of the actors involved.[58] The many problems of credibility in civil conflicts have been well documented, and credibility has been cited as the most important factor in both leading to civil conflicts and preventing their termination.[59] Because of these issues—nonstate actors must credibly commit to not resuming their armed struggle in the future, and the state must credibly commit to not destroying the former rebels once they lay down their guns—civil conflicts are notoriously difficult to resolve. Of the 287 civil conflicts that occurred between 1946 and 2005, for instance, less than 14 percent were ended by a peace agreement.[60]

There is an additional reason the resolution of intrastate and interstate conflicts differs. The resolution of interstate conflicts typically involves some negotiated settlement or peace agreement, but no central enforcement of such peace agreements occurs. For instance, when the Treaty of Versailles ended World War I and harsh provisions were placed on Germany for allegedly starting the war, there was no central authority that could enforce Germany's acquiescence to those provisions (something that Hitler seized on when he came to power, refusing to recognize the terms of the treaty as legitimate). With a negotiated settlement ending a civil conflict, on the other hand, "enforcers" of the agreement exist, but they are typically one of the warring parties. In order to come to an agreement and end the fighting, for example, the rebels might have to agree to give up their weapons to the government (or the former members of the government might be required to give up their power to the victorious rebels). Either way, the resolution of conflict is elusive because one side cannot credibly commit to refrain from using force in the future or reneging on the terms of a negotiated settlement.[61] Madhav Joshi, Erik Melander, and Jason Michael Quinn argue that the keys to a successful peace agreement in civil conflicts are provisions that avoid *disempowering* one side at the expense of the other.[62] The central impediment to resolving civil conflicts, then, is the fact that the enforcers of any agreement are likely to be the belligerents themselves.[63]

How does a noncredible actor such as a rebel group establish credibility and gain bargaining leverage against the state? After all, it is the rebels' weakness (their inability to strike effectively at the state) that undermines their credibility in the first place. How does a poker player demonstrate that they have the capabilities to win a hand? Successfully demonstrating such capability allows a player to engage in effective bluffing behavior. But without establishing a reputation of credibility over the course of many hands, what can a player with a weak hand do? Unfamiliarity between players can be an advantage since neither side has the information to classify their opponents as either credible or non-credible, so some players might play it safe and assume they are credible. But as we saw in the previous chapter, weak poker players have an option that allows them to immediately establish credibility: raising significant amounts of money on a single bet.

Such a strategy is particularly risky, though, for rebel groups and terrorist organizations precisely because they are so weak. In attempting to demonstrate their commitment and credibility, they often expose themselves and incur greater security risks to their organizations. The goal of many terrorist attacks, for instance, is to establish some baseline of credibility for the terrorist organization.[64] But it is the very act of establishing this credibility that subsequently puts the organization at great risk. Terrorist organizations, clandestine by nature, must "surface" to launch attacks and may leave a trail that helps the government hunt them down. Like poker players, the establishment of credibility brings with it significant, even existential, risks. But what is the potential payoff? A weak terrorist organization is often trying to establish its credibility not just with the government it is fighting but also with the broader population. Both the general population and the government may be uncertain about the organization's capabilities and resolve and may wish to see some demonstration before fully "buying" it as a credible threat. A successful terrorist act demonstrates that the group is capable of pulling off violent attacks and circumventing government security efforts and is committed enough to its cause that it is *willing* to use such risky tactics. Consequently, uncertainty over the group's credibility is reduced.

For weak actors, then, some sort of costly signal is required to establish credibility and to make their bargaining position effective. It is not surprising that after making a particularly credible display of its power and resolve with the attacks of September 11, 2001 (as well as earlier attacks against the U.S. Navy destroyer USS *Cole* and the U.S. embassies in Kenya and Tanzania), al Qaeda was able to "coast" on its reputation as a credible actor, even as its ability to conduct such attacks again was waning.[65] Within policymaking and academic circles, the severity of the threat al Qaeda posed had been debated during the 1990s and into the early 2000s. The 9/11 attacks, combined with a retroactive assessment of how the threat had been growing over the past decade, firmly established the organization as a credible terrorist group sincerely devoted to a cause and possessing the capabilities and willingness to achieve its goals.[66] As counterterrorism efforts expanded in the wake of 9/11, the group began to decline or at least morph into a different kind of threat that was far less capable of committing a 9/11-style attack than it had been. Despite this objective change in the group's capabilities, even a cursory reading of public statements by Ayman al-Zawahiri, the group's second in command under Osama bin Laden, gives the impression that the organization was *growing* as a threat. Al-Zawahiri repeatedly threatened U.S. interests domestically and abroad, and in some cases the group even threatened attacks on specific locations or at specific times, threats that rarely came to fruition.[67] Although the scarcity of successful attacks may imply effective counterterrorism efforts, it also suggests that al Qaeda was aware of its declining capabilities with respect to attacking the United States. Many of the public threats by al-Zawahiri and others, therefore, represent classic bluffing behavior. In some ways, the history of al Qaeda following 9/11 can be viewed as a long period of bluffing behavior by the organization.[68] But the organization would not have been able to engage in such behavior successfully without first establishing its own credibility. The result is that the general population and the adversaries of the group, such as the United States and the governments of western Europe, could never be fully certain that the organization was *only* bluffing.

This is a crucial point: even after an organization's effectiveness has been degraded through counterterrorism measures and other activities, it may maintain popular support and recruits based on the credibility established at earlier stages. This can be thought of as "resting on one's laurels." Poker players may similarly rest on their laurels by establishing significant credibility up front—even in a single hand—and then exploiting that credibility. A player who bets a great deal of money on a winning hand early may generate sufficient credibility that they expand their ability to bluff in later hands. This is the establishment of reputation, and it is something we address in greater detail in the next chapter.[69]

Credibility is a necessity for successful bargaining, and this is especially true for weaker actors in an asymmetric conflict since they are often inherently noncredible. But what about the stronger actor in such conflicts (that is, governments)? We have already noted that credibility is an important requirement for ending civil conflicts, but what is the importance of credibility prior to the termination of conflicts? The stronger actor wants to establish enough credibility regarding its capabilities and resolve that the weak actor (for example, an insurgent group) chooses to give up rather than face the prospect of total defeat. This has been the strategy of the Russian government in Chechnya:

to use overwhelming and indiscriminate violence against the Chechen rebels in an effort to establish credibility and deter future aggression. And by some accounts, this strategy has worked, particularly following summary executions and assassinations of Chechen leadership.[70] But again, terrorists and/or rebel groups frequently recognize this strategy and seek to exploit it by provoking the target government into a heavy-handed response. This is why many modern governments do not follow the overwhelming force strategy and instead try to balance their military efforts with campaigns to win the "hearts and minds" of the population. They, like the insurgents, must also concern themselves with their credibility in the minds of the general population. Strong actors must establish credibility about their willingness and ability to use force, but more important, they must establish credibility about their willingness to *not* use force. Demonstrating restraint is therefore of greatest concern to the stronger actor.

RANDOMIZATION AS A STRATEGY

We have now discussed the importance of bluffing and credibility in asymmetric conflicts, particularly for weaker actors. We have also seen how the ability to bluff depends on an actor's credibility, and vice versa. Credibility can be established in a number of ways. One particularly useful strategy is randomization, a tactic that is frequently employed by nonstate actors in asymmetric conflicts because it simultaneously generates credibility and the freedom to bluff. Guerrilla warfare, terrorism, and other tactics favored by relatively weak actors often contain some element of randomization for such purposes.

As the earlier example suggested, the best bluffing strategy is a mixed strategy where an actor bluffs only part of the time. Sklansky further notes that "a person who bluffs with approximately the right frequency—and also, of course, in [a] random way—is a much better poker player and will win much more money in the long run than a person who virtually never bluffs or a person who bluffs too much."[71] The key to success, then, lies not in just mixing the strategy, but in randomizing bluffing in a way that makes your behavior ultimately unpredictable to the opponent.[72]

If an actor acknowledges that it cannot take its opponent in a head-on fight (and in asymmetric conflicts, that is usually acknowledged at least privately among terrorists and insurgents), one strategy that allows a weak actor to break down a strong actor over time is to create the *perception* that a strike can be launched anywhere at any time. By launching attacks in a seemingly random fashion (with regard to location and timing), weak actors can generate high levels of fear and uncertainty, even when their capabilities are severely limited. Creating such a false perception is useful in two ways. First, it creates uncertainty and fear on the part of the stronger actor that they may not have the capabilities or information necessary to defend against such attacks. And second, it creates enough fear and uncertainty on the part of the population that they come to view the organization as much more capable than it actually is.

Interestingly, the fact that weak actors engage in seemingly random attacks was one of the earliest criticisms leveled at the proposition that terrorists should be considered rational actors. Critics charged that terrorists and terrorist organizations cannot be considered fully rational in the classic economic sense if they launch attacks that do not maximize their utility.[73] For instance, if an attack was chosen against a marketplace at random, it would not be rational if some more strategic target would give the terrorist organization more utility. What much of this criticism misses, however, is that randomization itself can be a strategy. While the specific tactical choice of a target may not maximize utility at that particular moment, the broader strategy of randomization may be the most effective way for the organization to achieve its goals.

Furthermore, what critics might deem "random" attacks have frequently been nothing of the sort. Nonstate organizations have often benefited from the *perception* that they are engaging in random selection of targets and attack times, when in fact they are carefully making choices to create that perception. Even a purely random set of events often does not *appear* to be random. For instance, if you have someone flip a coin twenty times but first ask them to predict what those twenty flips will look like, the average person will predict something like the following sequence:

H•T•H•H•T•T•H•T•H•T•H•H•H•T•H•H•H•T•T•H•T•T

There are exactly ten flips resulting in heads and ten flips resulting in tails. Furthermore, there are no sequences of consecutive heads or consecutive tails longer than two flips. The average person will make decisions like this, give or take a few flips, because this is what we think of as being truly random sequences.[74] With a 50/50 chance for either heads or tails, most people expect that the overall distribution will closely reflect the 50/50 probability, and they also expect that when heads or tails are flipped consecutively, the probability of hitting the same result on the next flip will decrease, as the distribution "corrects" itself.

An *actual* random sequence, however, usually does not appear as tidy as most people expect. A truly random series of twenty coin tosses might look more like the following:

H•T•T•T•T•T•H•T•H•H•H•H•T•H•H•T•T•T•T•T

In such a sequence, there are many more tosses resulting in tails than heads. Extensive, consecutive flips with the same outcome are also more frequent. There are more, and longer, clusters of both heads and tails in this truly random sequence. So our mental perceptions of random sequences do not typically align with what a random sequence actually looks like. Londoners experienced this problem during the Nazi bombing of their city in World War II. As the bombings wreaked havoc on the city, newspapers published maps of where each V2 rocket had hit. The maps appeared to show clusters of rocket hits, suggesting that they were aimed at specific targets.[75] Many Londoners used this information and deliberately moved their residences away from the clusters, perhaps only to fall victim to later bombings.[76] An analysis after the war revealed that even though the locations of the rocket hits *appeared* to follow a pattern, the distribution was entirely random.[77] This inability to spot either random or nonrandom distributions has important implications for the use of violence in asymmetric conflicts, and it has been exploited successfully by weak actors in such conflicts. Organizations only need to create the *perception* that their attacks are random to bolster their claims that they can strike anywhere and at any time.

Claude Berrebi and Darius Lakdawalla reveal possible evidence of such a strategy behind terrorist attacks in Israel from 1949 to 2004.[78] This span includes attacks from both the First and Second Intifadas, periods in Israel's history when it seemed like terrorists were capable of striking any target at any time within Israel's borders. Their analysis of the locations, timing, and target types of terrorist attacks, however, reveals that terrorists in Israel have been far more strategic, or at least more systematic, in their decisionmaking. Among their findings, they determine that areas with higher proportions of Jewish residents are at greater risk for attacks, as are symbolic government targets. But they also find that attacks are more likely near terrorist homebases and international borders, two findings that demonstrate that "random targets" are not randomly drawn from the population of all possible targets. They also find that "low-value" targets are less likely to be hit again following an initial attack. Many other studies have found discernible patterns in terrorists' selection of targets and timing of attacks.[79]

Despite these clear and measurable patterns, the attacks may *appear* to be random, something that greatly strengthens the terrorist groups' bluffing strategies. In fact, Richard Horsley argues that "terrorism must appear irrational and un-predictable in order to be effective."[80] Perceived randomness, in short, establishes credibility for organizations that otherwise lack it. Not surprisingly, terrorists frequently use phrases like "we can strike you any time we wish" because this kind of rhetoric, combined with the seeming ability to do just that, allows them to spread fear and achieve their goals. Did this strategy work for Palestinian terrorist groups? Although a variety of factors contributed to subsequent events, the Oslo peace process began after the First Intifada, and Israeli withdrawal from Gaza occurred after the Second Intifada. Randomization, then, can increase the effectiveness of bluffing behavior, and weak actors in asymmetric conflicts may be able to gain more bargaining leverage as a result.

At the tactical level, randomization has also benefited military combatants. During World War II, both the Axis and Allied forces began incorporating "dud" shells into their artillery bombardments. The practice actually grew out of a need to dispose of defective shells resulting from the production process. Rather than dispose of them at the production site, which was very costly, they were shipped to the front, where they were mixed into artillery bombardments on a random basis. When one of these duds landed behind enemy lines but did not explode, enemy commanders nonetheless were forced to expend resources to dispose of them, lest they be live munitions with time delays.[81] In this case, true randomization increased the overall effectiveness of the artillery campaigns.

The concepts and the strategies in poker are similar to those discussed here. The best strategy in poker is not to engage in truly random play in the sense that a player makes no strategic decisions. The best strategy is to play in a way that *accords with the adversary's notion of randomness.*[82] Recalling the modeling example from chapter one, a strategic player might distribute their folding and bluffing in a way that appears random. In other words, with a weak hand, a player might benefit by folding 50 percent of the time and raising (bluffing) 50 percent of the time. Not only is this a strategic way to establish some credibility and allow oneself the freedom to bluff, but it is also a way to avoid being modeled by the opponent. After all, one cannot model behavior without perceiving some pattern, and if the pattern appears truly random, then it will be nearly impossible to predict future decisions. The ultimate goal, therefore, is to get the other player to believe that you are valuebetting when you are actually bluffing, and only randomization and the use of costly signals generate enough credibility to do so effectively.

CONCLUSION

Randomization and bluffing not only are useful for weaker actors in interstate and intrastate conflicts but also may be their only realistic chance of defeating an adversary. As Sun Tzu argued, one of the best courses of action is to "attack [the opponent] where he is unprepared

. . . [and] appear where you are not expected."[83] This is particularly useful for those who cannot hope to attack a prepared opponent successfully. Similarly, any action that raises the *perceived* costs of continuing to fight on the part of the adversary or the *perceived* capabilities of the weak party only serves to improve the weaker party's bargaining position.

This has important implications for international conflict. While power parity among states may lead to a greater danger of conflict because it creates misperceptions and uncertainty, civil conflicts are, by definition, asymmetric. And it is this asymmetry that creates incentives for violence, including unconventional violence. While the efficacy of strategies such as terrorism has been heavily debated (Max Abrahms, for instance, suggests that terrorists rarely achieve their stated political goals), there are enough dramatic cases of successful terrorist campaigns to inspire others to use the same means.[84] And even when these groups do not achieve their goals, these strategies can play an important role in maintaining the organization.[85] While most observers believed in 2014 that ISIL was unlikely to establish a single, credible Islamic caliphate, the group's struggle against the governments of Syria, Iraq, and others helped shore up its recruiting and public support and led directly to its expansion, which would not have been possible without the high-profile violence that the organization employed.

This chapter has also spoken to the importance of credibility, which is based on past behavior and results in the development of reputations that can then be used to gain an advantage over opponents. Professional poker player Doyle Brunson demonstrated the value of understanding an opponent's reputation during the showdown at the 1977 World Series of Poker. During their game, there was a jack, a five, and a two on the board, and Brunson's opponent, Bones Berland, kept raising the bet. Although it would appear that Berland might have a pair of jacks, there were several other valuable combinations he might have held. For instance, he might have held a pair of pocket aces or kings. Brunson, however, called his final raise with a pair of queens, reasoning that he did not in fact have aces or kings. He won the hand since Berland was only holding a pair of jacks. He explained that Berland "couldn't have two aces or two kings because he never raised in early position with these hands before the flop."[86] In other words, by studying his opponent's tendencies against other players, he knew that Berland typically raised early if he had valuable pocket cards. This is, in fact, the appropriate play when holding good cards. Despite playing correctly, Berland shot himself in the foot by playing "with too much consistency."[87]

Credibility and successful deception, then, both require a skillful and careful development of reputation, and reputation can only be developed over time. In the next chapter, we move beyond the decision to use force and consider the consequences. How does the use of violence change combatants' war aims, and how do these aims ebb and flow over the course of a conflict?

| Chapter | **Game Flow and** |
| Three | **Reputation** |

Politics is war without bloodshed
while war is politics with bloodshed.
—Mao Tse-Tung

The lousiest poker players are the ones who direct all their efforts at winning a single hand.[1] These players disregard longer-term strategies and ignore how actions taken in the current hand may influence future hands. To this point, we have compared international bargaining to a poker game in which only one hand is played. We have assumed that two players have little to no information about one another and must make strategic decisions to achieve their goals in a single round. These assumptions are useful when examining some basic strategic concepts, but admittedly, this approach involves a great deal of abstraction from reality.[2] If international bargaining and conflict truly followed such a pattern, a simple lottery (or dice game) might be a better analogy than a game of poker: players place their wagers, and a completely random process determines the final outcome.[3] While randomness is an important factor in conflict, such a limited view ignores much of the larger strategic element in international relations. Poker, of course, is not typically played in a single hand. Arguably, the most interesting events in a game of poker occur well after the first hand, when players start to develop reputations and a "feel" for their opponents. One of the most critical parts of a successful poker strategy is understanding what makes an opponent "tick," or how they operate under certain circumstances (in poker parlance, a player's range).[4] Successful play requires not just a good hand but also "the ability to assess [an] opponent's style of play and what he is likely to do in a given situation."[5] Players intentionally and unintentionally develop reputations over time that influence the way other players interact with them. They may, for instance, develop a reputation for bluffing in inappropriate situations or betting aggressively at a certain point in the game (for instance, on the bet after the turn). Once a reputation has been developed, other players may change their strategies accordingly and, in doing so, develop their own reputations. The game of poker, then, is not limited to a single betting round with a subsequent reveal of the cards but is an ongoing, evolving process. The way a player behaves in the current hand may be influenced by their expectations about what is possible in the next hand.[6]

These points may seem fairly obvious when talking about poker. But in the study of international relations and international conflict, many theorists have assumed that strategic interactions occur in such a single-shot fashion.[7] Likewise, policymakers have made costly errors by treating strategic interactions with adversaries as a single event rather than as one episode in a series of events. For instance, the French and British effort to avoid war at any cost in 1938 led to the Munich Agreement, which ceded part of Czechoslovakia to Nazi Germany in return for a promise that Germany would no longer seek to expand its territory. Viewed as a single event, this agreement was lauded as a success by those who negotiated it. British prime minister Neville Chamberlain referred to the agreement as "peace for our time." But the bargain may have altered Germany's view of Britain and France and its own understanding of the bargaining dynamic between the European powers. During the next few years, Adolf Hitler seems to have been emboldened by what he saw as growing evidence of British and French desire for appeasement.[8] International bargaining, then, does not occur in a vacuum. But even the previous chapters in this book, for the sake of theoretical abstraction, largely assumed that international bargaining is an isolated event that ends with either a successful negotiation or some form of armed conflict. In such a view, conflict is therefore considered to be a "failure" of the bargaining process, divorced from previous and future bargaining.[9]

In this chapter, however, we move beyond this useful simplification and consider for the first time a bargaining process that takes place both during conflict and in successive bargaining scenarios. We examine how the bargaining process evolves during repeated interactions and during actual conflict, as information about players' capabilities and the credibility of their commitments changes over time and as players develop reputations based on their past behavior. We first consider how reputations are developed and how that development is inextricably linked to an actor's credibility. We then consider some of the more interesting types of reputations that international actors can develop, including for being unpredictable and for being unusually aggressive. Throughout the discussion, we examine the role that bluffing plays in the development of all strategies, especially as it affects a player's credibility. Next, we examine how reputations and information about one's adversaries evolve on the battlefield and how these changes influence the likelihood of conflict termination. Finally, we examine a tactical and strategic issue that influences both war onset and termination: the role of offensive and defensive advantages. Ultimately, this chapter focuses on the argument that bargaining and conflict are distinct manifestations of the same process.[10] Conflict is a continuation of bargaining, and conflict itself changes how actors view each other as well as their expectations for the future.

ESTABLISHING AND INTERPRETING REPUTATIONS

We have seen that credible commitments are among the most important factors driving the outbreak of conflict. But credibility is also key to understanding how conflicts are waged and how they end. We have assessed how credible commitments can be established between actors who are unfamiliar with each other and we have examined mechanisms (costly signals) by which international actors can establish immediate credibility. For poker players, establishing immediate credibility hinges on a player's betting strategy. Larger bets generally indicate greater levels of commitment and credibility, even if the bet is only intended to create the illusion of credibility.[11] But of course, most poker players do not play a single hand, just as most political actors do not interact on a single occasion and then go their separate ways (although many of them probably wish this were the case). Instead, most interactions between actors are part of an iterated series. That is, most actors engage with one another on a longer-term basis, and as such, they establish reputations based on their past behavior. They may also begin to identify behavioral patterns and reputations of their adversaries, using modeling strategies such as those discussed in chapter one.

Saddam Hussein's reputation for international aggression, for instance, was firmly established when he decided to launch large-scale conventional warfare against Iran in 1981. But it was his extensive *history* of aggressive behavior throughout the 1980s and 1990s, including his invasion of Kuwait and repeated violations of international law, that created significant credibility problems for him during the lead-up to the 2003 U.S. invasion of Iraq.[12] Similarly, the ongoing debate over who "started" the Cold War focuses almost exclusively on histories of behavior by the United States and the Soviet Union. From the traditional viewpoint, the United States did not view the Soviet Union as a credible actor because Moscow reneged on post–World War II agreements made at the Yalta and Potsdam conferences.[13] The revisionist view, on the other hand, emphasizes that the Soviet Union did not view the United States as credible because of the latter's support for tsarist forces during the Russian civil war.[14] Both viewpoints, however, emphasize that the ability to make credible commitments is established through past behavior and subsequently shapes actors' expectations about the future. Specifically, credibility in international bargaining shapes expectations about an adversary's likelihood of *refraining* from using force in the future.[15] Repeated interactions therefore have significant consequences for how actors behave, particularly as they shape actors' perceptions of credibility. And we will see that actors can use credibility (or the perception of credibility) to their advantage to achieve their goals in negotiations.

In poker, reputation is most accurately captured by the concept of game flow, "the pattern of decisions made over time, and how that pattern influences subsequent decisions."[16] Each player has their own game flow and can potentially model (and exploit) the game flow of other players as well. In games involving multiple rounds of play between the same players, those players will base their decisions not solely on the hand that they currently hold but also on the past betting behavior of their opponents.[17] The purpose of carefully crafting one's own game flow by valuebetting, bluffing, randomizing, and employing other strategies is to establish a reputation that can be used advantageously in the future. Qureshi refers to this as "bluffing equity."[18] In earlier rounds, a player can increase their equity, which can then be cashed in during later rounds.[19] So using reputation for strategic purposes is not as simple as betting a large sum of money to signal commitment. Players must wisely choose how to bet if they wish to establish a specific long-term reputation, and this will often involve bluffing to keep that reputation consistent.

We have seen that bluffing, when mixed wisely with valuebetting, can help foster a reputation for unpredictability. This is the single most important goal for a poker player: to remain unpredictable (or at least minimally predictable) to their adversaries. The best strategies in repeated play involve some balance of bluffing and nonbluffing behavior so that opponents have no reason to expect that one will be more likely than the other. Once a reputation like this is developed, the credibility of a player's commitments is enhanced. This is an important point—the goal is not necessarily to develop a reputation for always valuebetting, because that is unrealistic. To develop a reputation for *sometimes* bluffing and *sometimes* valuebetting with no apparent logic behind either, however, puts the opponent in a position where past behavior cannot effectively be used to predict future behavior.

To avoid a reputation for a particular strategy, then, the player's past actions must appear random. In the last chapter, we discussed ways in which some actors may create the illusion of randomness. In practice, it is surprisingly difficult to create a true image of randomness.[20] For instance, a reasonable strategy to avoid being classified as either a "bluffer" or a "valuebettor" would be to split your strategy 50/50 in relevant hands. That way, the other player would not have reliable information to predict the next hand. But a simple example illustrates why this is problematic.[21] A player might split his or her behavior in relevant hands as follows:

$$V \rightarrow B \rightarrow V \rightarrow B \rightarrow V \rightarrow B \rightarrow V \rightarrow B \rightarrow V \rightarrow B$$

While this appears to be perfect randomization, instead of saying the behavior is split 50/50 between valuebetting and bluffing, even a novice player would identify that on every even-numbered hand, the player bluffs. In other words, the player has a 100 percent bluffing strategy on even hands, which is exactly the predictability the player is trying to avoid. While this is admittedly a simple example, we can see how even concerted efforts to appear random can be deconstructed into basic, nonrandom strategies.

$$V \rightarrow B \rightarrow B \rightarrow B \rightarrow V \rightarrow B \rightarrow B \rightarrow B \rightarrow V \rightarrow B$$

In the above sequence, it appears that every second, third, and fourth hand involves a 100 percent bluffing strategy. So much for unpredictability! More intricate strategies, of course, are more difficult to discern, but the player using them must still struggle to avoid predictability. It should be obvious, however, from these simple examples that the only way to be *truly* unpredictable is to *truly* randomize your play. Many poker players and analysts of the game, in fact, have attempted to do just that—make their decisions between bluffing and valuebetting truly random.[22] If such a strategy could reasonably be implemented by a human being, it would probably be the single most effective strategy in the game of poker.

Many actors have demonstrated that developing a reputation for unpredictability can be an effective strategy. It was not necessarily clear to Britain and France in the 1930s, for instance, that Nazi Germany was an aggressive actor. When negotiating with Hitler over the annexation of Czechoslovakia, the British and French were unsure whether Nazi

Germany was valuebetting and demonstrating aggression or whether it was really a moderate regime making reasonable demands to incorporate German-speaking peoples into its territory.[23] In 2014, Russia appeared to deliberately foster a reputation for unpredictability. On one hand, Russia seemed resolved to interfere in Ukrainian affairs, annexing the Crimean Peninsula. But when the crisis had spread to the eastern Ukrainian territories of Donetsk and Luhansk, Russia seemed to indicate a willingness to restrain itself.[24] Reports suggest that the Russian military even engaged in a covert occupation of the territory, simultaneously achieving control of it while publicly suggesting that Russia had no interest in taking it over.[25] So by engaging in an aggressive and swift usurpation of the Crimean Peninsula, followed by a seemingly unresolved interest in the eastern portion of Ukraine, the United States, the European Union, and others were not sure if they were dealing with a resolved or an unresolved Russia. Both Hitler and Putin, by the way, would probably make excellent poker players.

This kind of reputation for unpredictability has also been particularly effective for rebel groups during peace negotiations. The Liberation Tigers of Tamil Eelam (LTTE), for instance, engaged in such a strategy during the 1990s and 2000s as it entered a peace process with the Sri Lankan government. Having already developed a reputation for using large-scale violence, it also appeared to be making significant investments in a peaceful resolution. Ultimately, the government was not sure which kind of organization it was dealing with—a violent terrorist group or a legitimate political organization seeking a peaceful solution. This strategy, which gave the perception that the organization did not fit neatly into a single category, worked to the group's advantage as it became clear that the LTTE was only using the peace process to rebuild its capacity to engage in violence.[26] The group, now with greater capabilities, subsequently resumed its violent campaign and increased its demands.[27] Similarly, in 2014, the Colombian government and the Fuerzas Armadas Revolucionarias de Colombia (FARC) seemed to be heading toward a final peace agreement. But as peace talks in Havana were moving forward, back in Colombia the FARC captured several top military personnel, including General Ruben Dario Alzate. This may have been a strategic act to make the Colombian government uncertain about which kind of organization it was dealing with in Cuba. Was the FARC an inherently violent organization or one that truly wanted peace? The immediate result was a temporary suspension of negotiations.[28] In short, demonstrating a willingness to engage in violence in the midst of a peace process may have served to increase the group's bargaining leverage.

Additionally, some members of an organization, displeased with a peace process, may engage in violence to try to sabotage or "spoil" it. Spoiling, which is used primarily to damage the reputation of another actor so a negotiated settlement cannot be reached, occurs when groups or individuals linked to one side oppose cooperation and launch violent attacks to undermine it.[29] Cooperation between actors can therefore put them "at risk from adversaries who may take advantage of a settlement, from disgruntled followers who see peace as a betrayal of key values, and from excluded parties who seek either to alter the process or to destroy it."[30] Spoilers use violence to influence an actor's beliefs about the intentions and commitments of its negotiating partner.[31] Violence launched in the midst of cooperation calls into question whether the partner is genuinely committed to peace. Spoiling, then, is a strategy used by third parties to create uncertainty and unpredictability to harm another actor's bargaining leverage.[32]

Spoiling raises another important issue. Much of our discussion has assumed that reputation is developed through iterated interactions between two actors. But others beside the two involved in negotiations are often aware of reputations and past behavior. For instance, in a game of poker, a player might gain a reputation for being aggressive, and this would be evident to both players and observers of the game. This insight has taken on new meaning for those studying international politics. Studies have shown that what happens between a single pair of states is not necessarily independent of what happens in other pairs.[33] In fact, the outcomes of bargaining and conflict between two states may have a dramatic impact on how each of those states bargains with others. Molly Melin, for instance, finds that the ability of two states to resolve a territorial dispute relies heavily on the states' observations of each other's behavior with respect to third parties.[34] In other words, states do not simply assign reputations based solely on their interactions with each other, but also on their observations of how each "plays with others." Adding other players to the equation can dramatically complicate players' strategies.[35] With more players in a pot, for instance, bluffing can be notoriously difficult because even a good bluff is not likely to convince *all* players at the table to fold.[36] Their decisions are also influenced by their expectations of the *future* of those third-party negotiations. Reputation, then, can be developed and observed in a variety of ways, and it dramatically affects the way actors interact. A good reminder for both poker players and international leaders is that *someone* is always watching.

REPUTATIONS FOR AGGRESSIVE PLAY

Let's now consider one particular kind of reputation, as well as its possible benefits and liabilities: a reputation for being aggressive or risk acceptant. As Clausewitz argues, the way in which a conflict is fought is proportional to the political goals at stake.[37] Although he acknowledges that the best strategy would be for a combatant to throw everything it has into winning a conflict, this does not happen in practice for two reasons. First, it is impossible to mobilize all of one's resources simultaneously to wage war. Second, and more important, combatants are usually unwilling to devote a great deal of resources to a cause that is only of limited significance. This is perhaps one argument for why the French, and later the United States, fought limited wars in Vietnam, in the sense that they refrained from deploying their full capabilities. For the French, maintaining a colony in Southeast Asia was something that had become increasingly unpopular at home. Popular disapproval of the war in Algeria a few years later also led to a limited military effort from the French.[38] For the United States, growing disapproval at home and a political objective that was questionable to many Americans influenced how the war was ultimately fought. So in practice, we typically see that states only put as much into the conflict as they see fit to secure a certain political objective.

A similar pattern applies in poker, where a rule of thumb is that the ratio of the opening bet to the ante should be around 1:1.[39] In other words, a player should bet only the amount they expect to win in return. An initial opening bet that is too low creates a ratio that approaches zero, while a bet that is too high creates a ratio that approaches infinity. And it is the latter of these two scenarios that we consider now: actors that clearly put far more skin into the game than is necessary or prudent. Such actors might be referred to as risk acceptant or aggressive. And despite Clausewitz's disapproval of these strategies, there are potential benefits to developing such a reputation under certain circumstances.

Risky or aggressive behavior is perhaps most obviously useful in disrupting how others play the game. Since conventional wisdom assumes that you put into the game what you expect to get out of it, making particularly risky or aggressive bets signals that you are not necessarily playing the game rationally. This can be particularly useful when a player is already in a losing position.[40] Such a reputation may create the impression that an actor is hard to subjugate. There were some psychological benefits for the UN/U.S. landing at Inchon, for instance, since it was thought to be a dangerous and counterintuitive place to launch an attack.[41] Given the geographical features and the complexity of landing forces there, it was a risky move. But Gen. Douglas MacArthur argued that the risk was worth it, since it might not only take the enemy by surprise but could also change the enemy's perception of fighting the combined UN forces.[42] Inchon, then, was a deliberately risky decision intended to change the allied forces' reputation.

Likewise, the Japanese rejected concessions from Russia in 1904, and the decision to ultimately engage in combat was part of a strategy of establishing a reputation so that outside powers would think twice in the future about challenging Japan.[43] The country, having recently built significant military and technological capabilities under the Meiji Restoration, was still viewed by many powers (including Russia) as weak and backward. In order to change course, Japan decided that the crisis over the Liaodong Peninsula was the perfect opportunity to change its own reputation. A series of possible concessions by the Russians were turned down by the Japanese, who seemed intent on fighting. They saw conflict itself as strategically important, as it would help to solidify their new reputation.

This was also the logic behind Gen. William Tecumseh Sherman's March to the Sea during the American Civil War. Arguing that the Confederacy would not voluntarily give up its fight, he intended to bring destruction to the civilian population and infrastructure as a means of convincing Southerners that the Union was too aggressive to be defeated.[44] The brutal campaign that Sherman waged in Georgia and the Carolinas, therefore, simultaneously reduced the enemy's resolve to fight and increased the perceived probability of a Union victory. It did so primarily by changing the Union's reputation to one of intense brutality, which in turn changed the Confederacy's expectations for the future.

The methods and tactics that an actor uses in actual combat are therefore crucial to the establishment and maintenance of reputation. This is one of the key underlying logics of terrorist campaigns. Even though most terrorist groups have no hope of defeating conventional forces head-on, by engaging in particularly risky and aggressive tactics, they may instead raise the government forces' perceived costs of fighting.[45] A reputation for aggressiveness, therefore, may convince more powerful actors that the price of staying in the game is just too high. Chechen resistance to post-Soviet Russian rule has followed this logic quite often, as Chechen separatists have engaged in aggressive and shocking tactics with the intent of signaling to the Russian government that they will not easily be subdued.[46]

In many games of chance, there is a similar benefit to appearing aggressive or engaging in risky behavior. This goes beyond just making large bets to establish credibility. Just as the methods and tactics used in warfare can influence the decisionmaking of other actors, the *way* in which one bets money can influence other players. An example of such behavior is the continuation bet, where a player *always* bets, for instance, following the flop (the first turn of the cards). This has the effect of raising the preflop bet, and it benefits players because they are aggressively taking the initiative.[47] Consequently, other players may not be able to determine whether a player is bluffing or valuebetting early in each hand, because the player always engages in the same action. In a way, this consistency is a form of randomness that appears to have no discernible pattern. In reality, such a strategy "masks" any pattern. But successful continuation bets, of course, first require that the player establish a reputation for always betting after the flop.

DOMESTIC BEHAVIOR AND AGGRESSIVE REPUTATIONS

Reputations are not developed solely within the context of a two-player game. Actors frequently judge the reputations and credibility of other actors by observing how they interact with third parties. One area in which reputations for aggressiveness are actively (and often unintentionally) developed are in relations between states and their own citizens. The way a government treats its own people often has significant repercussions for how other actors view that government.

In a series of articles, Mary Caprioli and Peter Trumbore explore the notion that a state's domestic behavior may influence how it interacts with other states. They pay considerable attention to "rogue states," a concept frequently referenced in popular political discourse.[48] Caprioli and Trumbore note that not only are rogue states commonly considered to be among the worst human rights abusers, but they also pose the most significant challenges to the global community. Using multiple measurement schemes to classify these rogue states, they find that the classic idea of a rogue state (a state that supports terrorism or seeks WMDs) is no more likely to be involved in, or to initiate, conflict than other states.[49] When they expand their analysis to examine how states treat their own citizens, however, they find significant relationships with interstate conflict behavior.[50] Using various measures and indices capturing state repression, ethnic discrimination, and the use of violence, they offer evidence that governments that abuse human rights and discriminate against minorities are more likely to be involved in international conflict and also more likely to be the first to use force in an international dispute.

Several other studies find similar relationships between domestic behavior and interstate conflict.[51] A state's ill treatment of its citizens, provided it is observable to outsiders, may inadvertently create a reputation of aggressiveness and untrustworthiness. Observable uses of violence at home influence a state's long-term reputation and impact its ability to reach international settlements. States that regularly commit violence against their citizens will likely engender a lack of trust on the part of other states. Arguments by U.S. leaders about why Saddam Hussein could not be trusted frequently referred to his use of chemical weapons "against his own people . . . Kurdish civilians in northern Iraq."[52]

More recent uses of violence against citizens should impact a state's international bargaining in the short run, as other states have immediate data points on which to judge the other's level of credibility. While anything that reduces credibility or information about a state's intentions should have a similar effect,[53] the use of violence should be particularly damaging to credibility because in bargaining scenarios, states are specifically judging commitments of others to not use force in the future to revise the terms of a negotiated settlement.[54] In evaluating the recommendations of a policy analyst, Robert Jervis says that "we should not be influenced by whether he beats his wife."[55] But in relations among states, we should be concerned (and many states are rightfully concerned) about what happens behind the curtain, because it provides valuable information about a state's credibility.

AGGRESSIVE REPUTATIONS AS LONG-TERM BRINKMANSHIP

Intentionally developing a reputation for aggressive behavior, on the other hand, is a form of brinkmanship. In chapter one, we discussed the Cold War strategy of mutually assured destruction as perhaps the most famous example of brinkmanship. The deterrent logic of MAD is that states can reduce the probability of going to war by first raising that probability. By pushing your enemy to the "brink" and demonstrating a determined willingness to use force (in the case of MAD, the use of nuclear weapons), the adversary should be less willing to risk conflict to get what they want. Some observers suggested in 2015 that the United States and China were playing such a long-term game in disputes over territories in the South China Sea.[56] Neither China nor the United States was immediately raising the prospect of war, but China's long-term reclamation projects in the Spratly Islands, as well as ongoing U.S. naval patrols through those islands, may have had a similar effect by cultivating a reputation for aggressive behavior on the part of both states.

The strategy of developing a reputation for aggressiveness may offer similar payoffs and risks as traditional brinkmanship. The benefits are potentially similar: if other actors view you as being overly aggressive and willing to engage in conflict based on their observations of your past behavior, they may be less likely to "push the envelope" and more willing to reach a compromise. The implicit threat of conflict, which is present in all bargaining scenarios, is much more explicit with actors that have already cultivated a reputation for taking aggressive actions. A long-term strategy of aggressiveness may be even more useful than short-term brinkmanship because adversaries have actual evidence that the other actor is willing to do what they say. Aggressiveness and the initiation of conflict in past bargaining scenarios greatly clarify an actor's resolve. In other words, uncertainty over another actor's resolve is reduced when they have demonstrated over time their willingness to fight.

Long-term aggressive behavior not only offers the hope of additional negotiating leverage but also may deter attacks from other actors. This behavior introduces the concept of defense by offense, or "offensive deterrence,"[57] a phrase coined by Henry Kissinger to describe Chinese behavior with respect to Taiwan. By being overtly aggressive against the island—especially in the 1950s, when the People's Republic of China occupied the Yijiangshan Islands and shelled the Matsu Islands in the Strait of Taiwan—the Chinese government demonstrated a willingness to use force over the settlement of the island. During the 1960s and beyond, China continued to "talk tough" with regard to Taiwan, but since it had already showed great resolve in the matter, observers were inclined to believe China's threats. According to Kissinger, the Chinese were actively engaging in "risk adjustment" through their aggressive behavior. The point was not to seek out a direct conflict with Taiwan or the United States, but rather to change the range of agreements that these two actors would find acceptable (and preferable to war).[58] Such a strategy is like the strategy of terrorism outlined in the previous chapter. Terrorists hope to shift the power distribution in their favor by eliminating certain bargaining options. Demonstrating a willingness, even an eagerness, to engage in conflict changes the bargaining options available to other actors and can ultimately change the power distribution. It is therefore reasonable to argue that since the 1950s, China has held the upper hand in ongoing negotiations over Taiwan because it has reduced the ability of either Taiwan or the United States to engage in particularly risky behavior. Kissinger argues that the use of Chinese forces in the Sino-Indian War of 1962 and the Chinese-Vietnam War of 1979 had a similar effect on relations between China and its adversaries.[59] Not coincidentally, there has never been major armed conflict over control of Taiwan. China's offensive deterrence seems to have worked, at least for the last seventy years. In one of the great ironies of human history, then, aggression can be an effective way to prevent conflict.

ENDING THE GAME

Clausewitz considered war to be politics by other means.[60] One of the implications of his statement is that once war begins, it does not end until the political goals at stake have been resolved in some way. War therefore ends "not because the states that are fighting are incapable of further fighting but because they agree to stop."[61] Likewise, most poker players do not play until they completely run out of money (pathologically compulsive gamblers notwithstanding). Instead, something changes during their play that causes them to reevaluate the wisdom of continuing. They may, for instance, decide that another player is too skilled and unlikely to be beaten often enough to justify continued losses, so the player may choose to exit the game rather than continuing on a disastrous course. Likewise, a successful player may want to continue but may observe changes in the game flow that suggest their luck is turning. They may prefer to walk away on top, rather than waiting to find out how their luck can change.

Gamblers must think about much more than just their initial bet. They must weigh their current resources against possible future events. What if the other player becomes more aggressive in later rounds or experiences a streak of particularly good luck? Could the current level of resources sustain the player through such circumstances? Or would it be best to avoid the risk altogether and walk away now? We will return to these discussions of how actors weigh potential risks and rewards in the next chapter, but for now, it is instructive to understand that players consider their own capabilities, and their own resolve, as their fortunes ebb and flow. Particularly sophisticated players will also reevaluate how their performance in one hand may affect their ability to successfully engage in strategies such as bluffing in future rounds.[62] Ultimately, the game is an evolving creature, and it ends when one or more players consider the future and decide the reward no longer outweighs the risk of continuing.

What causes states and other international actors to make a similar decision? Why do states that have already made the costly decision to invest their limited resources in a risky conflict voluntarily decide to seek peace or concede to their adversaries? It would seem that once one has made such a risky bet, it would be best to see it through to the end, but states rarely fight wars until one side is completely decimated.[63] Although a few debatable examples exist, such as the near-total defeats of Nazi Germany in World War II and the Confederate States of America during the American Civil War, they are few and far between. And Dan Reiter even argues that the Confederacy capitulated not because it had been decimated but because something changed in its calculation of the acceptability of potential postwar agreements and the benefits of those agreements compared to the cost of continuing to fight.[64] Most conflicts, however, end without a formal agreement, as one or both sides simply cease fighting under "unclear circumstances."[65]

Short of total devastation, then, what causes a state to signal that it is ready to sit down and negotiate an alternative to continued conflict? As several scholars have argued, the circumstances that lead to the outbreak of war are directly related to the causes of peace.[66] Whatever conditions must be present for states to choose the costly gamble of war must be absent to cause peace.[67] So something with respect to the conditions that caused the war in the first place must change during its course, ultimately leading to a termination of the conflict.

The literature generally suggests that two important factors drive the decision to engage in conflict: incomplete information and credible commitment problems.[68] A lack of information about an opponent's resolve or military capabilities can lead to miscalculations (and exaggerations) of one's own prospects for victory, ultimately leading some states to choose conflict rather than a bargained settlement. Similarly, when states cannot credibly commit to a course of action, other states may be willing to risk conflict rather than risk the possibility of the other actor reneging on an agreement in the future. The implication is that if states could solve these problems of incomplete information and credible commitments, there would be no reason to resort to violence, as some agreement can always be found that both sides would prefer to the cost of fighting.[69] Likewise, if two people could agree to amicably split a pot of money between them, there would be no need to play a game of cards. Of course, this is one of the most important differences between poker and war—games can be enjoyable on their own even where there is no money at stake. But if actors didn't have to worry about their opponent reneging on an agreement in the future (possibly trying to take their share by force), there would be no need to play the game at all. Conflicts, like games, end because one or both sides learn new information about the opponent's (or their own) capabilities or resolve or because new information is revealed about postconflict commitments. Ultimately, new information and changes in credibility may make it more beneficial to walk away than to continue accepting risk.

War, then, "does not suspend political intercourse or change it into something entirely different."[70] On the contrary, war is a continuation of the bargaining and betting process that occurs before conflict, and it changes as the available information changes during the course of the conflict. Once armies face each other on the battlefield, two things are likely to occur that alter their prewar calculations. First, opponents are likely to receive more accurate information about each other's capabilities and resolve. As Helmuth von Moltke, commander of Prussian armies during the Franco-Prussian War, once argued: "No plan of battle survives contact with the enemy." Once armies actually fight each other, the available information changes completely, altering not only assumptions about tactics and strategies but also prewar assumptions about strength and the willingness to fight. Second, as a war drags on, opposing sides are likely to receive additional clarification of possible postwar settlements and commitments. New information about any of these features may dramatically change an actor's willingness to continue fighting.[71]

Early treatments and theories of war focused on a prewar choice between settlement and conflict. Earlier in this book, we assumed that bargaining largely ends once conflict begins. But the current chapter has focused on how the bargaining process continues through the course of conflicts as actors develop reputations and learn more about their opponents. Thus, it is important to consider conflict as part of the bargaining process because conflict may, in fact, be an intentional bargaining ploy. R. Harrison Wagner argues that states often go to war specifically to get a better deal at the negotiating table.[72] In the summer of 1813, U.S. president James Madison approved the resumption of offensives against British forces in Canada. One goal of these actions was to give the United States more bargaining leverage during negotiations with the British government that were scheduled for that summer in Russia.[73] This was also the logic inherent in the Chechen resistance against Russia. By developing a reputation (on the battlefield and elsewhere) for being hard to subjugate, the Chechen leadership was pointedly trying to coerce the Russian government into making concessions it otherwise would not have considered acceptable.[74] At any given moment, the strongest negotiator is the one *currently* holding the gun to their adversary's head.

Additionally, as Wagner has pointed out, fighting a conflict necessarily changes the value of the fight itself.[75] As the fortunes of war shift, armies win victories and incur defeats. As one actor's fortunes improve, by default, their adversary's fortunes decline. And since we know that the bargaining range and the relative bargaining position of each actor are based on the power distribution between the two actors, even minor changes in that power distribution during a conflict ultimately influence each actor's leverage. More important, the prewar *perception* of that power range can be dramatically altered once two adversaries meet on the battlefield and the *objective* power distribution is made clearer.

These points about how power and the perception of power change over the course of a conflict are central to why this book has compared conflict to poker rather than a lottery or a roll of the dice. Conflict is not a matter of two parties failing to strike a deal and then making a bet on who will win or lose in a fight. If that were the case, bets would be placed, the dice would be rolled, and one side would win while the other side loses. The logical implication is that we would always see complete victories in conflict, with one side completely dominating the other.[76] We would also not see lingering issues after a war is fought, since one side would get what it wanted (that is, it would "win the pot"), while the other side would lose everything and be "put in its place." The power distribution would be clarified in such a decisive victory, and there would be no need or incentive for further conflict.[77]

But such victories are relatively rare, and it's debatable that there has ever been a truly decisive victory in the history of warfare. Although every military in every conflict throughout history has wanted to complete an epic "smackdown" of their opponent, smackdowns are exceedingly rare. Instead, the typical outcome is similar to what occurred at the end of the various conflicts fought between Russia and the Ottoman Empire during the seventeenth, eighteenth, and nineteenth centuries. Lingering strategic concerns about the Black Sea and ethnic and religious tensions, particularly in the Balkans, remained unresolved.[78] After each conflict, there was no decisive victory, so neither Russia nor the Ottoman Empire felt like a clear "winner" or "loser." But something *did* occur during those ten conflicts over a two-hundred-year period: in each, the relative value of fighting changed, encouraging one or both sides to give up the fight. For a variety of reasons, the Ottomans or the Russians decided that the value of fighting *this particular fight* did not match the expectations held at the onset of the conflict.

As the Russo-Turkish wars emphasize, war is not a costly lottery. Russia and Turkey did not place a prewar bet on who would win a decisive victory. Instead, they chose to place an initial wager and then adjusted their investment as each conflict played out and the relative value of continuing to fight increased or decreased.[79] War still involves an element (sometimes a great deal) of chance, but a key mechanism driving the onset, evolution, and termination of conflict is information and credibility, not chance alone. Through the intentional or unintentional cultivation of reputations during conflict, the information and credibility that actors had before a war are necessarily altered, clarifying the power distribution between actors. War, then, is a means of revealing information that otherwise would stay private. War is useful for actors to strategically establish their credibility and then use it to reveal private information to attempt to alter the bargaining range.

Of course, actors may unintentionally reveal information they wish to keep private, ultimately harming their bargaining position. During a conflict, incomplete prewar information may be revealed in such a way that convinces an actor that they do not have a chance at beating their opponent. More likely, they may be convinced that while they have a shot at victory, the costs of securing such a victory would be prohibitive. This is information they would not have had access to in the prewar bargaining scenario, especially if their opponent had significant incentives to misrepresent key information (such as capabilities, tactics, resolve, and so forth). This is the logic underpinning strategies of attrition.[80] The Confederate States of America and Nazi Germany are examples of actors that were ultimately convinced, over the course of a conflict, that the costs of continued fighting were too high. The optimism that accompanied the South's declaration of war against the Union and Hitler's confident march across Europe was based on a prewar estimation that these actors had the capabilities and resolve to achieve their goals (in fact, early in these conflicts, their opponents were convinced that they were facing a difficult challenge). Neither Nazi Germany nor the Confederacy, however, went to war anticipating that their enemies would ultimately invade their homelands, killing thousands of civilians in addition to destroying the industries that made up their economies. As such, their adversaries calculated that Sherman's March to the Sea and the firebombing of Dresden would credibly reveal information that would encourage these actors to give up the fight. And not coincidentally, following both these devastating attacks, the Confederacy and Nazi Germany voluntarily capitulated. In both cases, the defeated parties sued for peace two to three months following the attacks. Most historians agree that these events were crucial in bringing these conflicts to a close, and it was the information they revealed about the value of continued conflict that led to updated beliefs about the costs and benefits of fighting. If you can't credibly reveal your capabilities and resolve in prewar bargaining, it would seem that burning the enemy's home to the ground is sufficient.

CREDIBLE COMMITMENTS AND ENDING THE GAME

Why did the South choose to end the war when it did? Presumably, Southern military and civilian leaders recognized the tide had turned against their war effort, maybe even as early as the loss at Gettysburg in 1863. The financial and logistical support that the South enjoyed early in the war had begun to dwindle further by the winter of 1864.[81] Southern military leaders had few illusions that they could beat back the Union invasion, let alone that the Confederacy would conquer significant Union territory in the North. Reiter argues that the Confederates continued to fight, even in the face of diminishing returns, because of a credible commitment problem.[82] The North simply could not (nor did it want to) commit to a postwar agreement that involved an autonomous South of any kind. This was a necessity for the South, as it was the whole point of secession. But even if the North had offered such an arrangement, it was not a credible agreement to the South, which feared that the North would renege in the future and resume the invasion. The South, in turn, was not able to credibly commit to such an agreement because the North feared that eventually the South would look to expand slave-holding territories and resume aggressions. Reiter therefore argues that the South only agreed to end the war when it received some assurances of continued independence for Southern states (through the federalist system).[83] Fighting the war and seeing the horrors of Sherman's march changed the South's perception of the wisdom of continued combat. But the primary credible commitment problem was solved by promising continued independence, leading to the end of the conflict.

In many cases, credible commitment problems seem to drive the continuation of fighting. While the revelation of capabilities and resolve during conflict can affect the value placed on fighting, states' inability to credibly commit to a course of action *after a conflict ends* may prevent governments from seeking peace, no matter the current costs. In other words, credible commitment problems may cause states to make desperate gambles today to avoid a worse fate tomorrow.[84]

For example, Reiter examines how the Korean War ebbed and flowed during its three-year history.[85] Despite early victories, by September 1950, UN forces (led by the United States) had been pushed back to the far southeastern corner of the Korean Peninsula, outside of the town of Pusan. The forces had been so soundly beaten that they were considering making a final retreat to the town itself, where they would literally be cornered, to await their ultimate destruction. This new information about the relative power distribution of each side should have convinced the United States and its allies to sue for peace. But the opposite happened. As Reiter points out, U.S. demands became even more intransigent, and the goals of the fighting were revised from returning the peninsula to the prewar status quo (half communist/half democratic) to conquering the entire peninsula.[86] The key mechanism that prolonged the conflict, according to Reiter, was a problem of credible commitment.[87] Despite being in an obvious position of weakness on the battlefield, the UN forces decided to further gamble on the conflict; the thought of a wholly communist Korean Peninsula was unacceptable because the communist forces could not credibly commit to restraint in the future (in particular, Western countries were concerned that a communist Korean Peninsula would serve as a springboard for communist expansion into Japan, the Philippines, and other Asian countries, consistent with the "domino theory" popular at the time). The result, therefore, was a revised set of goals for the United States that would eliminate the communist government (and its credible commitment problem) entirely.

In poker, the first hand is the only point in the game at which a player may know *nothing* about their adversary. But poker, like international relations, is an iterative process, where opponents develop reputations and learn about each other over time. This process influences the way players play the game and the likelihood that they will "walk away," even with a loss. Reputation and past behavior, then, are often strong predictors of how a player may subsequently behave. They can also provide insight into when players are likely to voluntarily exit a game. All players, like governments before war, start a game with confidence and optimism. But the outcome of several hands of poker can quickly change a player's perspective. The same is certainly true of actors in warfare: the realities of war can change the relative value of fighting for one's goals.

OFFENSE, DEFENSE, AND BLACKJACK

Finally, we turn to an issue in international bargaining that is closely linked with the way in which conflicts are actually fought on the battlefield. This issue concerns the relative advantage that actors have over each other, depending on whether they will be fighting on offense or defending their own territory. Playing offense or defense can dramatically affect the fortunes of war and thus may influence whether actors will actually choose conflict rather than seeking a negotiated agreement.

In all conflicts, specific characteristics of the conflict tend to favor either the initiator or the defender.[88] This is true of not only general strategic considerations but tactical considerations as well. Clausewitz similarly argues that in warfare, at any given moment, one side has the advantage over its opponent (though this advantage is not always recognized and is frequently miscalculated).[89] Ted Hopf defines a tactical advantage as the ability to seize a particular piece of an enemy's territory, while a strategic advantage is the ability to seize "as much of an enemy's territory as is necessary to destroy its military potential."[90] These two characteristics are obviously not the same, and there are cases in which an international actor may have the tactical advantage but be at a disadvantage strategically. This was most certainly the situation for Egypt, Syria, Jordan, and other Arab nations prior to the Six-Day War. They massed their armies on the border with Israel, giving them a major tactical advantage, but their advantage was undermined by a preemptive attack from Israel. Hopf further argues that the perception of having a tactical or strategic advantage over your opponent can significantly influence the probability that an actor will choose armed conflict.[91] From the bargaining perspective, we can think of these advantages as increasing the relative capabilities of one actor over another. By studying tactical and strategic advantages inherent in defensive and offensive postures, we may be better able to predict the onset of conflict.[92]

For instance, where a potential defender has both a strategic and a tactical advantage, conflict should be far less likely because of a "double disincentive" for the attacker (and those that choose to attack under such circumstances might be referred to as "doubly stupid").[93] Many war theorists have argued that a U.S. attack on mainland China would put the initiator at both a strategic and tactical disadvantage, especially since it would bring forces into the line of fire of China's land-based cruise and ballistic missile technology before the mainland could ever be reached.[94]

While each potential conflict will be different in terms of the relative advantages of the attacker or the defender, certain periods in history have alternately favored either offense or defense.[95] The determinants of whether an era is generally favorable toward offense or defense is driven largely by tactical and technological innovations. Many scholars agree that tactics and technologies used during World War I generally favored defenders, helping to explain the stalemate that occurred on the western front of that war.[96] Likewise, World War II is considered to have been fought when offensive technologies and tactics were dominant. Today, many consider warfare to be entering an era when defensive missile technologies, for instance, are far more affordable and strategically valuable than offensive power projection capabilities, such as traditional air assets.[97]

There are undeniable advantages in certain circumstances to being on offense and particularly to taking the initiative against an opponent. For instance, launching a "preemptive" strike against an opponent can offer considerable benefits, even if only in the short term. While Israel seemed to be at a major disadvantage tactically with the Egyptian forces preparing for war in 1967, its preemptive strike (perhaps hours before Egypt was set to begin its attack) gave Israel a short-term advantage.[98] Israel, wiping out most of the Egyptian air force as it sat on the runway, seized the upper hand in the conflict. This was also the logic of the Japanese attack on Pearl Harbor in 1941. The Japanese understood that they were at a strategic disadvantage and that by going on offense, they could shift the balance of power temporarily in their favor. The logic of the attack was undoubtedly to earn a short-term advantage over the United States, as the Japanese leadership wagered that knocking out the U.S. fleet at Pearl Harbor would provide a six-month window to shore up their defenses in the Pacific.[99]

Such an offensive strategy has been the crucial advantage for many states over time. Stephen Van Evera points out that if a preemptive strike shifts the balance of power from 1.5:1 in favor of the defender to a ratio of 1.5:1 in favor of the attacker, the advantage might not seem that significant.[100] This is probably doubly true in cases such as Pearl Harbor, where the shift in the balance of power is decidedly short term. However, if the attacker only needs, say, a 1.3:1 advantage, such a shift is very significant.[101] A preemptive strike, then, may be the only chance that some actors have to defeat their opponents.

Thus, there are undoubtedly circumstances under which offense can be advantageous and can shift the balance of power. However, as we have seen, such advantages are often fleeting. Much historical evidence suggests that war often favors the defender.[102] From the Persian invasions of Greece in the fifth century BCE to Soviet and American military adventures in the twentieth century, history is replete with examples of superior forces suffering at the hands of less powerful adversaries defending their own territory. War frequently favors the defender for several reasons. First, unseating an opponent from their own territory requires a great deal more resources than is required to defend that territory. The relative distance from the homeland and resource base makes the invasion of foreign territory primarily a logistical exercise. War theorists have recognized this for centuries. For instance, Clausewitz argued that attackers are at an inherent disadvantage because they are required to move and protect a long supply line into enemy territory, while the defender's resources are readily available.[103] These disadvantages are magnified as an attacker must travel greater distances to defeat their enemy.[104]

For a useful demonstration of why defense offers key advantages over offense, we turn to the game of blackjack. Perhaps the first thing that any novice blackjack player learns is that they are playing against "the house," which is represented by the dealer of the game. They also quickly learn that the house has a built-in advantage over the players at the table. Unlike poker, players are not opponents of one another; each hand is strictly a two-actor, zero-sum game between the player and the house/dealer. Few players, however, bother to learn about the actual advantage of the house. In a standard game of blackjack, where the dealer has six decks, and assuming that the player uses a perfect basic strategy (the kind that is available on any blackjack strategy card), it turns out the game is structured so the house has a 0.55 percent advantage. This means that for every two hundred hands of blackjack, the dealer can be expected to win one more hand than the player. While these sound like fairly good odds, it emphasizes that the dealer (that is, the one defending the house's money) ultimately has a long-term advantage to which many players succumb.

The house is able to maintain the advantage because blackjack is ultimately a sequence of moves, and the player moves first. This means that when the player comes up with a competitive hand, the burden is on the dealer to beat that hand. But when the player "busts" (by going over twenty-one), the dealer is required to do nothing. In other words, players can defeat themselves, and the dealer can sit back and watch. Similarly, an attacker that is forced to mobilize large amounts of resources and personnel and then move them deep into enemy territory may never get past the transportation phase. Forces on the attack, for instance, might get bogged down in difficult geographical terrain before ever reaching their enemy. The defender doesn't have to do anything but still "wins" the conflict.

The second reason the dealer maintains such an advantage is because, as the defender, they have access to greater amounts of resources. Since the dealer is playing with the house's money, the resources at their disposal are almost limitless, especially when compared to the limited resources of the average player. This means that while the house's advantage may only arise once every two hundred hands, the dealer can *afford* to play the full two hundred hands and reap that advantage. The average player, on the other hand, is likely only able to play a limited number of hands that may result in significant short-term gains or losses. As former Las Vegas casino owner Bob Stupak once said, even if the house has only a one-thousandth of one percent advantage, given enough time, "that one-thousandth of one percent will bust the richest man in the world."[105] Those playing defense can afford to wait out their opponents because they have more ready access to resources. This is why many blackjack strategists recommend "hit-and-run" strategies that seek to earn quick rewards without allowing the house to reap its long-term advantage.[106] By contrast, the attacker must not only mobilize resources but also transport them across enemy territories. And static resources that are of great help to defenders, such as infrastructure, military bases, and so forth, cannot be mobilized or used by an attacker in a forward deployment.

One final advantage favors the defender: the political salience of defense. Over the course of history, when one country has invaded another, public support for the invasion has often been mixed. But in almost all cases, the defender enjoys a great deal of public support. This is because the goal of *existence* is a much more popular goal than fighting foreign wars. The salience of this goal, therefore, determines the intensity with which such conflicts are fought.[107] This helps to explain why colonial wars, such as the French and American wars in Vietnam in the twentieth century, often dragged on longer than others. Those on offense had only marginal public support, especially when fighting for such nebulous concepts as democracy, capitalism, or empire.[108] But the defending population, fighting for concepts such as independence, autonomy, or even existence, have demonstrated much greater resolve. Ultimately, while short-run dynamics may often favor the attacker, defenders are far more likely to win as a conflict drags on.

While many scholars and war theorists have argued convincingly that the relative advantages of attackers and defenders should influence the likelihood of conflict, it is less clear how these advantages should alter the prospect for war termination. While Hopf argues, for instance, that offensive tactical advantages lead to shorter wars and defensive tactical advantages should result in longer wars, the empirical evidence for such an effect is mixed.[109] For instance, if World War I favored the defender (with trench warfare being the most prominent example) and World War II favored the attacker (for example, the Japanese attack at Pearl Harbor), why did these two major conflicts last roughly the same amount of time? If the relative advantage of offense and defense is so important for how a conflict ends, why do we not see significant variations in war duration across those two conflicts? In short, there does not seem to be much of a connection between offensive/defensive advantages and how a war ends, unless those advantages somehow influence the information and credibility problems identified in the previous section. Most wars, as we have seen, do not involve the complete and total victory of one side over another, as might be expected if one side enjoys a clear strategic or tactical advantage.

CONCLUSION

This chapter has explored what happens when the guns start firing. The main conclusion is that the political process during war looks very similar to the political process that led to war in the first place. Even in the nineteenth century, Clausewitz recognized that the process that ultimately resulted in war was not fundamentally different from the process that occurred during the war or during repeated confrontations between states. The only real difference is that in the lead-up to conflict, actors are making educated guesses about the true capabilities and resolve of their opponents. Once war begins and armies meet on the battlefield, however, more information is revealed about these characteristics. Actors learn much more about their opponents (and often learn something about themselves as well). Further, as actors repeatedly engage each other over time, they intentionally and unintentionally begin to develop reputations that, in turn, influence their future interactions and the decisions that they make. Reputations influence future credibility and the ability to commit to agreements, as well as the general level of trust between actors.

This chapter has illustrated how the concepts of observed bargaining and conflict behavior, credibility, and reputation are inextricably linked. They are linked, most importantly, because international relations is an iterative process. Most governments, leaders, and political organizations play multiple rounds against each other. As we have seen, however, research and policymaking have not always treated conflict in such a holistic way and have instead considered conflict as the "end" of the bargaining process.

Understanding international bargaining and conflict from a holistic perspective is much more useful in developing policy solutions that might mitigate the probability and intensity of conflict. In particular, by facilitating more information about states' true intentions and preferences, we may be able to reduce the likelihood of conflict while increasing the chance that current conflicts can be ended. This is indeed the logic behind creating international organizations that facilitate information intended to reduce uncertainty about adversaries' capabilities and resolve among their members. But even with additional information, credibility problems can remain as a barrier to peace.[110] Even if actors agree today, fear of defection from an agreement in the future can preclude the resolution of issues and may intensify the nature of conflict. Mechanisms that enhance the future credibility of actors, such as third-party verification, monitoring, and "naming and shaming," can all potentially reduce this source of conflict.[111] Although increasing information and credibility between actors should reduce the likelihood of conflict, such efforts may not work equally across all actors and issues. Two actors may respond quite differently to the same information, a subject we examine in the next chapter.

Chapter Four	# Mistakes, Misperceptions, and Losing the Hand

All war is a symptom of man's failure as a thinking animal.
—John Steinbeck

In the preceding chapter, we considered why people defending their own territories are often successful. Many colonial wars throughout history demonstrated the remarkable ability of smaller, less well-equipped forces to successfully protect their homelands from more capable invading armies. The biggest military defeats in the history of Great Britain, for instance, occurred in far-off places such as America, Africa, and Asia against forces that were inferior to Britain's military might.[1] We have examined tactical reasons why defense is often more advantageous than offense, as defending armies have more immediate access to resources that don't have to be moved across large swathes of territory. But there is a simpler reason fortune often favors the defender. Studies in the natural sciences have shown that animals fight the hardest, often to the death, when they are trying to prevent losses.[2] When they are fighting to achieve gains, they do not fight as vigorously. There appears to be a base instinct common to all animals, including human beings, that causes them to weight losses more heavily than gains. This may be the main reason defending armies often achieve improbable victories: their resolve is usually much higher than that of their invading enemy. Human beings simply hate to lose. Regarding those who claim they only play for fun and don't care if they win or lose, professional gambler Frank Scoblete says, "People who spout this line of propaganda have never watched their own faces as they lose bet after bet. . . . I have yet to *see* a person who is losing *look* happy about it. . . . Losing is not fun, period. Winning is fun."[3]

In this chapter, we consider the possibility that human beings do not always behave as perfectly rational individuals in the economic sense of the term.[4] If people are perfectly rational, they should value a piece of territory equally, regardless of whether that territory is gained or lost. Instead, human beings often place differing values on the same issue, depending on their specific circumstances. India, for instance, probably places a higher value on maintaining its current territory in the Kashmir region than Pakistan places on gaining new territory in the region at India's expense. The reverse is likely also true.

The image of a gambler down on his luck pushing his remaining chips toward the dealer for one final hand is a familiar one. Counterintuitively, many gamblers will bet more aggressively, even with objectively weak hands, when they are further in the "hole." At the exact moment when it would be prudent to conserve their resources, gamblers often act increasingly reckless. In gambling parlance, this behavior, known as "going on tilt", is described as "betting stupidly, and big, in an heroic, but idiotic, attempt to get back [the player's] losses."[5] The game of craps seems to result in players going on tilt more frequently than any other casino game, including poker.[6] Conversely, it is common to observe a gambler who is on a hot streak, winning hand after hand, abruptly walking away from the table. The purpose of walking away is to conserve the winnings that one has earned. But with significant winnings, players can actually *afford* to take more risks, though they frequently choose not to do so. History is full of examples of military commanders who, after winning important battles against their opponents, failed to follow up and deliver the critical blow. Some consider that the Union had an opportunity to end the Civil War earlier by routing Gen. Robert E. Lee's army after the Battle of Gettysburg.[7]

Gen. George Meade, however, allowed Lee to escape across the border to Virginia, and the war continued for two more years. At the exact moment when Meade had the upper hand against the Confederacy, he seems to have become more conservative, seeking to avoid further risks.

How do we explain these seeming contradictions—that actors might value an issue more when they are down on their luck and place comparatively less weight on the same issue when they are in a good position? Until now, we have considered conflict—including its outbreak, development, and termination—with the basic assumption that states and/or decisionmakers are rational actors. That is, we have assumed that international actors weigh the costs and benefits of each possible action and then select the course of action that offers the highest net value or the highest expected utility. But "throwing good money after bad," as the down-on-his-luck gambler is likely to do, rarely offers the highest expected utility.

In this chapter, we relax the assumption that actors are perfectly rational. Although the assumption of rationality has provided important insights into human behavior, including international conflict behavior, it is limited in its explanatory power. An approach known as *prospect theory* offers an alternative to the basic assumption of perfect economic rationality.[8] This theoretical framework will allow us to look more closely at the often puzzling decisions made by policymakers, particularly in such high-stakes circumstances as international negotiations and violent conflict. Prospect theory does not necessarily undermine the insights we have already examined.[9] Bargaining breakdowns, which occur because actors are uncertain about the true balance of power or the resolve of other actors, still represent the immediate source of all conflict. But prospect theory offers a more nuanced understanding of how this uncertainty may be generated. It offers a wealth of information on why actors make biased decisions, and bargaining theory explains how these decisions may ultimately contribute to conflict. In chapter six, we discuss whether these two approaches are compatible, but for now, we focus our attention on prospect theory.

Importantly, prospect theory does not explain personality quirks. In other words, it doesn't explain someone "throwing good money after bad" by just categorizing that individual as risk acceptant. Instead, it explains behavior as a result of the *context* in which actors operate rather than the idiosyncrasies of the actors themselves. Context can have a dramatic influence on how an actor views the world, and vice versa.

This chapter examines a range of implications, including how context influences perceptions and how these perceptions ultimately influence human behavior. First, we will briefly examine the history and purpose of prospect theory and the types of incongruous behavior that it helps explain. We will focus on the role of losses and potential losses in the decisionmaking calculus of states and leaders, and we will examine why such losses are weighted more heavily than comparable gains. We will then consider a range of biases that occur because of the overweighting of losses, and how this is likely to influence outcomes, including the probability of conflict. Finally, we will discuss how some specific biases, including the attribution of intention and initial bias, can dramatically influence relationships between states.

THE PROBLEM WITH EXPECTED UTILITY

The discussions in this book so far have relied on the framework of rational choice theory. Rational choice and its most common version, expected utility theory, have been used for centuries as methods of explaining human decisionmaking in all areas of life, including both war and gambling. In fact, the approach was developed in the eighteenth century by French mathematicians as a way to understand (and win) games of chance. French noblemen asked the mathematicians to analyze various forms of gambling and come up with the most effective strategies. This pursuit led to a great deal of trial and error, and the basics of what we know as rational choice theory were born, focusing on how individuals can use information about probabilities and costs and benefits to make decisions that maximize their utility.[10] Assuming that actors are rational offers a number of advantages, even though rational choice, like any theory, involves abstracting from reality to better understand some phenomenon of interest. In this case, rational choice theory has offered a better understanding of human decisionmaking despite its limitations.[11]

A basic assumption of rationality, for instance, has helped scholars explain the decision to use terrorism. Without the assumption that terrorists are economically rational individuals (that is, they seek to maximize their utilities), we might conclude that terrorists are simply irrational, "crazy" individuals. But operating from the assumption that terrorists are economically rational individuals—that they have "well-ordered preference rankings" and they employ strategies to achieve their preferred goals—we see how even terrorism can be a rational strategy.[12] Importantly, the term rationality refers to strategies, not goals. So even if their goals appear crazy or unattainable, terrorists are not necessarily irrational. The only thing that matters in understanding terrorist behavior is whether their strategies are logical choices in the pursuit of their goals. Studies show that terrorism is often a last resort for individuals and organizations that initially sought to achieve their goals in other ways, suggesting that terrorists weigh the expected utilities of their actions.[13] Considering human behavior from a rational choice perspective has therefore given us quite a bit of leverage in understanding even extreme behavior such as terrorism. Understanding how terrorists make decisions and why they choose certain targets, methods, tactics, and strategies over others has led to important insights that have bolstered counterterrorism efforts.

Similarly, assuming the rationality of one's opponent in a game of poker is a useful approach that has been responsible for many of the basic insights in poker theory. Assuming that an opponent has very limited goals—winning the current hand and/or winning as many hands as possible—offers the insight that there are limited (and partially predictable) strategies that the opponent can employ in pursuit of those goals. This makes strategizing against opponents more straightforward than it would otherwise be. Strategizing against opponents in international relations, by comparison, is much more difficult because actors can have a wide variety of goals and strategies to achieve them.[14] Nevertheless, assuming the basic rationality of state and nonstate actors has produced the kind of insights about bargaining and conflict that we examined in previous chapters.[15]

But the strength of the approach is also its key weakness. Rational choice theory implicitly assumes that actors have sufficient information to make informed decisions and select the correct option, even though the theory is about making decisions under conditions of uncertainty.[16] In fact, the most popular form of rational choice theory is referred to as expected utility theory because it assumes that actors are capable of correctly weighing the expected utility of every possible option and selecting the decision that offers them the highest possible utility. To make such informed decisions implies that the actor is, in fact, fully informed. In other words, the actor must have enough information about various options and their relative costs and benefits to be able to make the correct decision. Jack Levy contrasts this with situations of complete uncertainty (the actor has no information) and of perfect certainty.[17] Expected utility theory assumes that actors deal with risk (an action may or may not produce the desired result) by assigning probabilities to certain outcomes, assigning payoffs to each outcome, and calculating which action produces the most beneficial result. It therefore assumes not only that human beings have the information necessary to compare each option and its associated probabilities and payoffs, but also that the human brain can process all this information in an unbiased manner. Expected utility theory assumes that decision-makers have enough information to make the correct decision and that they don't make mistakes.

These rather large assumptions are the focus of most criticism of the rational choice approach. The assumption that human beings face no impediments in calculating expected utilities and that they always make the perfectly logical, unbiased choice is simply too large for many scholars who have sought to understand human decisionmaking.[18] As Daniel Kahneman, Amos Tversky, and others have argued, human beings are not perfectly rational because our cognitive processes limit our ability to properly process information.[19] Instead, we make decisions through a variety of cognitive shortcuts that often represent a departure from rational behavior.[20] Rational choice theory assumes that not only do human beings have sufficient information to make the appropriate decision, but that they also have unlimited time in which to weigh the options. The reality, particularly in high-stakes scenarios such as gambling and international relations, is that humans often work under much greater informational and time constraints. The approach also assumes that there are no processing limitations *within the mind* of those making decisions. Even with access to the greatest amount of information and with sufficient time, humans often make decisions based on subjective things such as past experience and fears.[21] Sometimes, in fact, decisions must be made based *only* on this kind of subjective information. In situations where available information is severely limited, the only thing a decisionmaker may have to inform their decision is their own experience, or "gut instinct."

Even with access to perfectly objective information, though, decisionmakers often choose options based on similar decisions and outcomes that have occurred in the past, whether or not such comparisons are warranted or even useful.[22] This is one reason first-time encounters between players often do not conform to standard expectations of behavior and why the outcomes are often different from the outcomes of repeated games.[23] When players have had prior interactions, they have more information about their opponents, but ironically, they may also develop more significant biases in their decisionmaking process (we examine the consequences of such biases later in this chapter). The events of 9/11, for instance, resulted in unprecedented behavior by the U.S. government, from foreign military adventures to dramatic changes in domestic political institutions, on the basis that the event itself was unprecedented. Although the United States had been the target of terrorist attacks for decades, the intensity and nature of the attack were seen as an entirely new game with an entirely new enemy.[24] Because of this perception, the United States did not respond to the event in the same way it had to other attacks in the past.

If the inability to account for subjective and biased interpretations of information is a major criticism of expected utility theory, another point of contention may be even more troubling for the approach. The problem is most apparent when viewed in the context of gambling behavior by individuals. Daniel Bernoulli, considered the father of modern expected utility theory, noted that people do not always base their decisions on the absolute expected value of the payoffs of their options.[25] They frequently take into consideration the likelihood of actually achieving each payoff. This led to the insight that human beings often seek to maximize their overall utility rather than simply pursuing their highest expected payoff. The bargaining approach that we explored in the first few chapters is based largely on this understanding. When threatening violence to achieve their goals, states don't consider only the expected costs and benefits of conflict; they must also take into consideration the likelihood of actually winning a conflict (which, in turn, is based on their own capabilities and resolve).[26]

The main implication of assuming that human beings try to maximize their utilities is that, for the most part, we should observe people avoiding gambles with large payoffs when the *probabilities* of those payoffs are small. However, this is wholly inconsistent with the popularity of some games of chance, such as state lotteries, where the payoffs are disproportionately large and the probabilities of winning are disproportionately small.[27] Even so, proponents of expected utility theory developed a solution to this inconsistency by categorizing those willing to play such games as risk acceptant.[28] A risk-acceptant individual has a convex utility function, meaning that the individual derives increasing marginal utility as the potential payoff increases. But if we assume that an individual is risk acceptant, how do we square their willingness to gamble with the propensity to buy insurance? The purchase of insurance involves the exact opposite logic as gambling on a lottery. Individuals spend small amounts of money on insurance in an effort to avoid catastrophic losses that occur with low probabilities. Expected utility theory has a built-in explanation for this, by assuming an individual that buys insurance is risk averse. But expected utility theory cannot reconcile these two ideas. In other words, it can explain risk-averse and risk-acceptant behavior, but *not by the same individual*.[29]

Another simple illustration from gambling emphasizes this paradox.[30] Imagine a game of high-stakes poker between two sophisticated professional poker players who are equally matched in skill, disposition, and so forth. After one round of play, they are even equal in the amount of money that they have in their coffers; they both have $300,000 at their disposal. However, when they began playing, Player A had $100,000, while Player B started off with $500,000. The important question is, "Are they equally happy?"[31] Even though they currently have the same amount of money, are their expected utilities for winning really the same? The answer is no, and this gives us more insight on why actors, including international decisionmakers, make the decisions that they do.

PROSPECT THEORY

The insights from expected utility theory, while useful, must be further conditioned. While the theory is a useful abstraction that helps us understand limited issues related to human decisionmaking, expected utility offers "no way to represent the fact that the disutility of losing $500 could be greater than the utility of winning the same amount."[32] The preceding examples also suggest that not everyone will find the same utility in winnings and that the amount of utility they place on such matters depends greatly on the context in which they are operating. The reason two individuals might not place the same value on, say, $100,000 is not their own idiosyncrasies. In fact, the insight here is that two very different people placed in the same context would likely make *the same decision*. Instead, the focus is on the context and the exogenous endowments that actors have prior to being faced with a decision. This is not the same as categorizing people as risk acceptant or risk averse but instead focuses on some fundamental tendencies of *all human behavior*.

Prospect theory, developed in an effort to address many of the perceived shortcomings of expected utility theory, is responsible for these insights about human beings reacting differently under different circumstances. Instead of objective outcomes, prospect theory views all outcomes as either gains or losses given some "reference point" and then determines the likely decisions that human beings will make based on this information.[33] Prospect theory offers a theoretical framework to explain decisionmaking and takes into account, above all, human beings' natural aversion to losses. This aversion is summed up in a general principle for poker players: "When one alternative will have slightly bad consequences if it's wrong and another second alternative will have terrible consequences if it's wrong, you may be right to choose the first alternative even when the second is slightly favored to be the correct play."[34] In other words, this kind of conventional wisdom demonstrates that the best play is not always the best play. The best play is often the *least bad* play.

Whereas expected utility theory requires that we only know the static state of wealth for an individual, prospect theory requires that we also know the reference point—outcomes that are improvements over the reference point for an individual are considered gains, and those below the reference point are considered losses. The central prediction generated by prospect theory is that people tend to become more risk acceptant when they are in a bad position.[35] When an actor has already lost a great deal, they are likely to make worse decisions (that is, decisions that do not conform to expectations of rationality). This is the logic behind the phrase "throwing good money after bad," as a gambler suffering significant losses may unwisely spend quite a bit of money to salvage their position. In fact, one "system" of gambling, designed to improve a player's standing in the long run at any game, operates on this principle. The d'Alembert system is a simple strategy that requires the gambler to increase their bets after every loss and decrease their bets after every win.[36]

Recall that prospect theory makes no attempt to explain behavior based on personalities but focuses exclusively on the context. Accordingly, the same actor in two different situations is likely to behave differently, even when facing the same objective probabilities and payoffs. Figure 4-1 depicts the logic of how actors weight losses and gains relative to one another.[37] This famous visual depiction of prospect theory is known as the *S* curve. On the *x* axis is the outcome in terms of losses or gains. So for a gambler, we might have losses in increments of $100 on the left-hand side of the graph and comparable gains on the right-hand side. The *y* axis indicates the psychological value attached to each outcome, with points at the very top of the graph representing highly positive values and points on the very bottom of the graph representing highly negative values.

Figure 4-1
The Value of Losses and Gains in Prospect Theory

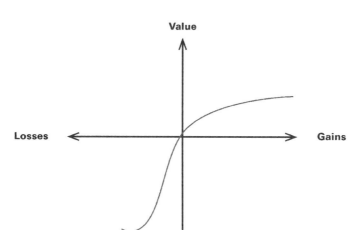

The most basic information that can be gleaned from the graph is that an individual places negative psychological value on losses and positive psychological values on wins. The *S* shape of the graph also indicates diminishing sensitivity for gains and losses. This captures the fact that losing the first $100 often leads to a steeper decrease in psychological value than losing $100 when the player has already lost, say, $1,000. Similarly, winning $100 when you have nothing increases your psychological value at a faster rate than winning $100 when you already have $1,000. Finally, the curve is not symmetrical—the steeper slope in the bottom left quadrant indicates a greater sensitivity to losses than comparable gains. The behavior of human beings, like that of other animals, is influenced more by the prospect of losses than gains.

The *S* curve does a nice job of capturing some of the key assumptions of prospect theory. But what are the implications beyond the observation that people don't like to lose? One important implication is that people prefer a "sure-thing" gain to a chance of winning a large sum. Recall the example of bluffing strategies that we considered in chapter two. In that scenario, two players are making their final wager before the final card on the table is revealed. The pot is currently at $120.

Remember also that if Player A never bluffs and Player B never calls, then Player A would bust eight times and win just twice, for an average of $24 per hand. If instead Player B called every time, Player A would win, on average, $48 per hand. So the system of never bluffing would produce an average of $36 per hand.

The important information here is the potential gains and losses for each player. While always bluffing produces the highest potential payoff ($120 per hand), it also holds the risk of the greatest losses ($48 per hand). Given that the 1:2 bluffing strategy guarantees the player $36 per hand, which strategy should they choose? The optimal strategy is considered optimal not because it returns the highest potential gains but because it offers the highest possible gains while avoiding significant losses. On average, we would expect that an individual given these options would likely choose the sure-fire $36 per hand rather than risk the $48 loss per hand. But prospect theory suggests that we must also know how the player was faring in previous hands. If Player A has suffered a series of significant losses already, they might be more likely to choose the option that holds the possibility of a gain of $120 per hand, despite the risk of enormous losses.

A more straightforward example is worth considering here.[38] Imagine that we give players the option of playing a game of poker or simply splitting a fixed amount of money. As we have seen, the reason

Table 4-1
Bluffing Strategies Revisited

Player A Bluffs	Player B Calls		
	Never	50%	Always
Always	$120	$36	–$48
2:1	$72	$36	$0
1:1	$48	$36	$24
1:2	$36	$36	$36
Never	$24	$36	$48

players often decide to play a game of chance, and the reason states often fight wars, is that they cannot amicably agree on a way to split up an existing amount of money or territory. Should it be 50/50, 70/30, or should the players think of some other way of dividing up the goods? In many cases, particularly greedy actors may go for an all-or-nothing approach. But instead of offering the chance to divide the goods through conflict (or a game), the players are given the following two options: option A, in which each player is given $50 to bet, with the caveat that they *must bet the entire $50 on a single hand*, or option B, in which each player is given $50 and they do not play the game, which would they choose? With the structure of the game changed so that the amicable division of wealth is *guaranteed,* the likely outcome also changes. Since the bet is all or nothing, each player has the chance to win a total of $100. This is twice as much as they would expect from option B, but option A also holds the possibility of ending up with absolutely nothing. Given that possibility, being assured of $50 starts to sound like the better option. An important implication for human behavior is that ending up with nothing is a particularly unattractive option when there are *certain* ways of gaining something, even if the gain is relatively negligible. While the chance of winning $100 sounds good, the worst outcome is coming up empty handed, and human beings, under most circumstances, will choose the sure-fire reward of $50. While the $50 is unlikely to change an individual's wealth significantly, it highlights the fact that human beings "just like winning and dislike losing."[39]

The additional implications for human behavior, and for decision-making in international relations, are fairly significant. Since people attach unusual weight to negative events over positive events, even minor negative events can overshadow the most positive of events, yet the reverse is rarely true. As one psychology study explains it, a single cockroach in a bowl of cherries will completely disgust most human beings, and they will not be interested in eating the cherries. On the other hand, a single cherry in a bowl of cockroaches does not improve one's impression of it.[40] Similarly, the human mind responds more quickly to words and concepts that connote something negative than ones that connote positive images. Loaded words such as *terrorism* and *war* are likely to attract more attention than the words *cooperation* and *peace*.[41] No doubt, this peculiarity of human thinking is understood well by those in the journalism business.

Researchers have gone so far as to estimate a "loss aversion ratio," which expresses how much an individual must gain to balance the possibility of a loss. Through a series of experiments, researchers determined that the average person has a loss aversion ratio in the range of 1.5 to 2.5.[42] In other words, if you offered the average person a gamble that involves the possibility of losing $100, most people would need the gamble to also involve a chance of winning $150 to $250 to consider the bet worthwhile. In general, though, most people need some added incentive to place a wager, and unlike the implications of expected utility theory, most people are not indifferent to an equal loss and gain.

THE ENDOWMENT EFFECT AND OFFENSE-DEFENSE

If human beings are generally averse to losses, and if they prefer sure bets to risky gambles, it logically follows that they should be particularly attached to the *things they already possess*. In other words, human beings place greater value on the resources they already own than on equally valuable resources they do not own. This is known as the endowment effect, and it is one of the most important implications of prospect theory. And it is another explanation for why fighting an offensive war is riskier than fighting a defensive one.

The endowment effect was identified by Richard Thaler, who observed that one of his professors in graduate school often behaved contrary to what expected utility theory would predict.[43] What made the observation all the more interesting was that his professor was a conservative economist in one of the most conservative economic departments in the country (in other words, someone who subscribed wholeheartedly to classic economic theory, including expected utility). Thaler observed that the professor, who was a wine connoisseur, would rarely sell a bottle from his own collection. In fact, he would frequently buy bottles of wine that were $35 or less but would not sell a bottle from his collection unless it was worth $100 or more. There was a disconnect, therefore, between his maximum buying price ($35) and his minimum selling price ($100), which is not how a classic economist should behave. Expected utility theory would predict that he should always be willing to sell and buy at the same prices, presuming that the bottles were in fact valued correctly. But being so averse to selling his own bottles unless they were particularly valuable indicated to Thaler that ownership of the bottle increased its value for the professor. In other words, while the professor might buy a bottle for $20, he would refuse to sell the same bottle if it was in his possession.

Experimental evidence also supports the existence of an endowment effect.[44] In one experiment, participants were given tokens and were allowed to trade them as if in a stock market (the tokens could be redeemed for cash at the end of the experiment).[45] The trades mostly conformed to expected utility theory. But in another version of the experiment, half of the participants were randomly chosen to receive a coffee mug at the beginning of the experiment. The mugs were attractive gifts bearing the insignia of the participants' university. Participants were asked to estimate their selling price for the mug, and those without mugs were asked to write down how much they would pay for the mug. The average selling price was nearly twice the average buying price. Human beings simply do not want to give up what they already own.[46]

We have noted that human beings and animals demonstrate greater enthusiasm and resolve when defending their own territory and possessions than they do when seeking to acquire someone else's possessions. We might therefore expect the endowment effect to influence the kind of bargaining scenarios laid out in chapter one. Recall that with two states bargaining over some divisible good, their bargaining range is determined by their capabilities and their resolve. The endowment effect can be expected to primarily influence their resolve (that is, how important the matter is to them). Bargaining over something already in one's possession should result in a smaller bargaining range than bargaining over something that neither side currently "owns."

Let's consider both of these potential scenarios. Imagine first that two states are bargaining over a piece of territory that neither of them currently possesses. For instance, a topic of growing importance to the international community is control of the Arctic regions and the natural resources there. In addition to the resources, the Arctic is considered to be of direct strategic significance to the United States, Canada, Russia, Norway, and Denmark.[47] But despite the importance of the Arctic to these countries' futures, there is no single treaty governing its management, leading to an increasingly salient bargaining game between many of the world's most powerful countries.[48] Figure 4-2 depicts this generic scenario. Two states are bargaining over a divisible good, and they have some given capabilities and resolve, which ultimately determine the bargaining range—the set of bargains short of war acceptable to both sides. The bargaining range is the area between the two lines in the figure (refer to chapter one for a more in-depth discussion of these principles).

But what happens when two states are bargaining over territory that one of the states already controls (at least partially)? For instance, think about the bargaining that has occurred between Israel and its neighbors over territory that was ceded to Israel during the Six-Day War. Syria would like to resume control over the Golan Heights, and Jordan would have preferred to receive the territory it lost in the West Bank. But after the Six-Day War, bargaining over these territories meant explicitly negotiating over areas that were controlled, albeit unofficially, by one of the states in the negotiations. Israel, having newly acquired the territory, demonstrated an immediate attachment to the areas and seemed particularly averse to losing the territory to its enemies.[49] This scenario is much more complicated than that in the Arctic, precisely because Israel and its neighbors are negotiating over *current* endowments. According to prospect theory, a state like Israel should be particularly averse to giving up the territory, even if it were offered territory of comparable value elsewhere.

Figure 4-3 shows the likely change in the bargaining range compared to the previous scenario. Since the endowment effect gives the territory added importance and value in the mind of its current owner,

Figure 4-2
Bargaining over Unclaimed Territory

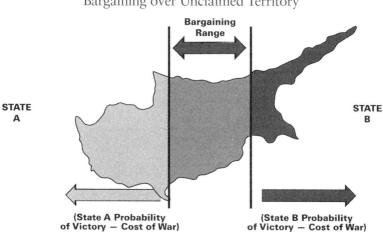

Figure 4-3
Bargaining over Territory Controlled by One Side

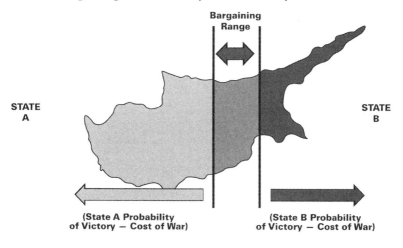

their resolve is likely to be particularly high over the issue. This lowers the overall costs of an expected conflict for that side and shrinks the bargaining range relative to the first scenario. As a result, there are fewer acceptable bargains for both states short of war, and the overall probability of conflict is higher. Comparing the two scenarios offers hope for cooperation in areas like the Arctic but may justify some of the pessimism about cooperation in areas like the Golan Heights.

One extension of the endowment effect is that actors may also place higher value on endeavors in which they have already invested quite heavily. In other words, if an actor invests a large amount of money in the stock market or some other financial investment, they may place greater value on that particular investment, even compared to earning the same amount from some other source. If this is true, the aversion to losses may produce the phenomenon known as "attachment to investment."[50] Actors may be averse to losing their initial investments and may value recouping that investment above all else.

What kind of behavior are we likely to see in someone who has already invested heavily in a single endeavor? Prospect theory argues that human beings are generally averse to losses, and their proclivity to take risks depends on the relative losses and gains they are facing at any given moment (that is, we must understand their reference point). Facing the possibility of significant losses, someone who is attached to their investments (having technically already "lost" the money) is more likely to engage in further risk-taking and "loss-chasing" behavior.[51] These are the individuals who may throw good money after bad if their investment looks as though it may be lost. This is the exact logic of prospect theory, which argues that those who have already suffered great losses will accept greater levels of risk because they are attached to the investments they have already made and wish to avoid further losses.[52]

Two specific types of actors are often required to invest a great deal of capital and are likely, at any given moment, to face the possibility of significant losses: entrepreneurs and military leaders.[53] Because of the nature of their positions, they are likely to engage in particularly risk-acceptant behavior. Success in business or warfare often requires investment of substantial amounts of money, resources, and—in the case of military leaders—human lives. Further, business and war are frequently marked by downturns in fortune (which is why it is beneficial to be "thick-skinned" in these professions). Entrepreneurs and military leaders, in other words, often are in situations where, having already invested heavily and operating in a domain of losses, they choose to accept greater levels of risk. Their reference point ultimately determines their course of action.

There are many examples of decisionmakers who, when faced with great losses, willingly accepted greater risk in their foreign policy decisions. This is frequently referred to as "gambling for resurrection," and it occurs most often in the middle of ongoing conflicts.[54] In fact, Hein Goemans suggests that certain types of states are particularly likely to gamble for resurrection, and his theory owes a debt to prospect theory (although he does not explicitly acknowledge this).[55] He argues that moderately repressive regimes are the most likely to engage in risk-taking behavior when the cards are not in their favor, because they face the greatest potential for punishment at home. Fully authoritarian regimes face no serious punishment at home because they have a firm grasp on power. And democracies offer peaceful leadership transitions, even if a leader performs incompetently in war and foreign policy. But not only do moderately authoritarian regimes, according to Goemans, face threats at home (because they do not have complete control domestically), but their leaders are also likely to face severe punishments, including torture and execution, if they are overthrown.[56] To avoid such a fate, he argues that these leaders will accept greater levels of risk in warfare. This process is based on the logic of prospect theory because it suggests that the leaders facing the greatest potential losses (particularly of their own lives) are the ones who will engage in the riskiest behavior. This argument is illustrated by Germany's perplexing decision to continue fighting World War I in 1916–17. While many have suggested that Germany was in a good position to sue for peace after winning millions of square miles of territory in the east, Goemans argues that Germany's leaders faced a significant potential for punishment at home because of their failure to secure territorial gains in the west.[57] This failure, and the perceived threat it posed to their power, led Germany to increase its war aims (that is, increase its risk) precisely when it was in a position to negotiate a victorious peace.

Iran's foreign policy decisions with respect to the Yemeni civil war in 2015 are another illustration of how attachment to investment and aversion to losses can help explain counterintuitive decisionmaking. During the early part of 2015, Iran faced a series of real and potential losses in foreign policy; it was deeply involved in negotiations with the West over its alleged nuclear program, for which it had been sanctioned. As a result, Iran's economy had been declining for years,[58] and a serious downturn in oil prices during 2015 only compounded the economic woes.[59] In addition, the Syrian civil war and ISIL threatened to topple Iran's two most important allies in the Middle East, the governments of Syria and Iraq.

Facing some of the most serious foreign policy losses in the nearly forty-year history of the regime, Iran took unprecedented steps to insert itself into the Yemeni civil war. By all accounts, if Iran were operating from a purely rational position, it would expect little utility from involving itself in another regional conflict. Not only was military involvement prohibitive in terms of direct costs, but entering the Yemeni civil war also threatened to antagonize two of Iran's most hated rivals, Saudi Arabia and the United States. But instead of avoiding another foreign entanglement, Iran made numerous efforts to supply the Houthi insurgency in Yemen with resources, manpower, and weapons. Allegedly, Iran made multiple attempts to bring in loads of weapons by air and sea, in spite of Saudi warnings that doing so would expand the conflict to a regional war.[60] Iran also apparently attempted to bring in the weapons on a merchant vessel in one of the tensest moments of the conflict, as the United States dispatched an aircraft carrier and a destroyer to intercept the ship.

In short, involving itself in the Yemeni conflict risked pulling the Iranian regime into a massive conflict at a moment when it was least able to fight such a conflict. But like a gambler reeling from a series of bad hands, the Iranian government may have been desperately looking to shore up its allies in the region (the Houthis) precisely because it was losing on other fronts. In this way, the Iranian decision seems less puzzling and fits with the process of decisionmaking outlined in prospect theory. Acquiring a Shia-dominated ally in Yemen may have been a way to salvage its potential losses elsewhere.

WINNING, LOSING, AND U.S. PRESIDENTIAL DECISIONS

Examples of U.S. foreign policy decisions during the twentieth century further emphasize the important role that reference points play in the decisionmaking process. In one of the few comprehensive studies of foreign policy to explicitly examine decisions through the lens of prospect theory, Rose McDermott analyzes a series of seemingly counterintuitive decisions made by U.S. presidents.[61] She selects scenarios in which the decisions made were contrary to what we would expect based on the logic of expected utility theory. McDermott focuses on prospect theory as an explanatory tool and stresses that the idiosyncrasies of each president or administration are not satisfactory explanations for the decisions that they ultimately made. She notes that "risk-taking behavior is based not on the individual predispositions of a particular leader, but evolves out of a cognitive response to a situation that constrains the way options are interpreted and choice is made."[62] If risk taking were simply a function of one's individual personality traits, we would expect some presidents to always make risky decisions, while others would always be more cautious. But examining the individual does not provide sufficient evidence to explain their behavior, because McDermott selects cases in which the *same* president alternately made conservative and risky decisions. It is therefore something about the context in which the leaders operate, she concludes, that helps explain their decisions.[63] And notably, changing contexts explain why a single president's propensity for taking risks may vary over time.

McDermott examines both risk-acceptant and risk-averse behavior by two U.S. presidents—Dwight D. Eisenhower and Jimmy Carter. For Eisenhower, McDermott argues that perhaps the riskiest foreign policy decision of his tenure was his decision to deny the existence of the U.S. spy plane program after the Soviet Union downed a U-2 spy plane and captured its pilot, Gary Powers.[64] Why was the decision to deny the program so risky? If Eisenhower publicly lied about the program (which he ultimately did), keeping up the facade in light of Soviet allegations would involve substantial risk. This required him to lie to the American public, as he repeatedly called the allegations false and made the long-standing argument that only the Soviet Union engaged in spying. Eisenhower's decision may have seemed fairly straightforward, but it held the possibility of the greatest backlash from the public and even of direct armed conflict with the Soviet Union. McDermott concludes that it was by far the riskiest of the options available to the president.[65] But the Eisenhower administration nonetheless decided to accept the risk, claiming that the alleged spy plane was in fact a weather balloon that had strayed into Soviet airspace. Ultimately, the ruse was exposed and Eisenhower suffered on all fronts: not only was the program revealed to the public, but he also had to admit the program's existence to the Soviet Union.[66]

On the other hand, during the 1956 Suez crisis, Eisenhower surprised many when he chose not to back the British, French, and Israelis during the conflict and even demanded their withdrawal.[67] This decision, arguably a very conservative and risk-averse decision, seems even more surprising in retrospect. Eisenhower's decision to remain neutral was ostensibly driven by his desire to avoid conflict with the Soviet Union as well as to avoid being seen as imperialist in the developing world as the Cold War ramped up.[68] But many have argued that, at least in 1956, the United States was still largely seen as the world's sole superpower. The Eisenhower administration was therefore in a position to achieve whatever it wanted in the crisis, as the Soviet Union would probably not have become involved.[69] Yet Eisenhower chose to remain neutral and abandoned his former allies in one of the more risk-averse decisions in American history.

McDermott uses prospect theory to explain these two puzzling decisions by the same U.S. president, which fall on the extreme ends of risk taking.[70] She argues that Eisenhower's decisionmaking at these two points was a function of the immediate context in which he operated. In short, in 1956, during the Suez crisis, Eisenhower was operating in a "domain of gains," while just a few years later during the U-2 incident, he was making decisions in a "domain of losses."[71] His reference point, therefore, largely determined his subsequent behavior.

In the case of the U-2 incident, Eisenhower was already in a losing position because the program had been exposed, and the United States had been publicly implicated by Soviet premier Nikita Khrushchev.

For most of the 1950s, the United States was able to successfully maintain the illusion that the Soviet Union was the only one that would engage in such underhanded deeds as spying against former allies. The Eisenhower administration perpetuated an image that the United States would not spy on the Soviet Union, let alone provoke a conflict. But that changed with the allegations of the spy plane program. To make matters worse, the Soviet Union had captured the American U-2 pilot and was threatening to hold a public trial. Eisenhower, then, had no good option in such a situation. If he admitted to the program, it would call into question much of the decisionmaking of the administration over the past decade, and if he lied about it, the truth might be exposed anyway, causing even greater reputational damage. In such a dilemma, prospect theory predicts that actors become more risk acceptant, and in fact, Eisenhower "doubled down" on his lie that the program did not exist and the United States never engaged in intelligence collection against the Soviet Union. Instead of taking the relatively safer option and admitting to the existence of the program up front, his ultimate decision risked not only infuriating the Soviet Union but also undermining the credibility and popularity of his administration. Notably, this is one of the turning points at which Americans began to express significant distrust of their government.[72]

During the Suez crisis, on the other hand, Eisenhower made a relatively "safe" decision by remaining neutral and even demanding that the British, French, and Israelis withdraw. Thus, the overall willingness of Eisenhower to accept risk cannot explain his behavior in both the U-2 incident and the Suez crisis. Instead, Eisenhower was in a relative position of strength during the Suez crisis and felt no pressure to take unnecessary risks. The administration was at the peak of its domestic popularity, and the United States was still the dominant superpower following World War II. Operating from a "domain of gains," then, Eisenhower saw no need to risk conflict with the Soviet Union, despite the likelihood of victory in any such conflict.[73] The decision to remain neutral was a function of the Eisenhower administration's reference point in 1956, just as the decision to take great risks during the U-2 incident was in 1960.

McDermott examines a similar pair of cases during the Carter administration in the 1970s. In one case, Carter's decision to refuse the shah of Iran medical treatment in the United States represented an unusually risk-averse course of action. Admitting the shah on humanitarian grounds might have been a fairly noncontroversial move, but McDermott argues that the Carter administration was in a position of strength in early 1979 and did not want to jeopardize either its relative popularity at the polls or its relationship with the new Iranian regime.[74] Only after these two situations deteriorated did Carter reverse course and admit the shah. By late 1979, when relations with Iran were at their low point and Americans had been taken hostage at the U.S. embassy in Tehran, Carter's behavior became particularly risk acceptant.[75] Given the options for how to resolve the hostage crisis, Carter arguably took the riskiest option available in staging a covert rescue mission.[76] Not only did the action represent a departure from Carter's public commitment to nonmilitary solutions, but the decision to fly American helicopters into Iran to retrieve the hostages also risked the deaths of the hostages or, even worse, a full-scale armed conflict with Iran.[77] But reeling from a series of domestic and international setbacks, Carter risked everything to salvage the situation. Like Eisenhower, then, Carter seemed to make conservative decisions when he was operating in a domain of gains and riskier decisions when he was operating in a domain of losses.

While these cases seem to illustrate the central principles of prospect theory, it is worth considering a possible counterexample: the behavior of Adolf Hitler and Nazi Germany prior to World War II. Many historians and analysts have held that Hitler and Nazi Germany became most aggressive when they were, in fact, at their strongest reference point. In other words, contrary to the expectations of prospect theory, Hitler may have engaged in the riskiest behavior when his regime was at its strongest rather than its weakest.[78] A common theme in much of the analysis on the origins of World War II in Europe is that Germany decided to invade Poland, and subsequently the Soviet Union, only because it felt it was strong enough to do so.

But even this seemingly conventional wisdom has its counterarguments. Hitler's decision to initiate aggression against Poland in 1939 may have resulted from recognition not of Germany's strengths but of its growing weaknesses.[79] Hitler and the Nazi regime leadership believed that the economic and political strength that Germany experienced during the 1930s had actually peaked earlier in the decade.[80] Hitler saw the Soviet Union, on the other hand, as a state that was rising in power at the same time that Germany was beginning its decline.[81] Due to fear of a rising Soviet Union and a desire to seize any advantage that might be diminishing by the day, Hitler believed that it was time to strike Poland. Similar logic figured into his plans to invade the Soviet Union. It seems, then, that Nazi Germany may have considered its reference point and, seeing itself in a domain of losses, chose a risky gamble with its invasion of Poland. Reference points and aversion to losses, then, help further explain why preventive wars occur and why states often feel the need to seize an offensive advantage.

THE DANGER OF OVERWEIGHTING PROBABILITIES

The existence of so much "conventional wisdom" about Nazi Germany and World War II illustrates another implication of prospect theory. Because of human beings' overwhelming aversion to losses, we tend to overweight the probability of highly unlikely events occurring.[82] This is why the case of Nazi Germany is frequently cited in contemporary debates about international relations. Popular political discourse often includes arguments referring to certain international actors as the "next Hitler" or warning of the dangers of appeasement because of what occurred prior to World War II in Europe.[83] But it should be obvious that Nazi Germany and World War II are both outliers on practically any dimension, and the probability of a similar case or a similar conflict is undeniably low.[84] Yet World War II is probably the most cited historical example in discussions about international conflict. By contrast, research suggests that the probability of near-certain events is frequently underweighted, and so decisionmakers often ignore them when making decisions.[85] International decisionmakers, then, often consider the worst-case scenario and pay unwarranted attention to it, even when the chances of it occurring are negligible. They often ignore key information about the most likely scenario when making decisions, which has the powerful effect of significantly biasing those choices. And it further explains how misperceptions about capabilities and resolve may occur, ultimately leading to a narrower bargaining range and a higher probability of conflict.

One reason human beings tend to overweight such unlikely events is because they often represent the most "vivid" examples.[86] Human beings are biased toward events and decisions that invoke more vivid images and are more accessible in their minds. For instance, consider which of the following two statements describes the most likely scenario: statement A, the United States will enter a conflict with Russia in the next two years, or statement B, the United States will enter a conflict with Russia in the next two years over Russian aggression in Ukraine. While there is one important difference between these two statements, research suggests that most people would select statement B as being the more probable scenario out of the two because it conjures a concrete image in the mind.[87] It provides a scenario that is much easier to visualize—it might invoke Russian forces moving across a border on a map or images from previous Russian incursions into Ukraine. Either way, the scenario is more visual than the more "academic" statement A. When an option is more representative in this manner, the human mind tends to ignore actual probabilities.[88] Selecting statement B as the more likely scenario ignores the fact that the probability of a conflict between the United States and Russia over a *specific issue* (statement B) cannot be greater than the probability of conflict overall (statement A). It may be equally as likely (if we assume that Ukraine is the *only* issue over which the two can fight), but it can never be more likely. Nevertheless, people may estimate the probability of conflict in statement B as being higher, demonstrating how decision-makers often misjudge the likelihood of an event occurring if it is more easily accessible in the mind.

This is one reason that references to Nazi Germany and World War II are almost inevitable in contemporary debates about international politics, particularly in those areas where conflict is more likely.

During the series of regional conflicts involving Russia that began in 2008, comparisons to Nazi aggression prior to World War II were repeatedly made.[89] Similarly, negotiations over the nuclear programs of Iran and North Korea have often been compared to diplomatic efforts prior to Germany's 1939 invasion of Poland, with the dangers of appeasement being a popular refrain.[90] Even China and its aggressive moves in the South China Sea have been compared to German expansion in the 1930s.[91] While these cases may have little resemblance to that of Nazi Germany, it is easier to summon because it is such a concrete and widely known example. This phenomenon has even given rise to a tongue-in-cheek theory; Godwin's Law states that as political discussions grow longer, "the probability of a comparison involving Nazis or Hitler approaches 1."[92] So while cases such as Nazi Germany, World War I, and World War II are outliers on nearly every dimension of international relations and international conflict, they are probably the most cited examples supporting a variety of political arguments. It's easy to imagine people in the fourth century BCE similarly comparing every issue to the Battle of Marathon and the Peloponnesian War, despite the fact that Greece did not experience conflicts of such magnitude ever again.

OTHER SOURCES OF MISPERCEPTION AND BIAS

Endowment bias and the overweighting of unlikely events are a few of the biases and misperceptions that result from human beings' inability to adequately process the information they are given. But a host of other common biases have been documented with respect to human decisions. Prospect theory and its extensions have provided great insight in this area; prospect theory is ultimately about decisionmaking, but making decisions involves using judgment. Judgment, in turn, is a fallible human process that is wildly "susceptible to biases."[93] These biases can dramatically disrupt the decisionmaking process, which, in the realm of international relations, can derail negotiated agreements and lead to a higher probability of conflict. Since decisionmaking is not simply a matter of calculating objective expected utilities, conflict may be more likely than we even think. It is not enough, therefore, to simply understand the "operational milieu," or the world in which the policy will be carried out.[94] We must also understand the "psychological milieu," or the world as the actor sees it.[95] And these two concepts, as we have seen through the lens of prospect theory, are endogenous. In other words, when two players have been sitting at a table for a long time playing repeated hands of poker, there are two realities: the objective reality of the game as it exists and the reality of the game *as the players see it*. Importantly, these two realities are not necessarily the same, and there are important implications for the decisions that players ultimately make.

One reason actors may view a situation differently than the objective reality is the attribution of intention applied to other actors in the game.[96] An actor's observable action—movement of troops by a state, or a display of frustration by a poker player, for instance—may take on different meanings to different players if they ascribe different intentions to the action. If the movement of troops is viewed as a defensive measure, for instance, other actors are likely to react differently than if the movement is viewed as a preparation for a first strike. Similarly, a display of frustration from a poker player may result in different strategies by other actors if it is assumed to be a bluff instead of a genuine display of frustration. One common example is the teacher faced with equally poor performance by two students on the same exam.[97] If the teacher attributes the performance to laziness in one student and to a serious learning disability in the other, the teacher is likely to respond to them in different ways.

The attribution of ill intentions or the intention to cause harm can have serious repercussions for how others respond. A psychology study found that people faced with the same observable behavior by their partners responded differently based on how they perceived the intentions of the partner.[98] Those who viewed their partner's behavior as being intended to harm them were angrier and more likely to retaliate in some way. On the other hand, those who saw the same observable behavior but did not attribute an intention of harm were far less likely to show anger or retaliate. In the same way, states are likely to respond differently to the same observable behavior if they perceive such behavior as stemming from different intentions. This, of course, was the center of much of the debate in U.S. policy circles during the Cold War concerning the Soviet Union. In particular, seemingly aggressive Soviet moves following World War II, such as attempts to revise the agreement over the Dardanelles Strait and a delay in removing troops from northern Iran, contributed to confusion about Soviet intentions. Were these decisions intended to put the Soviet Union in a better position to expand farther? Or were they simply meant as defensive hedges against other powers that might expand at their expense?

It is therefore a difficult proposition in international relations to label any behavior as either "aggressive" or "peaceful," because both intentions may produce the exact same observable behavior in many cases. This is like trying to model an opponent's behavior in poker and to determine whether their actions constituted bluffing or were genuine. In many cases, poker players (like states) never learn the true intention of their adversary because they might fold before the cards are actually revealed. They must rely on their *perception* of what their opponent's intention was, which contributes to further bias regarding the type of opponent they are actually playing. Either way, when a state views another's actions as being intentionally hostile, it is likely to respond in an exaggerated, even aggressive, fashion regardless of whether the original action did any harm.[99]

Notably, the differences in opinions about Soviet intention produced two dramatically different views on how to manage the U.S. relationship with the Soviet Union.[100] Those who viewed Soviet actions as hostile and aggressive often proposed some form of deterrence.[101] Threats and demonstrations of force, according to this line of reasoning, could successfully raise the expected costs of continued Soviet aggression and prevent conflict. On the other hand, those who argued that Soviet actions were defensive in nature, or that Moscow was truly afraid of Western aggression, often subscribed to spiral theory.[102] This view held that threats and demonstrations of force would only make the Soviet Union more insecure, leading to aggression and hostility where none may have previously existed. There are plenty of cases throughout history where deterrence theorists seem to have been correct and plenty of cases where spiral theory seems to explain events well.[103] The variance in the success of these measures, then, is caused by the extent to which perceptions about intentions were correct. Both the context in which actors operate and their relative misperceptions and biases can contribute to a breakdown in bargaining and a higher probability of conflict.

The fact that the United States ultimately interpreted Soviet intentions as hostile and the way the Cold War subsequently played out suggest additional biases.[104] Once the Soviet Union was seen as hostile, it was difficult to change this perception among U.S. policymakers, even if Soviet intentions objectively changed over the years, as is often argued. This is known as initial bias, and it can occur whether the initial attribution of intention is incorrect or correct. Initial impressions, particularly that another actor is hostile, cause others to assimilate "ambiguous and even discrepant information" to that impression.[105]

We have seen that credibility can influence an actor's reputation and, in turn, can influence the outcomes of repeated interactions. Initial bias suggests that an actor's reputation does not necessarily have to be objective. Other actors can interpret their behavior in a way that is erroneous but nonetheless contributes to a long-term reputation that is difficult to reverse. As with comparisons to the Nazis and World War II, when an initial bias is based on an overweighted probability, the chances of reversing that impression, however inaccurate, can be very small. In other words, an actor's experience in previous interactions with one player may continue to bias their interactions with *other* players in the future. This is why comparisons to Hitler and World War II are frequently made by the countries that dealt most directly with Hitler. Those interactions have continued to dominate political thought and discourse many decades later. Personal experience, then, predisposes actors to viewing subsequent experiences (even unrelated ones) through the lens of their initial impressions.[106] As Robert Jervis puts it, "Dealing with one kind of adversary will increase the chances that other adversaries will be seen as similar."[107]

Finally, a related problem known as projection bias may significantly hinder the decisionmaking capabilities of actors. Projection bias is a common bias, particularly in poker, but it is also evident in international relations.[108] It is the tendency to view the intentions and thought processes of others as being similar to one's own. Conservative players of poker, for instance, will be more likely to view others as conservative, and particularly aggressive players will be more likely to view others as aggressive.[109] Obviously, this was not the case with the relationship between the United States and the Soviet Union, which often viewed the "other" as radically different. But it is cautionary for understanding perceived "allies," since our strongest allies are often presumed to think about issues the same way as we do.

CONCLUSION

Success in poker relies on the player's ability to accurately assess the following questions: "How great is the risk? How great is the reward? Is the reward great enough to justify the risk?"[110] These are also the keys to managing a smart foreign policy. But the systematic biases and cognitive errors that we have discussed in this chapter pose serious threats to our ability to answer these questions accurately. Human beings frequently make suboptimal decisions, even when provided abundant information on their potential choices. Many circumstances are just too complex and time-sensitive to allow for a perfectly rational decisionmaking process. Introduce incomplete information into these complex and time-sensitive circumstances, and human beings are likely to make even more erroneous decisions. From the betting table to the battlefield, there are a number of situations in which suboptimal decisionmaking may occur. We have also seen that suboptimal decisions are likely to be made when the stakes are particularly high, as with a gambler who has already lost large sums of money or a general who has already sustained grievous battlefield losses. This is why always assuming the perfect rationality of actors can only provide us with a limited understanding of the decisions that they make.

Some of the biases we have examined include initial bias, where an actor's first impression of another actor (rightly or wrongly) persists and can influence their decisions, even when the objective circumstances have changed. Overweighting bias causes human beings to assign particularly high probabilities to rather unlikely events. And a host of additional biases can affect decisionmaking, such as planning bias, when decisionmakers are overly optimistic about the time in which they will complete a given task. There are a number of examples in the history of conflict when leaders thought that military objectives could be achieved in a small window of time, but after implementation, that time stretched out into years and decades beyond their initial estimates.

One of the most concerning implications of the biases examined in this chapter is that they can influence actors and situations simultaneously. With all of these potential sources of bias and misperception, it can be difficult to accurately predict decisions, which makes it difficult to plan strategically. And even if we know the true intentions and capabilities of other actors, we often don't fully understand our own intentions.[111] President Kennedy, for instance, threatened to retaliate militarily against the Soviet Union if a U.S. U-2 spy plane was shot down.[112] When a U-2 was actually shot down during the Cuban Missile Crisis, Kennedy completely reversed course and decided not to threaten force against the Soviet Union. Robert Jervis argues, however, that this was not a matter of Kennedy bluffing. Indeed, there is evidence to suggest that he fully intended to retaliate at one point but simply did not understand his own intentions or resolve.[113] If actors do not know their own intentions, we have a bleak prognosis for the probability of conflict since bargaining is more likely to break down when actors misjudge capabilities and resolve—including their own.

It is therefore "insufficient" to examine a situation and predict how an adversary will react. Instead, "one must try to empathize with a variety of possible outlooks, any one of which could be a true representation of the adversary."[114] A simplistic look at the costs and benefits of conflict, then, does not provide sufficient explanation for why conflict happens. Instead, understanding how adversaries make decisions—and how they make mistakes—is the only way to obtain a comprehensive picture of the likelihood of conflict.

Importantly, misperception and bias can come from various sources, including from deliberate manipulation. It follows that if bias can raise the risk of conflict, then actors may find benefit in creating and exacerbating bias on the part of other actors. Deliberate reinforcement of biases and misperceptions is an important reason for the persistence of terrorism, although this can be true of any endeavor in which people are asked to fight for a cause.[115] The way in which many Islamist terrorists are educated—in the Wahhabi schools of Islam, for instance—consequently influences their perceptions of other actors and their willingness to die for their cause. In other words, it raises their own resolve while also fostering biases about other actors' positions and intentions. Any "brainwashing" or propaganda campaign is aimed at achieving the same goal: enforcement of biases that raise the risk of conflict.

The issue of planning bias provides an additional insight into conflict that will be explored more fully in the next chapter. One important reason people are often more optimistic than the situation warrants is the role of random events. Initial planning estimates are frequently inaccurate because the decisionmaker is unable to predict random occurrences that may throw off their timetable. So even if we are equipped with an objective understanding of the costs and benefits of each actor's potential decisions, and even if we understand the contexts that can change those costs and benefits, we are still unable to predict how future random events may influence outcomes.

Russians and Roulette

*I have neither the time nor the inclination to differentiate
between the incompetent and the merely unfortunate.*
—Gen. Curtis LeMay

In the previous chapter, we examined a range of biases and cognitive errors that influence decisionmakers. World War I is perhaps the
most frequently cited example of a major conflict stemming directly
from such errors. Popular explanations for its outbreak often focus
on the mutual optimism of European leaders on the eve of the war.[1]
While some scholars have disputed just how optimistic the key players
were, anecdotal evidence suggests that many of them were confident
the war would be short and would work out in their favor.[2] Kaiser
Wilhelm II famously told his troops, "You will be home before the
leaves have fallen from the trees." This apparent optimism was not
just a side effect of the war but also an important clue in understanding why it occurred in the first place.[3] In almost every international
conflict throughout history, examples can be found of overconfidence
and unwarranted optimism by decisionmakers. States have frequently
gone to war against one another with leaders expecting positive returns,
even though it is impossible for both sides of a conflict to simultaneously reap a positive utility.[4]

Planning bias is one explanation for this seemingly irrational outlook. Human beings tend to dramatically underestimate the difficulty and time needed for completion of tasks and instead "make decisions based on delusional optimism rather than on a rational weighting of gains, losses, and probabilities."[5] Anyone who has hired a contractor to work on their house has probably experienced the unpleasant results of planning bias. Contractors are notorious for making more optimistic projections regarding the time needed to complete a project than is warranted. Likewise, in contracting and many other economic transactions, cost overruns are a common occurrence.[6] Human beings suffer from less catastrophic forms of planning bias in their day-to-day lives as well. Just about everyone has made the honest mistake of thinking they could complete a task before noon, and instead the task ends up stretching out across the entire day (or several days).

Why do we continue to see optimistic projections from leaders, even when the objective reality (at least in retrospect) is quite different? Why do seemingly careful and rational human beings, especially professionals who have done their job a thousand times before, still make incorrect projections? We have already seen two reasons why the projections of international decisionmakers often don't align with reality. First, as described in chapters one through three, basic information problems cause states to miscalculate the true capabilities and resolve of their opponents. Second, as described in chapter four, human beings are prone to making cognitive errors that exacerbate the problems caused by incomplete information. This chapter explores a third reason why it is difficult for human beings to accurately predict the outcomes of their decisions: randomness. Even if decisionmakers had perfect information and suffered from no cognitive biases, it would still be impossible for them to predict how random, unforeseen events might influence outcomes.

Recall the Fundamental Theorem of Poker, which suggests that if a player plays the game exactly how they would play if they could see their opponent's cards, they will win. But what if the opponent also plays as if they could see the other's cards? Obviously, both players can't win. The game is now distilled down to a purely random process.

The winner is simply the player who draws the best card. So even with perfect information, or perfect analysis of one's opponent, an element of chance remains that often makes victory elusive. This is particularly true in the realm of international bargaining and conflict scenarios, where a range of seemingly unrelated factors can dramatically influence the course of events. Professional gamblers, by contrast, are aware of the role of chance and explicitly account for it when making their projections.[7] But even sophisticated players often fail because they do not fully respect the role of randomness. Many players ignore the part it played in their past victories because they "tend to have an overinflated sense of their own skill," which, in turn, is often a direct product of past success.[8] Our brains tend to attribute success to our own skill and ingenuity, ignoring the uncomfortable possibility that we were simply "lucky."[9] But if luck was responsible for part or all of those prior successes, a player's future decisions likely will be based on incorrect interpretations of past outcomes.

In poker, randomness is largely limited to the order in which cards appear in the deck, but in international relations, infinite sources of randomness can ultimately affect real-world outcomes.[10] In 2011, when Osama bin Laden was in Abbottabad, Pakistan, the U.S. military began planning a mission to either capture or kill him. For several months, they meticulously crafted a plan and a variety of contingency plans. Those involved in the raid trained intensively during these months, preparing for many of the identified contingencies. The mission also benefited from brand-new technology: transportation would be facilitated by two MH-60 Black Hawk helicopters with previously undisclosed stealth technology.[11] The mission planners and participants, then, benefited from every possible technological advantage and months of careful planning.

The mission, of course, was a success. But it almost failed. During the raid, one of the Black Hawks crashed just outside bin Laden's compound, seriously jeopardizing the mission. Instead of being deposited directly into the compound, the team on board was forced to exit the crash and breach the compound walls. Later analysis revealed that the helicopter crashed because of a combination of unusually high temperatures and the design of the compound walls, which caused an unexpected updraft of air that toppled the Black Hawk's tail rotor.[12] In short, the crash was caused by an almost freakish set of minor circumstances, nearly impossible to predict ahead of time. And yet this combination of minor, unpredictable factors almost jeopardized the entire mission.

A single random event or series of events, then, can have dramatic implications for the outcomes of our decisions. Such events are by definition unpredictable. In this chapter, we examine the often uncomfortable and unfortunate reality that "the empirical world contains a stochastic element."[13] In other words, in human interactions, including international bargaining and conflict, there is an ever-present element of randomness, the size and variance of which can have dramatic effects on the outcomes that we observe. Ultimately, this calls into question our ability to predict with any great accuracy where conflict will occur, how it will play out, or how it will end. In this way, international bargaining and conflict may more closely resemble a spin of the roulette wheel than a game of poker.

WHY OUR BRAINS DON'T DEAL WITH RANDOMNESS

Perhaps the scariest thought many of us have is that we have little control over the events that affect our lives. It is also disturbing to think that major events, particularly those in international relations, might occur not because of some discernible causal process but instead might be driven primarily by randomness. Human beings have spent centuries trying to understand why conflict occurs and to develop procedures and institutions to prevent it. But if randomness plays a large role in past events, our ability to predict the future is severely limited. Despite how much we have invested in understanding conflict, our ability to predict it has probably only marginally improved. Unfortunately, the most consequential human endeavors often involve a great deal of randomness.[14] Notably, two fields that involve the greatest amount of randomness are also the most intensely studied: war and the financial markets. In trying to predict future events in these fields through the use of quantitative data, scholars have often acknowledged and accounted for the role of chance. Statistical techniques such as multivariate regression that are intended to isolate the average effect of one variable on another (the effect of economic growth on the probability of war, for instance) explicitly incorporate an "error term" that captures "noise" or randomness. But even this formal incorporation of randomness may do us no favors if we incorrectly specify the causal process, underestimate the extent of randomness, or both.

The single most important problem that this causes is an inability to predict the future based on past events.[15] If we improperly attribute events to causes that do not exist, we cannot use those causes as a basis for prediction. Imagine someone who wins their first bet at video slots (supposedly a purely random game) trying to explain to someone else their "strategy" for victory! This is important because the implied purpose of analyzing past events, such as conflicts, is to try and gain some predictive leverage over future events. If our understanding of past conflicts, however, is significantly biased, we cannot predict the future. Consider the opponent modeling that we discussed in chapter one. Our ability to predict our opponent's future strategies in a game of poker relies on an accurate understanding of their behavior in previous rounds of play. We note where the opponent bluffs and where they valuebet in an effort to make projections about their likely behavior in the future. But this kind of opponent modeling implicitly assumes that all of a player's actions are *intentional*. What if, however, we were playing against someone with cognitive issues that prevented them from designing and implementing an intentional strategy? What if that individual was making decisions on a purely random basis (in other words, there was no strategy behind the decisions)? Such random play could result in the same outcomes we would expect based on our predictive modeling. If so, our interpretation of past behavior would be worthless, and we would be unable to predict future behavior. Consider a less extreme example: we are playing a first-time poker player who knows enough to understand the rules of the game but is in no way sophisticated enough to design their own strategy or analyze the strategy of other players. In this way, their performance may approximate pure randomness (particularly in a fast-paced game) that appears to have a strategy behind it but really does not. In such a scenario, trying to model the opponent's strategy would be completely futile.

In behavioral economics, this tendency to ascribe meaning to random past events is known as hindsight bias. It is a fact of human life that when two events coincide in time and/or place, we cannot help but attribute some causality between the two.[16] Our brains are not designed to either identify or understand randomness. This does not preclude the possibility of causal events occurring, but it means that when truly random events do occur, our brains have a difficult time telling the difference. Truly nonrandom events often display no discernible pattern, while truly random events can *appear* to follow some pattern. For example, a well-known observation, Benford's Law, argues that the distribution of digits in many data does not appear truly random, at least not in the way that we expect random distributions to look.[17] In fact, in large collections of data, the numeral one appears as the first digit about 30 percent of the time, with diminishing frequencies for the other digits. This observation allowed investigators to identify a financial scam perpetrated by Kevin Lawrence in 2002.[18] Lawrence had raised money from private investors to back a chain of health and fitness clubs that in reality consisted of a single converted bowling alley with "a few pieces of fitness equipment."[19] Meanwhile, Lawrence and his partners used the investments to fund their own lavish lifestyles. After suspecting a scam, authorities analyzed the accounting of the investment firm and noticed that the numbers in the accounting sheets didn't follow Benford's Law. In other words, the faked accounting looked *too* random, and investigators were able to infer that the numbers could not, in fact, be random. By trying to fake randomness, the scammers inadvertently alerted investigators.[20]

How does the limited ability to spot either true randomness or true causality impact our ability to make important decisions? Since many of our decisions are based on past experiences, and since hindsight bias and our inability to spot randomness influence our perception of past

events, it follows that our interpretation of current events and our prediction of future events will both be biased.[21] Perhaps nowhere is this
more likely than in the realm of international relations, where decisionmakers frequently make explicit comparisons to previous situations,
contexts, conflicts, and actors. Politicians in particular base many of
their arguments, positions, and agendas on past events. If the causes
of these events are misinterpreted (or if the cause is simple randomness), their policy prescriptions will be significantly biased. Leaders are
particularly likely to misunderstand or ignore the role of randomness
because these key decisionmakers "tend to be uncomfortable with
explanations that point to the importance of chance or blunders."[22]
After all, what kind of individual in a key decisionmaking role would
begin with the a priori assumption that their actions do not matter or
that key events might be driven largely by randomness? On the contrary,
such individuals are probably more likely than others to assume that
events occur because of *deliberate actions*. And even if they recognize
the outsized role of randomness, there are political incentives to down-
play it. In short, for all human beings, but especially those who are
responsible for making decisions of this nature, "chaos and confusion
are not intellectually and psychologically satisfying explanations."[23]

The very thought of a lack of control over events, especially significant events, is therefore anathema to many actors. And given that
decisionmaking in international relations occurs within a strategic
framework, such actors have a difficult time seeing and understanding
randomness in the behavior of *other* actors. Leaders frequently overestimate the extent to which their adversaries have control over a single
policy.[24] Human beings usually prefer to ascribe the actions of an
adversary to some Machiavellian purpose and design, even when the
adversary has simply bumbled their way through the decisionmaking
process. During World War I, for instance, Friederich von Holstein saw
every ambiguous event as evidence of a grand British conspiracy against
Germany.[25] And while it is popular to ascribe a Machiavellian design
to Adolf Hitler (especially after reading *Mein Kampf*), Germany in the
1930s and 1940s seems to have been the exception to the rule. Not

only do international actors typically lack a grand strategy, but they also are unable to effectively employ the strategies they have designed because of various constraints placed on them.[26]

Actors usually have grand *preferences,* but they often respond to events as they occur (and often in a biased fashion). After the Russian annexation of Crimea in 2014, for instance, many key decisionmakers and observers argued that it had been Russian president Vladimir Putin's plan all along.[27] They saw the annexation as the culmination of a series of intentional, strategic maneuvers, as if Putin had been playing a game of chess. But others saw the event as nothing more than Russia's opportunistic response to events that had taken place in Ukraine.[28] While the unrest that occurred in Ukraine during the Euromaidan Revolution may have been instigated by Russia, the possibility remains that much of the political situation in Ukraine resulted from a series of related but unintentional occurrences. Analysts of such events, however, often "overestimate the extent to which other countries are pursuing coherent, rational, goal-maximizing policies, because this makes for more coherent, logical, rational explanations."[29] If this is the case, erroneously assuming the annexation of Crimea was planned and directed by Moscow undermines our ability to predict similar events. On the other side of the coin, many Russians see what happened in Ukraine as evidence of a plot by European nations and the United States. This has similar implications for Russian decisionmakers trying to predict the future behavior of their adversaries.[30]

Robert Jervis offers some stark illustrations of how decisionmakers have ascribed causality, intention, and purpose to adversary actions that were actually just random or unplanned.[31] In 1966, for instance, during the Vietnam War, inclement weather caused American forces to suddenly cease their bombings of Hanoi and Haiphong. The pause was an unplanned tactical decision that responded to unpredictable changes in the physical environment. This did not stop the North Vietnamese, however, from attributing greater purpose to the decision. They interpreted the change in American behavior as an indication of support for the ongoing peace process.[32] And during World War II, many unpredictable events that damaged Allied war efforts, such as equipment failures and accidents, were frequently attributed to sabotage by a German fifth column. Like the "gremlins" that were invented to explain the occurrence of random, unfavorable events in aircraft at the time, German saboteurs were used as an excuse for nearly anything that went wrong behind Allied lines. But in almost all cases, these unfavorable events were a result of Allied organizational problems, natural disorder, and randomness.[33] In other words, decisionmakers in international conflict situations often take random events and try to fit some model about their opponent to the data. Actors may be reacting not to their opponents but rather to random circumstances.

Closely related to the improper attribution of intention is a cognitive bias that causes actors to improperly attribute unity of purpose to adversaries. We often assume that a group of individuals, such as a government or an insurgent group, is more unified and cohesive than is actually the case. Nowhere was this more evident than in the days following the 9/11 attacks against the United States. Experts, pundits, and policymakers almost immediately spoke of al Qaeda as a monolithic, united group of individuals with a strong constancy of purpose. This was a natural way to interpret the events of 9/11 (at least with hindsight bias) because such a spectacular attack seemed to require significant cohesion and agreement. Not long after the attacks, however, additional information came to light about the nature of the organization and planning for the attacks, and the group turned out to be far more fragmented than many assumed. Even the decision to execute the attacks was not without internal controversy. In fact, part of the purpose of the attacks may have been to end infighting within the organization.[34] In other words, any unity of purpose existing in al Qaeda was *because* the attacks were a success. The success of the attacks, on the other hand, was not a reliable indicator of unity of purpose. Observations about the unity of military alliances suffer from the same problem. Actors typically assume greater unity among their adversaries than is really the case, just as the Japanese assumed a deep military cooperation between the United States and Britain prior to World War II that did not exist.[35]

RANDOMNESS AND PERCEPTIONS OF SUCCESS

Many politicians, generals, and other decisionmakers are uncomfortable with the possibility that randomness plays a large role in how events unfold. Professional card players might be even more uncomfortable with this possibility. In spite of an explicit random element to the game, poker players, particularly those who have achieved ongoing success, often attribute that success to their own decisionmaking and ingenuity. When they beat an opponent, "luck" is rarely credited. Instead, their strategy or their ability to outthink their opponent is considered the reason they win.[36] When poker players lose, on the other hand, "bad luck" is almost always the culprit (this is also frequently the case for "unlucky" generals, stockbrokers, and other professionals). But luck is arguably the dominant factor in poker, and intentionally so. During the World Series of Poker in 2014, Connor Drinan and Cary Katz faced off. At the end of the final round of play, just before Drinan and Katz saw the river, both were holding the same pocket cards—a pair of aces. Of course, each player thought he had the upper hand, but the outcome was to be determined by pure luck. Since they would make the same hand based on the numbers of the cards, only the suit could actually make a difference, and it did. With the final card, Drinan drew a flush, and Katz lost his unprecedented $1 million buy-in.[37] While strategy and analysis of one's opponent certainly contributed to the two players' ability to *reach* the finals, the actual outcome depended on a random event: which card was next in the deck. The roles of strategy, reputation, and bluffing had reached their limit, and the game was stripped down to its random component.

Investors in the stock market are plagued by the same problem, although a number of strategies help them overcome the perils of randomness in equity investing.[38] Specific investment strategies are designed, for instance, to reduce exposure to random fluctuations in a single sector. An investor might diversify their portfolio so that unexpected random changes in the utilities sector have a minimal impact on their overall financial picture. An investor might also implement strategies to reduce their exposure to such randomness in a single company.

But even with diversification, the investor will be susceptible to overall randomness in the market.[39] Randomness always plays a role that cannot be avoided, no matter how intelligent and forward-looking the investment strategy.

How seriously should we take the possibility that randomness influences the course of international relations and conflict? Clausewitz was perhaps the first scholar of war to formally argue that randomness plays an important part in how nations interact and fight wars.[40] He introduced the term "friction" to capture all the events and factors that cannot be predicted when fighting wars. This includes many of the factors that have traditionally been thought to be uncontrollable by humans, such as weather. But it also includes factors that, while manipulable by humans, may nonetheless be unpredictable. Clausewitz argues, for instance, that adverse changes in troop morale can have an outsized effect on the ability to prosecute a war.[41] Such a shift in morale, while sometimes predictable, can be caused by random occurrences such as weather patterns, breakdowns in communication, and other similar events. According to Clausewitz, "Friction is the only conception which, in a general way, corresponds to that which distinguishes real war from war on paper."[42] Randomness, in other words, is what separates theory from practice.

One dramatic example of the difference between real war and war on paper is the decision by the Carter administration in 1979 to attempt a rescue of American hostages from the U.S. Embassy in Tehran. This was a particularly controversial decision once the plan was revealed to the public, especially because it had failed.[43] The failure of the operation, known as Operation Eagle Claw, owed a great deal to randomness. Some of the key planners, including President Carter and national security advisor Zbigniew Brzezinski, argued that the operation would have succeeded if it weren't for "a strange series of mishaps," including unpredictable weather patterns and equipment failures.[44] While the rescue attempt had been intricately planned, it quickly ran into trouble when rotor problems forced one of the RH-53 helicopters to land in the middle of the desert. The remaining seven helicopters were blanketed by an unpredictable weather phenomenon known as a *haboob*, a sandstorm with especially fine particles of sand. Poor visibility caused one of the other helicopters to abandon the mission, and another made it to the landing site but was crippled by damage in its hydraulic system.[45] With only five of the original eight helicopters functional, the entire operation was scrapped.[46] Carter and his administration were heavily criticized when details of the mission's failure were revealed the next day at a press conference. The possibility that fifty-two U.S. hostages might have been safely rescued were it not for freak weather patterns and equipment failures is a stark example of the role of randomness. Further, these random events and the subsequent failure of the rescue attempt impacted relations between Iran and the United States for years to come. Random events, then, can have far-reaching effects that thwart even the most intricate of strategic plans.

Charles Perrow details how random events can disproportionately influence subsequent outcomes in his book *Normal Accidents*.[47] He argues that in complex systems, "accidents" are inevitable. In other words, mistakes, random occurrences, and other unpredictable events are simply a fact of life. The rate of these accidents and random occurrences only increases as systems grow more complex. This is one argument against states having multiple military alliances—more military commitments increase the probability of mistakes and random events that could pull a state into war.[48] According to Perrow, even small mistakes and miscalculations can have a cumulative effect on subsequent events so that the causal path may be entirely diverted.[49] Some leaders have recognized the powerful role that unplanned events play in historical outcomes. In his book *Strategy and Compromise*, Samuel Eliot Morison argues that in warfare, the side that makes the fewest mistakes is the one that usually wins.[50] Similarly, Simon Ramo argues that the difference between great and "ordinary" tennis players is that the great ones make fewer mistakes.[51] He sees the game of tennis, in fact, as being largely determined by the number of such mistakes that occur in a match.

The failure of Operation Eagle Claw also illustrates an especially pernicious implication of hindsight bias. What if the helicopters had failed but the operation succeeded nevertheless? What if the special forces involved in the rescue attempt found an alternate way of getting into Tehran and completing the mission? It seems unlikely that the strategy would have been deemed a failure; on the contrary, the operation would likely have been hailed as a success precisely because the strategy was bold and daring and because those involved overcame significant obstacles. The problem with this alternative reality is that the strategy does not differ from the real-world events. The only thing that differs is the outcome of success versus failure. Hindsight bias causes human beings to judge the soundness of a strategy based on the outcome. When an outcome is positive or produces the desired results, we infer that the strategy used to get there was sound and well thought out.[52] When an outcome is unfavorable, we assume that the strategy was not sound and usually infer some level of incompetence on the part of the decisionmakers involved. This is particularly true in the stock market, where investors frequently earn great profits through luck alone. In fact, the investment strategies of some of the most "successful" investors, when examined closely, appear reckless and borderline incompetent. Likewise, some games of poker make "fair players into good players by accident."[53] Consistently aggressive players are unlikely to be successful in an ordinary game of poker, but in games where the ante is very high, their style of play will often lead them to victory (despite the fact that they have not adjusted their style to the structure of the game). Nonetheless, we tend to judge investors and poker players by how much money they make rather than how they make it.[54] And we judge military operations not by the sophistication of their strategy and planning but by the outcome.

The common perception that Operation Eagle Claw was a bad plan is a direct result of the failure of the mission. We have seen the danger of inferring causality when there is none. This is especially true when the outcome is a result of a series of random events (or when a random event leads to a large change in subsequent, nonrandom events). But the failure of the Iranian hostage rescue was arguably not caused by strategic shortcomings but by a series of unpredictable events that occurred during implementation of the plan. Ironically, the common link in both the 1980 rescue attempt and the 2011 raid that killed Osama bin Laden is the mechanical failure of the helicopters involved. If this was the most significant complication in each respective operation, how can we infer that the strategy in 1979 was flawed while the strategy in 2011 was sound?

The real danger of hindsight bias lies not in our interpretation of past events but in how we apply these interpretations to our expectations about the future.[55] When decisionmakers misinterpret the causes of historical events, or when they infer causes when there is only randomness, they tend to apply these erroneous interpretations as "lessons learned" in future situations. Yet even if we draw accurate conclusions about the causes of past events, that does not necessarily mean we can predict future events. Even with accurate retrospective modeling, our ability to predict the future is severely limited. Meteorologists, for instance, can explain with great clarity why a weather pattern occurred three days ago but may still be unable to accurately predict tomorrow's weather.[56] The Yom Kippur War came as a dramatic shock to Israel and the United States, despite a wealth of intelligence on the movements of the Arab nations and lessons learned from the Six-Day War, mainly because analysts failed to update their models as information changed.[57]

THE ERROR TERM

We are significantly limited in our ability to predict the future of international bargaining and conflict based on past events alone. We have seen two important reasons why this is the case. First, we cannot perfectly predict human behavior, because human decisionmaking is subject to bias. Further, these biases are exacerbated in situations of incomplete information. If human beings do not weigh their decisions rationally and fail to choose the best option based on relative costs and benefits, it is difficult if not impossible to predict their choices. Second, random events disproportionately influence outcomes. The implication is that even if human beings were perfectly rational under all circumstances, we would still be limited in our predictive capacity, because random events are by definition unpredictable.

Nevertheless, scholars have developed theoretical frameworks for modeling human decisionmaking in international relations contexts. The frameworks are intentionally abstract; they do not claim to explain decisionmaking in all circumstances of international relations.[58] But despite these explanatory limitations, such theories often provide considerable leverage by focusing on a few key variables (or a single variable). For instance, the bargaining approach discussed earlier focuses exclusively on the capabilities and resolve of actors, and the amount of information that we have about each, as an explanation for the occurrence and manifestation of conflict. While this approach leaves quite a bit out (hence, the abstraction), it has still provided us with important insights about how these variables influence conflict. The predictive capacity, though, remains limited.

International relations scholars have also used statistical regression techniques to validate their theoretical models. This approach, which has long been used in the natural sciences as well as economics, allows researchers to identify the relative effect of several variables on a dependent variable of interest. If we consider a bivariate model (in which there is a single independent variable and a single dependent variable), we can easily test a hypothesis with some basic data. For instance, we might hypothesize that countries whose economies grow at a faster rate are more likely to fight wars. We might then collect data from the previous year, measuring each country's change in its gross domestic product (GDP) and also determining how many wars it fought. If we collected data for six countries, the data might look something like table 5-1, with the first column showing each country's GDP change and the second column indicating how many wars that country fought in the previous year.

As it turns out, the regression equation that best summarizes the data in table 5-1 is *Number of Wars* = 0.89 + 1.00 (*Change in GDP*). The regression equation tells us that, on average, a one-point increase in a country's GDP is correlated with the country fighting an additional war in a given year. This is hypothetical and in no way resembles real data. But if these were real data, we might be tempted to use the regression equation to predict who will become entangled in wars in the

Table 5-1
Hypothetical Data on State Economies and War

Country	Gross Domestic Product Change	Number of Wars
Vietnam	1.9	3
China	2.2	3
France	1.1	2
Colombia	0.2	1
Cameroon	1.0	2
Russia	2.2	3

future. If we project, for instance, that the United States is going to end the year with 2 percent growth in its GDP, we would predict that it will fight three wars by the end of the year.[59]

But the basic regression equation does not give us the full story. Scientists, including political scientists who study international relations, have long recognized a random element to the outcomes that we see in the real world. Thus, the basic regression equation includes one final element, the error term, which captures the inability of the rest of the equation to perfectly predict the outcome variable.[60] In other words, it captures how far off the actual predictions of the regression model are from the data themselves. A large error term indicates that our equation doesn't have much predictive capacity, partially due to the role of randomness.[61]

The error term is so important in statistical studies of conflict because it is the only piece of information that acknowledges the relative influence of random occurrences on our outcome of interest. It is also important because it allows scholars to "explain away" randomness, treating it as a nuisance, in much the same way that diversifying a portfolio allows investors to hedge against randomness in a single company's stock valuation. Some scholars of international conflict believe the relative influence of randomness, however, is much higher than we prefer to admit. Erik Gartzke, for instance, argues that contemporary studies of conflict processes do not adequately explain the role that randomness plays.[62] According to him, even knowing the relative size of the randomness does not ultimately tell us whether conflict is more or less likely. Even if we account statistically for randomness when modeling why conflict occurs, we still have no reason to believe that randomness makes conflict *more*, rather than *less*, likely. Similarly, over the long run, every poker player should draw the same proportion of good and bad cards.[63] Some random events should therefore make conflict more likely, while other events should make it less likely. As a result, rationalist explanations for why war occurs may be "theoretically indeterminate."[64]

To develop an accurate model of why war occurs, then, a simple regression equation with an error term would seem insufficient. Conflict may truly be unpredictable, even if we explicitly acknowledge that randomness plays a role. Similarly, poker is unpredictable because although a player may acknowledge the role of randomness, they still don't know whether the random placement of the next card will help or hurt them. In poker, much of the outcome relies on deliberate, rational decisionmaking of the players. But ultimately, the reason poker is so difficult to predict, and hence the reason it remains an attractive game for risk seekers, is the deliberate "introduction of a randomizing element."[65] There is no need, however, to introduce a randomizing element into international relations scenarios; it already exists, and it generates a far greater level of unpredictability than a simple card game.

Put in different terms, if uncertainty and incomplete information are constant features of international conflict, we can never know the true causes of war. Hindsight bias causes us to see patterns in previous events that do not exist. That is essentially what the regression model does—it fits a model to past data that may be inaccurate or inappropriate. If events are solely influenced by random occurrences, there is no causal model that fits the data. If there is any level of uncertainty or incomplete information *after* a conflict occurs, we have no way of knowing what actually caused it. And in most cases, the true causes will be highly contextual.[66] In other words, "What explains international conflict—what leads states to war or to peace—are precisely those factors that cannot be anticipated, that are unique to each event."[67] This is like trying to predict the prices of stocks, bonds, and commodities.[68] While price changes may be predictable to some extent, the biggest changes in prices are caused by large "shocks." By definition, these shocks are unpredictable and stochastic. With this kind of random element, trying to predict stock prices is ultimately a losing game, and it may also be a losing game trying to predict conflict.[69]

A simple illustration emphasizes the indeterminate nature of randomness.[70] Imagine that two states are negotiating over a piece of territory much like the example we saw in chapter one. The key variable of interest (other than their probability of winning a hypothetical conflict) is each side's resolve. In other words, the bargaining hinges largely on the costs each side is willing to incur to get what it wants. The resolve of the other player, however, is almost always unknown. And as with President Kennedy during the U-2 incident, actors often don't even know their own resolve. But let's assume that State B has an accurate understanding of its own resolve. State A, on the other hand, is unsure of the costs State B is willing to incur to get what it wants. With this lack of information, State A must make an "educated guess" about the kind of actor it is dealing with. Is State B the overly aggressive type that is willing to incur disproportionately high costs to gain even a small concession? Does it lack resolve altogether and is just bluffing? Is it somewhere in between, as most actors probably are? State A doesn't know, but it needs to guess. The best strategy for State A is to make an offer that would satisfy the "average" state (probably a state with an average level of resolve).[71]

Now assume that if State A makes too low of an offer, State B will launch a war in response. If the offer is too high, State A concedes too much, but war is avoided. So the strategy to target the "average" state is the most efficient in this case. And the ultimate likelihood of war depends on what type of state B actually is. If it has a lower than average cost of war, and State A makes an offer to satisfy the "average" state, State B will choose to go to war. But if State B has a higher than average cost of war, State A's same offer will result in peace. The key insight here is that either event (war or peace) is equally likely, since

State B's true cost of war is private information that even the negotiating process cannot fully reveal. This means that our ability to predict conflict may be further constrained if we are not able to say whether random events make peace more or less likely. So while statistical regression and other means of identifying causal processes can explicitly account for random error, they are not helpful if we don't know whether the randomness has a positive or negative effect on the final outcome (conflict).[72]

Gartzke is correct in drawing attention to the stochastic element of human decisionmaking, including in the realm of international conflict. Randomness can significantly disrupt our ability to understand and predict outcomes that we see in international relations. But contrary to what Gartzke argues, there is still good reason to believe that randomness, in the context of international negotiations specifically, may lead more often to conflict than peace.

In a previously published study, I argued that research on international conflict has often failed to properly account for randomness and error.[73] We typically model the process by which conflict occurs as nonrandom. Even though we include an error term when testing our hypotheses, we usually treat it as a nuisance rather than trying to understand the forces (both random and nonrandom) that influence our dependent variable beyond our simple models. A typical statistical model of conflict includes a hypothesis such as "Countries with greater levels of economic development are more likely to start wars than countries with lower levels of economic development." This is a very clear hypothesis, and it is relatively straightforward to collect data on economic development and the number of wars that a country starts and compare the two to obtain an average effect. But we do not properly account for how random events may influence the probability of governments making mistakes and miscalculations (that is, the probability that they will launch wars when it is not in their best interest).

In the study, I analyze specifically how power distributions between military alliances influence the likelihood of states making mistakes (and launching wars).[74] I argue that when the power between two military alliances is roughly equal ("power parity"), these mistakes are far more likely than when one alliance is much more powerful. When the power distribution is relatively even, states are not sure of their relative advantage. As such, a wide variety of events, including random events, may result in miscalculations of force that lead to war.[75] The results of the study show that when there is power parity, variance in the size of the error term is greater, suggesting more mistakes and miscalculations.

So why might this increase in variance actually lead to more conflict (rather than more peace)? Very simply, international bargaining always involves the threat of conflict—it is the tool used to achieve one's goals in negotiations. The bargaining process that we saw in chapter one is based on the (at least implicit) threat of military force. It is the instrument of conflict that is used to coerce and/or deter another state. When mistakes and miscalculations are made, therefore, the mistake is literally over the appropriate use of military force.

Additionally, if we think of the absence of militarized interstate disputes as indicating some level of peaceful resolution (even unintentional), the empirical results of the study demonstrate that such outcomes are less likely at power parity. I subsequently demonstrate that the greater variance in the influence of randomness ultimately results in a higher probability of conflict overall. So more equal power distributions lead to a greater number of mistakes, which consequently increase the probability that states will launch wars against each other. In other words, more uncertainty at power parity leads to more errors, and more errors lead to more conflict. The study also finds that errors are less likely when the military alliances involve more democratic members. Democracies are better at communicating credible intentions to their alliance partners and adversaries, which in turn reduces the number of mistakes and lowers the probability of conflict overall.[76]

An important conclusion here is that while randomness is unpredictable, we may be able to identify causes (such as power distributions) that ultimately influence the likelihood of random events occurring, as well as the relative effects of those random events. For instance, one implication of the study is that public military cooperation among democratic states may be particularly useful in deterring conflict. Every year, the United States participates in the Balikatan war games with the

Filipino military. Not only is the alliance between the United States and the Philippines public knowledge, but also such exercises are held with great openness, with the specific intention of deterring states such as China and North Korea from launching conflicts.[77] If these exercises succeed at credibly communicating intentions, capabilities, and resolve, there is less room for mistakes and miscalculations by North Korea and China and ultimately a lower probability of conflict overall.

RANDOMNESS AND LONG-TERM TRENDS IN CONFLICT

Randomness doesn't just pose a challenge for our ability to explain and predict specific cases. Our broader historical understanding of how conflict has evolved may also be biased as a result of randomness. This is the premise of a study by Pasquale Cirillo and Nassim Nicholas Taleb that argues that our attempt to identify trends in conflict over time may be futile.[78] Recall from our discussion in chapter one that conflict is an exceptionally rare phenomenon. Despite the amount of policy, media, and academic attention devoted to understanding conflict, it ultimately is not something that occurs often. Of course, the destructiveness of even a single conflict probably warrants all the attention. But Cirillo and Taleb question some of the conclusions that have been reached about the relative destructiveness of international conflict over time.[79] Examining the relative dearth of interstate war in the past ten years, for instance, we might conclude that interstate conflict is on the decline. Judging from figure 5-1, which is based on data from the Uppsala Conflict Data Program (UCDP), this appears to be part of a broader trend in which the frequency of interstate conflict has been waning in the post–World War II era. It certainly appears from these data that conflict is becoming less likely (at least since the 1960s and 1970s). Of course, many theories have been developed to describe this apparent trend: the spread of liberal political and economic ideals,[80] the success of international peacekeeping efforts,[81] and changes in how human beings perceive war.[82]

But using these relatively peaceful few decades to make bold predictions about the future of war is dangerous. As Jack Levy and William Thompson point out, human beings have previously made this kind

Figure 5-1
Interstate Wars since World War II

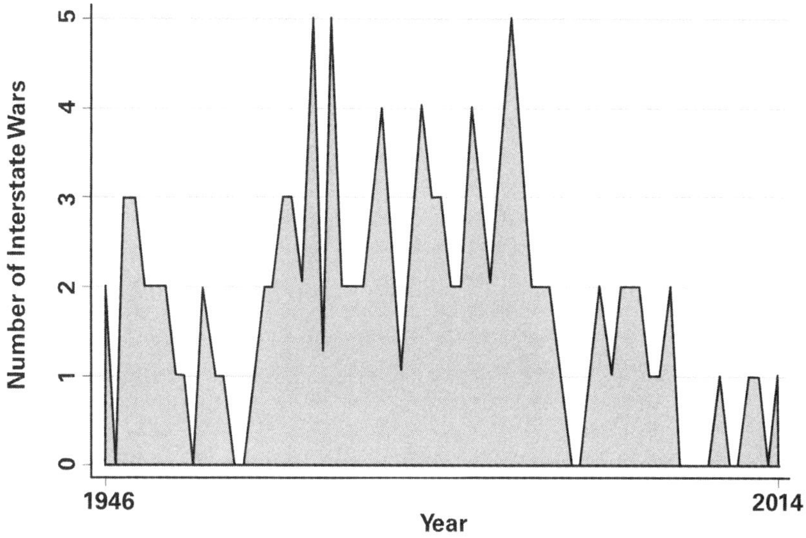

Source: Uppsala Conflict Data Program

of mistake. In fact, they note that "our counterparts in 1912 had even more grounds for optimism about the prospects for peace than we do today," yet only a few years later, a global conflict completely engulfed many of the nations of the world.[83]

Even the trend itself is highly debated. Some scholars argue, for instance, that focusing on the frequency of war is misplaced, and that we should instead be examining the rate of war deaths. One study finds that there is no change in war deaths in the past fifty years.[84] Cirillo and Taleb examine data on casualties from warfare extending back to the first century, and they find the opposite trend: the data suggest that the average number of casualties from war has steadily *increased* over the past two thousand years.[85] While war may be less frequent, it appears to have grown more destructive over time. But when the data are rescaled according to a popular method in studies of war casualties, the conclusions are reversed.[86] When the casualties are rescaled to the world's population, the average number of casualties from war appears to *decline* over time. All of this suggests that our confidence in drawing broad conclusions about trends in international conflict over time may be misplaced. If we think that war has become *less* destructive over time, we might argue that human beings have a greater understanding of the true costs of war than we did centuries ago. Or perhaps conflict has declined because the international system gradually became state-centric and those states, in turn, have increased their cooperation. If we look at the data and see that war has become *more* destructive over time, we also have a number of ready explanations: the increased lethality of military technology, or perhaps greater competitiveness by humans over increasingly scarce resources.

But if we can't even agree on what the trend is, how can we draw causal inferences about what is driving it over time? And how can we rule out the possibility that the trend is a largely random process? This is exactly what Cirillo and Taleb argue: any explanation about how conflict has changed over time suffers from significant hindsight bias.[87] They assert that our tendency to ascribe a single causal process to conflict over a period of millennia amounts to nothing more than data mining. The unfortunate reality is that *there may be no explanation at all*. While there are certainly causes and influences that drive individual conflicts, the possibility that there are one or two factors that have influenced all conflicts over the course of two thousand years is simply improbable. And it ignores the role of randomness in why conflict occurs.[88]

Cirillo and Taleb find that using the sample mean of war casualties to identify trends over time is not appropriate, because most analyses assume a normal distribution.[89] On the contrary, conflict data (and casualty data specifically) are composed of many very large events (like the An Lushan Rebellion and World War II) as well as many very small events. As a result, the mean is undefined. Without a defined mean, there is "no particular trend, [which contradicts] a popular narrative about the decline of violence."[90] Instead, the occurrence of certain casualty levels follows something closer to a random process. Cirillo and Taleb estimate the average "arrival times" of conflicts with specific casualty levels and find that certain types of conflicts tend to occur after specific periods of time.[91] For instance, over the past two thousand years, the average time between conflicts that kill five million people is about sixty-eight years. Figure 5-1, however, only shows data for a period of about sixty years. So it is understandable that a conflict that kills five million people may not show up in such a limited sample of the data. This is concerning, because there has been much talk about the "long peace" after World War II (with a variety of explanations for this relative period of peace, as we have seen).

In short, the absence of such an extreme event, even during a prolonged period, does not mean such an event is unlikely to occur in the future. Since time trends typically underestimate the probabilities of such extreme events, we must be careful about the conclusions that we draw and, in the case of conflict, our resulting complacency. A similar complacency existed during the "long peace" of the nineteenth century, when comparatively fewer international conflicts were waged.[92] Intellectuals and policymakers during the nineteenth century formulated a number of explanations for why warfare had seemingly become extinct, but these explanations were worthless once World War I began.[93] The implication is that although we may be living in a peaceful time relative to other periods, there may be no general trend in the frequency or severity of conflict, and "the very large event could just be behind the corner."[94] In other words, our psychological need to ascribe causal trends to conflict may blind us to the true risk of such events occurring.

DOGS PLAYING POKER THAT DON'T BARK

The rarity of interstate and intrastate conflict leads to an additional problem that plagues our ability to draw inferences from past events. According to the UCDP, there have been only four cases of interstate conflict in the past ten years, and several of these are debatable.[95] Another way to think about it is that there are far more instances of conflict *not* occurring than occurring. This is a potential problem for understanding conflict if we try to draw causal inferences using only information about *cases where conflict occurred*.[96] When explaining conflict, we rarely if ever take into account the cases where war could have or almost occurred but failed to materialize. These "nonevents" contain important information that is missed if we only examine actual wars.

The tendency to draw conclusions about war based only on the wars that have occurred is a form of survivorship bias, a common problem where we attempt to create causal explanations by only looking at the cases *still left in the sample*. In other words, we ignore information about cases that don't show up in the data (that is, nonevents). For instance, if we wanted to know the secret to success in high-stakes poker, one strategy would be to select a sample of players who have won the World Series of Poker. After all, these individuals are commonly considered to be among the most successful players in history. We might then examine each of these players in detail and look for similarities in their personal traits and philosophies. We could create a survey and ask each of them the same questions—how they bet under certain circumstances, or what their view is on the appropriate conditions for bluffing. We might even ask about their personal habits. If we found that all the players in the sample, for instance, take a nap just before a big game, we might begin to draw some conclusions. We might go so far as to say that taking naps before games is the reason these players were successful. If we found several similarities among the group, we might begin to think that we have a set of fairly reliable predictors for what constitutes success in poker.

But in doing so, we would be making an important logical error: succumbing to survivorship bias. By focusing only on those players who have reached the upper echelons of the poker world, we would be missing a great deal of information. Two particularly important missing pieces would be the common traits of *unsuccessful* poker players and the traits that seem to be common to both winners and losers. If any of the observed traits are common across both unsuccessful and successful players, we can't conclude that they influence success at all. But we can't know any of this unless we observe information on a wider sample of players than just those who won the World Series of Poker.

A classic example of survivorship bias occurred during World War II that had significant implications for the U.S. war effort. The issue was chronicled by Abraham Wald, a statistician interested in improving the survivability of American bombers.[97] He looked at data on the damage sustained by bombers that was compiled by Navy researchers after the aircraft had returned to base. The researchers gathered information on where the bombers were most frequently hit by enemy fire and then recommended adding reinforcements to those areas. Wald noted, however, that this method of analysis was missing an important piece of information. By looking at data on only those aircraft that had returned, they were unwittingly identifying the areas where the bombers could be hit *and still survive.* The crucial question, Wald pointed out, was where had the *downed* bombers been hit? Wald subsequently concluded that the areas where the returning bombers had *not* been hit represented the spots most likely to down a plane, and he recommended reinforcing these areas instead.[98]

Survivorship bias hinders our ability to draw meaningful conclusions about past events, yet it permeates decisionmaking in many human endeavors. Like our example of successful poker players, there seems to be a cottage industry devoted to identifying the common traits of the most successful investors in the stock market. One bestseller, *The Millionaire Next Door,* has gone through multiple reprints due to its enduring popularity.[99] The authors interview a group of very wealthy investors and try to identify the common traits that have predicted their success. Even worse, multiple books claim to identify the secrets of a single investor—Warren Buffett—and promise to divulge how you can apply his traits and philosophies to become a successful investor. If drawing conclusions from a small sample of "survivors" is inherently biased, trying to draw conclusions based on a single case is nearly useless. Yet that is what many policymakers and leaders often do, comparing current world events to World War II or the Iranian Revolution or some other high-profile case. While it is undoubtedly useful to understand those cases, and it is probably even useful to examine the practices of Warren Buffett, they do not offer a comprehensive picture of what drives war or success. Perhaps even more concerning is the possibility that wars and individual success can be driven largely by randomness, in which case our ability to draw conclusions from these events is further limited.

When we study the onset of conflict, we frequently make the logical error of focusing narrowly on those cases where war actually occurred. We unwittingly ignore all the crucial information that exists in cases where war never occurred or was successfully prevented. This problem has often been compared to the "curious incident of the dog in the night" detailed in the Sherlock Holmes short story *Silver Blaze* by Sir Arthur Conan Doyle.[100] In the story, Holmes is examining a crime scene where a famous race horse had been kidnapped the previous night. As they are discussing the crime, a Scotland Yard detective asks Holmes if he noticed anything particularly interesting, to which Holmes replies, "The curious incident of the dog in the night-time." The detective remarks that the dog did nothing the night before (in other words, the dog was not heard barking during the time the crime was thought to be committed). Holmes replies, "That was the curious incident." His conclusion is that whoever kidnapped the horse must have been familiar to the dog since it didn't bark. Many of our efforts to determine the causes of conflict have us looking for the barking dog—the big, explosive conflict. But in reality, the best information is often buried in times of peace, when the dog did not bark.

Some modern statistical analysis of conflict has avoided this problem to some degree by also examining cases in which conflict *might have* occurred but ultimately did not. But this kind of analysis is still dependent on the available data, and our data collection frequently suffers from survivorship bias as well.[101] For instance, imagine that we hypothesize that war is caused by aggressive actions on the part of leaders. If we then try to collect data to bolster our argument, we already have a built-in bias. Media reports, state documents, and other materials where we would look for information on the behavior of leaders will be heavily biased toward those incidents where their behavior is particularly aggressive (presumably because this type of behavior is "sensational"). By comparison, there is relatively little information available on those times when a leader's behavior was not aggressive and did not warrant attention. But like the dog that didn't bark, ignoring these nonevents, whether in the collection phase or the analysis phase, removes crucial information from the equation.

ROULETTE AND THE PROBLEM OF TRUE RANDOMNESS

Randomness plays a much larger role in international relations and international conflict than we would like to acknowledge, but we should not *overstate* its role. There is no better example of the tension between randomness and nonrandom factors than the history of a game that was designed to be perfectly random: roulette. The roulette wheel was intentionally designed to strip away the elements of strategy present in other games of chance such as poker. Theoretically, there is no room for strategy in roulette and no illusion of control (although people nonetheless believe they can control the outcome through superstitious behaviors). But just as pure causality is often an illusion in conflict, pure randomness is also an illusion at the roulette table. Even the game that is designed to be unbiased frequently results in biased outcomes.

The game was introduced in Paris in the late eighteenth century to specifically address the problem that other games of "chance" were not based on chance alone. The perception was that existing games of chance were inherently unfair to gamblers because some people might have built-in advantages. *Pure* randomness was seen as the only way to level the playing field (even though pure randomness takes away the role of skill and strategy). By the end of the eighteenth century, the game of roulette had become wildly popular because of this perceived fairness.[102] But more than one hundred years later, a man named Joseph Jagger discovered that the perception of true randomness was, in fact, an illusion.

Jagger, an amateur mathematician, hired six assistants in 1873 and went to Monte Carlo to play roulette at the casino there. He tasked his assistants with recording all the outcomes of roulette wheel spins in the entire casino, which they did for five weeks. Analyzing the data on a single wheel, Jagger noticed some irregularities. Specifically, he noticed that some of the numbers on the wheel came up more frequently than others, which should not occur if the game was truly random (theoretically, there should be an equal probability of all numbers coming up). This suggested that the wheel was actually unbalanced, physically favoring some of the numbers over others. In practice, it is nearly impossible to create a perfectly randomized wheel. There will always be some physical defect or bias that throws off the randomness, even if slightly.

Recognizing this, Jagger began playing the wheel and betting heavily on the favored numbers. He was able to win substantial amounts of money for a full week before the casino caught on to what he was doing. When he came into the casino the next day and began betting as usual, he started losing large amounts of money. Jagger couldn't figure out why his strategy, which had been foolproof, was now failing spectacularly. But then he noticed that a small scratch on the side of the wheel, which he had seen thousands of times after staring at the wheel for a week, was no longer visible. When he realized this, he looked around the casino until he found another wheel with the exact same scratch. The casino, wise to his methods, had switched the locations of the tables overnight.[103] Again, we see how randomness is difficult for human beings to understand, let alone replicate. In all endeavors, including gambling and conflict, bias may exist where it initially appears there is none.[104] The key to success is recognizing when the wheel is producing near-random results, and when there is a systematic bias that can be analyzed and exploited.[105]

CONCLUSION

At all levels of international relations and in all contexts, leaders often experience an "illusion of control."[106] Although decisionmakers develop strategies, analyze their opponents' strategies, and calculate their most advantageous course of action, they still make mistakes for two important reasons. First, human beings are prone to cognitive biases that prevent them from identifying the best course of action under circumstances of uncertainty. Endowment bias, planning bias, overconfidence bias, and hindsight bias—all logical errors that we have discussed—are examples of inherent cognitive limitations that influence how we make decisions. Second, even with perfect information about the present, we can never fully predict random events that may occur in the future. Ultimately, this means that we can never accurately predict where and when conflict will occur. We can never accurately predict how a battle or war will be waged or won. And we can never accurately predict how a conflict will end. But we continue to believe that these things are within our control if we are just smart enough or well prepared enough. Similarly, poker players may believe they can ultimately control the course of a game if they just play smart enough and "outthink" their opponents. Poker players, though, are susceptible to the same kinds of biases and errors as world leaders. They are also susceptible to the whims of randomness. Bobby Baldwin, for instance, lost the 1981 World Series of Poker when his opponent outdrew him with 21:1 odds.[107] As a result, "In any moment, the factors over which [players] exert genuine conscious influence are small."[108]

This illusion of control continues to influence future events because decisionmakers use past outcomes to inform their future decisions. If those past events are even partially the result of randomness (rather than intentional influence alone), subsequent decisions will be highly biased. Success in particular causes people to assume causality and intentionality. We subsequently tend to appraise the strategy used in reaching a successful outcome as being sound. By contrast, some sound strategies can produce unsuccessful outcomes. For instance, in many respects, terrorist strategies are arguably sound, though terrorist campaigns are rarely successful in achieving their stated goals.[109]

These are inherent cognitive "defects" that influence decisionmaking at all levels. Even statisticians who are experts on the subject of probability—in other words, people who have an intimate understanding of the role of randomness—can often be found at the card tables in a casino. Some have even been known to consult fortune tellers. This goes against everything that these experts know and teach.[110] No one, then, is immune to these errors or the underestimation of randomness, but if we can be more aware of such limitations and also seek a comprehensive understanding of nonrandom influences, we may be able to better manage conflict in the future.

Conclusion

*Never, never, never believe any war will be smooth and easy,
or that anyone who embarks on the strange voyage
can measure the tides and hurricanes he will encounter.*
—Sir Winston Churchill

In light of the topics covered in this book, it is worth reconsidering the famous assertion by Helmuth von Moltke that "no plan of battle survives contact with the enemy." We have seen that military plans and strategies do not survive for a variety of reasons. The traditional interpretation of Moltke's quote, especially by military strategists, is that even with sophisticated strategic planning, once armies actually face each other on the field of battle, their carefully crafted strategies can easily come undone. On the battlefield, political and military leaders learn new information about the enemy's capabilities, as well as their strategic and tactical decisionmaking, and they learn about the *true* resolve of their own forces and civilian population. All this new information can change, and ultimately destroy, even the best laid plans. This book has focused on some of the more prominent challenges in international conflict, including the informational challenges to which Moltke referred. But as we have seen, efforts to either avoid or win wars are complicated by more than just a lack of information.

Even with "bulletproof" strategies, basic cognitive errors can prevent leaders from making the optimal choice in many situations. Human beings still make mistakes and often behave in ways that do not conform to classic notions of rationality.[1] One of the most famous poker games in history illustrates how cognitive errors can trump sophisticated, strategic decisionmaking and pose significant difficulties for predicting human behavior. In the late nineteenth century, U.S. senators Daniel Webster and Henry Clay reportedly played a game of poker with unlimited stakes. Clay had nothing in his hand—just a single ace—and Webster made a large initial bet. Even though he could not hope to compete, Clay subsequently raised Webster's bet in what might be described as the ultimate bluff. Following the initial raise, the two men engaged in a series of additional raises and reraises until the pot stood at $4,000 (a sizeable pot even now, but a small fortune in the nineteenth century).[2] When it was Clay's turn to bet, instead of raising again, he called Webster's raise. When the men revealed their hands, Clay was defeated by Webster, who held only a pair of twos.

Clay's decision to call Webster defies logic, which is one reason the veracity of the story is sometimes questioned. As one commentary on this legendary game puts it: "Each clearly and correctly suspected the other of bluffing. Still in no case should either player have called, for neither could reasonably have desired to match his low hand against even a bluffed hand. No amount of knowledge of each other's bluffing tactics could justify anything but infinite raising or retirement without seeing."[3] In other words, the strategically optimal decision under these circumstances (that is, the optimal decision according to game theory) was for Clay to either fold, avoiding any further losses, or to continue to reraise Webster indefinitely.

So what explains his seemingly irrational decision? It is possible that Clay simply did not understand the basic principles or strategic dynamics, but the situation was not complicated in terms of the possible outcomes and their associated probabilities—particularly for a player such as Clay, who had a long-standing reputation as a smart high-stakes poker player. The only explanation seems to be that he simply made an error in judgment. Perhaps he had a biased interpretation of Webster's thought process and expected that Webster might also have failed to make a hand. In that case, Clay's ace would have won. Or perhaps he had become averse to any further losses (but even folding would have been a better choice if this were the case). Either way, he made a suboptimal decision because of some cognitive error, and he paid the price. The point of many of the gambling examples used in this book has been to demonstrate that even a relatively simple game like poker is difficult to predict because of complex cognitive processes that result in human error. The Clay-Webster game was straightforward and the most likely outcome would have seemed predictable, yet Clay made a massive blunder.

Finally, as if strategic and cognitive challenges were not enough, even the most intelligent and rational actors are still defeated by chance. One poker professional says, "Expert players do not rely on luck. They are at war with luck."[4] The most experienced and strategically minded players know that their careful play can be undone by one unlucky draw (or one lucky draw by their opponent). Nothing throws off plans at the card table like chance, and nothing ensures that military plans die on the battlefield like random, unpredictable events. Chance is the most important reason why the best poker players do not consistently win games and why we often see wild and surprising outcomes in international conflict. And perhaps the most dangerous aspect of randomness is not how it disrupts plans today, but how it distorts our plans for the future. When we ascribe causality to events that have occurred in the past, we tend to use those causal models to interpret current and future events. Ascribing specific causality to past events is always risky, but if those events are largely a result of randomness, our predictions for the future will necessarily be skewed and often dangerously wrong.

In some ways, gamblers and international decisionmakers frequently resemble the pigeons in B. F. Skinner's famous series of experiments.[5] Skinner provided food to a group of pigeons at random intervals. Despite the fact that there was no pattern in the timing of the food's appearance, the pigeons seemed to develop "superstitious" behaviors. One pigeon would repeatedly turn in a counterclockwise circle until the food appeared. Another would thrust its head into the corner of the cage until the food showed up. Although the outcome (the timing of the food's appearance) was a completely random process, this did not stop the pigeons from apparently believing that their idiosyncratic behavior was causing the food to appear. Similarly, people who frequently play games of chance often develop "gambler's tics," or patterns of behavior that they believe lead to success. Shuffling the cards in their hand in a specific way, always ordering the same kind of drink prior to playing, and other behavioral tics are some examples.

Like the pigeons in the experiment, human beings—especially those dealing with complex subjects such as political negotiations and conflict—often take comfort in the illusion of causality. A particularly insidious form of this illusion is the "hot hand fallacy," or the simple belief that success predicts success. In other words, outcomes are thought to have a causal effect on subsequent outcomes. The hot hand fallacy is probably most evident in games of pure chance, such as craps. When a player rolls successfully, particularly in succession, it is not uncommon to see gamblers flocking to the table to wager on the player with the "hot dice." But even in games that are not purely based on chance, such as poker, there is a common perception that players can get "on a roll," and as such can expect their success to continue. In basketball, a game where success is largely (but not entirely) dependent on skill, the hot hand fallacy is referred to as "streak shooting." It is widely believed that a basketball player who makes their most recent shot or several recent shots is likely to make the next shot. But evidence suggests that previous successful shots do not predict future success, and if anything, players are *less* likely to make their next shot after a successful shot.[6]

Unfortunately, this kind of dangerous thinking permeates public policy decisions, including foreign policy and military decisions. Many armies have been doomed by the common wisdom that "we won the last war, so we will we win the next one." The U.S. military's initial struggles in Iraq in the mid-2000s were largely a result of assuming past success would predict future success.[7] Even Helmuth von Moltke was probably familiar with the hot hand fallacy, as he personally witnessed the overwhelming German success in the Franco-Prussian War give way to poor decisionmaking in World War I. In short, success does not predict success, and attributing random outcomes to strategic decisionmaking is a dangerous game.[8]

WAR GAMES AND PREDICTION

What do the combined challenges of strategy, cognitive biases, and randomness tell us about international conflict? First and foremost, they suggest that we must consider all three to reach a comprehensive understanding of international issues. Many analyses of historical events, particularly those of warfare and military decisionmaking, focus exclusively on strategic considerations. But we have seen examples of leaders ignoring the larger picture at their own peril. Second, the combined challenges suggest that we should be suspicious of any claims to "predict" or "foresee" the future in any aspect of international relations, but particularly in warfare, where all three elements are intensified. The difficulties of prediction were illustrated by a series of war games called Hegemon that the Potomac Foundation conducted in the summer of 2015. Top-ranking military officials were invited to participate in the game, which involved a simulated military crisis in the South China Sea. While the game was designed specifically to capture the strategic aspect of decisionmaking in such a scenario, the way the game unfolded demonstrates how complex and unpredictable such situations can be. Although the basic parameters of the game were relatively simple (and can be used to simulate any kind of international situation), "just as in real life, events build upon themselves like fractals. Players bluff and second-guess others' intentions, alliances are formed and broken and decisions need to be made in a fog of uncertainty."[9] This kind of complexity means that there is room for cognitive errors and random events to take over the course of the game, and the outcomes are a testament to this complexity. Participants actually played many iterations, and the outcomes varied widely from one game to the next. In half of the games played, the result was violent conflict, while in the other half, the crisis did not lead to war. In other words, if we were tempted to use the results of the games to predict real-life outcomes under such circumstances, the game is no more useful than, say, flipping a coin. While unpredictability is a feature of all international relations, it is particularly true of circumstances such as those simulated in the game, where the stakes are high and decisionmakers do not have much time to reflect on their choices. Recall that as stakes increase in poker games, players' behavior can become unpredictable as they risk increasing sums of money, even on marginal hands.[10] But the Hegemon games should be a cautionary tale for those claiming to predict where conflict will happen next, how it will play out, or how it will end. Even a simple game with clear parameters is difficult, if not impossible, to predict. How then can we hope to accurately predict the outcomes of real-life conflict situations, which are infinitely more complicated and involve aspects completely unknown to the participants?

RATIONAL PLAY STILL PAYS OFF

While we have focused on the complications caused by cognitive errors, as well as randomness, it is important to emphasize that strategy still works. Like the example of the roulette wheel in chapter five, systematic biases exist in many forms that we often overlook, and the experienced and strategically minded actor may be able to exploit these biases to their advantage. Despite the doubt we have cast on prediction, it is important to remember that international relations often follow discernible and predictable patterns if we assume that actors are rational. The lesson of this book is not that we can *never* anticipate the moves of an adversary or plan around them. Actors are still responsible for their own choices and actions, which means that, ultimately, they determine the outcome. Furthermore, while it may be difficult to predict broad trends in international relations or predict conflict in all cases, it is easier to anticipate the moves of a single adversary and plan accordingly. In other words, although challenges such as randomness make perfect prediction impossible, they do not preclude us from better managing conflict through a combination of experience and skill. Louis Pasteur, noting that randomness exerts a strong influence on events, also argued that "chance favors the prepared mind." And one professional gambler sums up success like this: "For what is true of any war, or any endeavor in life for that matter, is also true of gambling—winning is a combination of timing, skill, and luck. But luck favors those who have the skill and timing. Luck favors the prepared. So in our war against the casinos, we must be totally armed with the best strategies and the proper mental attitude."[11] Despite seemingly insurmountable challenges, rational, strategically oriented actors are still more successful than those who do not think strategically. This is why a 2008 study on poker found that beginners who received pointers on the game prior to playing were more successful than those who didn't.[12]

One reason the "prepared" actor benefits more is that experience and skill allow them to acknowledge and successfully manage the risk generated through randomness. In poker, over the long run, every player will draw the same proportion of winning and losing hands. Randomness alone therefore levels the playing field. But experts use their experience and skill to minimize their losses when drawing bad hands and maximize their profits when drawing good hands.[13] The beginner or novice, on the other hand, is not sophisticated enough to manage risk in such a way and as a result will not be as successful. The successful poker player or military leader resembles, in many ways, long-term investors who implement strategies to diversify their risk.[14] This does not preclude them from sustaining short-term losses, even large losses, but they can significantly improve their financial position after enough time has passed. Such investors are different from the flashy investor who hits the jackpot on a single investment and subsequently claims to have a superior understanding of the markets.[15] These investors are less like expert poker players and more like video slots players who hit it big thanks to exceptionally (and often fleetingly) good luck.

Preparation, experience, and an understanding of strategic dynamics can also be an important hedge against players whose decisionmaking can be described as "irrational" or whose cognitive limitations lead them to behave in ways that are largely unpredictable. Theoretically, if two players play a game according to the principles of perfect rationality, and all other conditions are equal, the players should break even in the long run. Neither side has an advantage in such a scenario. But if one player plays irrationally (that is, does not make optimal choices), an adversary who plays rationally should be able to come out ahead.[16]

While irrational or illogical choices can surprise and diminish the position of adversaries in the short term (the landing at Inchon seems to have done that to North Korean forces), given enough iterations, rational and logical play can eventually put the player in an advantageous position. Over the years, the focus on the game between Henry Clay and Daniel Webster has been on the irrational decision made by Clay. But this focus misses an important point: Daniel Webster made a series of rational choices. In other words, Webster continued to play exactly as he should have (and exactly as Clay should have), and this adherence to strategic principles paid off for him eventually. Webster won the game.

While this book has focused on how cognitive biases and randomness can disrupt strategic principles and planning, it is important to remember that not all success in gambling or war is random. Sometimes the experts win precisely because they are experts! But we must distinguish between successes due to expertise and luck. Ultimately, though, strategy has a role to play. And under many circumstances, sticking to basic strategic principles is the most useful approach. Some of the best poker players know that while it is important to consider a variety of factors, sometimes it is more beneficial to "abandon psychology altogether and rely on game theory."[17]

A ROLE FOR BOTH EXPECTED UTILITY
AND PROSPECT THEORY?

This book (particularly chapter four) has skirted the decades-old debate about the compatibility of expected utility theory (and other forms of rational choice) with prospect theory. While a detailed analysis of this debate is outside the scope of this book, it is worth reconsidering. A review of much of the literature in the debate suggests that the two approaches are not compatible.[18] Expected utility theory assumes that actors make decisions based on only two factors: preferences and probabilities. Actors examine their possible choices and weight their utility by the probability that it will produce the desired outcome based on their own preferences. The actor then selects the choice with the highest expected utility. The choice that an actor is likely to make only changes when their preferences change and/or the probabilities of the outcomes change.

The cornerstone assumption of expected utility theory is that actors have perfectly transitive ordinal preferences. In other words, an actor can rank their most preferred outcomes, and the removal of a possible outcome from that list should not change the order of the remaining outcomes. By contrast, prospect theory assumes that an actor's ranking of preferences changes depending on the context or situation. Prospect theory, unlike expected utility theory, focuses on concepts such as reference points as determinants of preferences. Rather than being exogenously determined, preferences in prospect theory are highly fluid. Actors' likely choices change when their preferences change, which can occur based on the given context.

An ongoing debate in economics and other fields is whether, given these important differences, the two approaches are ultimately irreconcilable. While this book has ignored the debate for the most part, the discussion has demonstrated that insights from both approaches are worth taking seriously, and they are both potentially useful in understanding international relations and conflict.[19] In the introduction, I mentioned that the analysis of international relations has been compared to studying an "onion" or "boxes within boxes," with different levels of aggregation, units of analysis, and problems at each layer. Our exploration of conflict processes would suggest that while an expected utility approach may be most appropriate at one level, prospect theory may provide more leverage at other levels. Because of prospect theory's focus on reference points and relative gains and losses as determinants of preferences, it would seem that it cannot be fully integrated into an analysis based on expected utility theory.[20] Even so, many scholars have successfully incorporated insights from prospect theory into expected utility theory or have used both simultaneously to understand different aspects of the same problem. Some have suggested that the two approaches can be combined into an overall analysis of "weaker forms of rationality."[21] Others have even recommended the development of a hybrid approach, a "behavioral game theory," incorporating most if not all of the insights from expected utility and prospect theory.[22]

Decisionmaking in the real world probably incorporates elements of both theories. As several scholars have noted, it is difficult in practice to determine if previous choices in international relations were driven by one or the other, as the outcomes often look identical. Saddam Hussein's invasion of Kuwait, for instance, is easily explained by expected utility theory. Given the massive debt that Iraq incurred during the Iran-Iraq War, combined with falling oil prices (allegedly driven by Kuwait's overpumping of oil), it can reasonably be argued that Saddam's choice to invade offered the highest expected utility. His apparent disbelief of Saudi and American threats of retaliation seem to make his decision even more logical. But at the same time, it can be argued that the invasion plan was far riskier than other options and did not actually offer the highest utility given the potential costs. In such a case, perhaps the only way to explain the decision is to invoke prospect theory. Given massive debt and the prospect for further losses, perhaps Saddam was in a domain of losses and "rolled the dice" in a gamble for resurrection. Neither approach, then, gives us a definitive answer. But perhaps the answer does not need to be mutually exclusive; insights from both approaches may be necessary to get a complete picture of what happened.

In the same way, it is necessary to understand both strategy and an opponent's cognitive processes to be successful in poker. While expected utility and prospect theory may not be compatible in a strictly academic sense, it is useful for international decisionmakers and gamblers to keep the principles of both approaches in mind. Poker players do well, for instance, when they understand the basic concept of utility optimization that is central to game theory. But players also benefit tremendously by understanding how an opponent's preferences and behavior may change depending on how the game has played out to that point. If a player ignores either basic strategic principles or the psychology of their opponent, the result will likely be failure. Likewise, it is not sufficient for states and their leaders to analyze opponent preferences in a vacuum, although this can provide important information. They should also examine how their preferences may have been influenced by recent history (or ancient history, if there is merit to the idea of initial bias). States and nonstate organizations that suffer setbacks at the hands of their enemies, for example, might take drastic actions that do not accord with expected utility theory. Such seemingly irrational actions might be more in line with the predictions of prospect theory: actors throw good money after bad when placed in a desperate situation or domain of losses. While many implications of expected utility theory can be justified by real-world examples, prospect theory also seems valuable in explaining many of the outcomes that we see (such as the contradictory decisionmaking of the Eisenhower and Carter administrations).[23] Just as in the game of poker, then, scholars and policymakers should not jettison one approach altogether but should consider the explanatory value of each in specific circumstances and at specific levels of analysis. Just because one approach does not adequately explain a single case or set of cases does not mean that the approach does not hold value in other cases. And even though expected utility theory, game theory, and prospect theory all seem to provide value in their own ways, the "tool kit" of the analyst and the policymaker should not be limited to these approaches. In international relations, important insights have come from a variety of approaches, including constructivist and other nonrational choice schools of thought.

HOW TO IMPROVE YOUR GAME

What, if anything, do these lessons about chance, strategy, and human error offer us? Is there a better way to manage international relationships so as to reduce, rather than increase, the probability of violent conflict? In chapters one through three, we examined many of the strategic concerns that international decisionmakers must consider. States and their leaders often ignore many of these issues at their own peril. But analyzing the strategic situation and deftly playing an opponent may result in a successful outcome that avoids armed conflict. Even mastering the strategic situation, though, does not promise success, because strategic situations are by definition situations of incomplete information. The lack of information about opponents' capabilities and resolve leads to uncertainty and makes such decisionmaking particularly challenging.

It follows, then, that more information means less war. Anything that increases the amount of available information will likely reduce the probability of conflict. Recall the Fundamental Theorem of Poker: to succeed in poker, a player must play their hand in the same way they would play if they could see their opponent's card.[24] If opponents at the poker table could see each other's hands, games would be less likely to result in costly and unnecessary betting. And the best (and most controversial) way to win at blackjack is to count cards, a strategy that increases a player's information about the house's capabilities.[25] Card counting is a method of mental accounting to determine which cards likely remain in the deck, thus increasing the player's information and reducing the role of randomness. Card counters can subsequently avoid unwise bets and focus on winning the hands where the odds are significantly in their favor. Similarly, if international actors knew what their adversaries were willing and able to accomplish to achieve their goals, there would be little room for escalatory strategies that often result in warfare. But as some scholars have argued, informational asymmetries alone do not fully explain why conflict occurs or how it manifests itself.[26] Indeed, in a game of Texas Hold 'Em, knowing the adversary's pocket cards would not necessarily prevent additional betting. The luck of the draw in the community cards could change the situation in favor of one player at the expense of the other. The shadow of the future still complicates matters, even if there is complete information about current capabilities and resolve. For the same reason, political actors might find themselves at war even if they have complete information in the moment; while an agreement could be reached today, they must also be able to credibly commit to not using force in the future to revise the terms of a deal. This, as it turns out, is perhaps the most complicated issue that prevents peaceful resolution.[27]

In addition to increasing the amount of information available, managing conflict scenarios also requires the facilitation of credible commitments. Plenty of evidence suggests that one of the most important ways that states can bolster the credibility of their commitments is by institutional design.[28] Domestic political institutions can be used to restrain decisionmakers in a way that signals greater reliability and makes their international commitments more believable. Domestic political institutions can also be designed to foster transparency, increasing the amount of information available to external observers. Military alliances among democracies, for instance, tend to be more reliable, and their alliance partners are less likely to renege on the terms of their security agreements.[29]

Democratic institutions facilitate credible commitments and transparency, but in practice, mechanisms that accomplish these goals can be developed in a variety of institutional settings (including nondemocratic settings). Specifically, states' commitments are far more credible when institutions are able to align actors' self-interest with the public good, when they restrain actors, and/or when they provide monitoring mechanisms to ensure compliance with agreements.[30] Each of these mechanisms tends to be strongest in democratic systems, but they can all be managed within a variety of institutional contexts. In turn, the design of the institutions influences how governments interact. For instance, "electoral systems favoring an emphasis on collective goods bolster [international] multilateralism."[31] When institutions at home emphasize the provision of public goods, such as security and economic growth, states seem to externalize these domestic norms when dealing with other states.[32] Additionally, when institutional characteristics reduce leaders' ability to make major policy changes (such as revising the terms of an international treaty or alliance), the commitments they make today are more credible.[33] The resulting stability of domestic preferences makes international commitments more credible.[34] Where governments are not constrained by such procedural mechanisms, leaders should have an easier time backing out of agreements, since few checks and balances or significant political opposition might exist to prevent such a unilateral move. All this creates additional uncertainty on the part of an adversary and raises the risk of conflict. Finally, institutional mechanisms that increase accountability allow states to better signal their intentions and resolve to other states.[35] This is because higher accountability results in greater costs for governments that back down from their commitments or that handle foreign policy in an incompetent manner. Again, while such institutional mechanisms are more common in democracies, other types of regimes, including autocratic regimes, can facilitate higher levels of accountability and reliability through similar mechanisms.[36] Finally, it should be noted that while states have the ability to create such mechanisms, it is markedly more difficult for nonstate actors to generate credibility.

Changing the domestic political structure of another state may therefore offer hope of reducing conflict, but in practice, it is a difficult and controversial option (and is likely to require armed conflict in the short term). It is comparatively easier to design international institutions in a way that facilitates credible commitments and increases information among members. These measures, however, are necessarily limited because of the anarchical nature of the international system. Since there is no central enforcement body in the international system, measures that work at the domestic level (such as institutionally restraining decisionmakers) are far less applicable at the international level. Nevertheless, international institutions have successfully been used to incentivize peaceful state behavior and the fulfillment of commitments. For instance, power-sharing arrangements, such as the rotating presidency of the Council of the European Union, ensure that all member states are invested in the organization and give them incentives to cooperate and follow the organization's rules. Further, this manufactured reciprocity leads to consequences for not following rules. Fear of reputational costs for noncompliance deepens member state commitments.[37] International institutions also facilitate cooperation by reducing transaction costs and providing information about members, reducing the kind of uncertainty that can lead to conflict in the absence of such institutions.[38] International institutions have also been successful by providing monitoring and verification mechanisms. Although enforcement is almost nonexistent in the international system, organizations that monitor states' behavior, such as the International Atomic Energy Agency, may be able to better manage potential conflicts. After verifying noncompliance with an international agreement, organizations have been able (with mixed success) to alter state behavior by "naming and shaming" violators.[39] But combined with the other mechanisms available to international institutions, evidence suggests that organizations such as the International Criminal Court have been successful in generating credible commitments among their membership, reducing many possible points of conflict.[40]

Even when enforcement is out of the question, institutions can therefore help "manage" conflict by altering the strategic environment.[41] But can they also help manage problems generated through randomness? This ever-present factor in international relations poses challenges even when information and credible commitments among actors are particularly high. Further, randomness is far more dangerous in international relations than in poker because it involves both known and unknown events. As Clausewitz pointed out, there are infinite sources of "friction" that can completely undo military and diplomatic strategies.[42] But while this problem can never be fully overcome, increasing information in the system also reduces the probability of unexpected events occurring. The chance of mistakes and random events that threaten peace can be reduced by managing uncertainty, and increasing information is the best way to do so.[43] Transparent military exercises and military agreements can help manage uncertainty, reducing the probability that an adversary misunderstands intentions or miscalculates its advantage. Increasing information and transparency, then, is one of the most important ways to prevent conflict. While skill at decisionmaking is constant, "knowledge is variable" and offers one of the best hopes for changing the situation from one of likely conflict to one of likely peace.[44]

Ultimately, though, the threat of randomness is the most important reason that predictions in international relations are never foolproof. We can manage randomness, but we cannot eliminate it. As we have seen, randomness poses a significant problem when we interpret the future based on incorrect interpretations of past outcomes. This hindsight bias is particularly dangerous when past outcomes were largely the result of random processes. Makers of foreign policy need to be conscious of hindsight bias and instead develop policy by evaluating the success and failure of past strategies based on their internal logic rather than their outcomes. The internal logic of Operation Eagle Claw seemed to have been relatively sound, but the failure of the outcome undermined the important lessons that might be drawn from the event. Likewise, a guide to playing blackjack admonishes, "Don't alter your strategy based on prior results."[45] The basic strategy in blackjack offers the best hope of maximizing winnings in the long run. It is the soundest strategy available, so when a player abandons it because of a few bad hands, they do so at their own peril.

FRAMING THE BET

Finally, cognitive limitations of actors, while posing significant challenges for conflict resolution, also offer important opportunities. In particular, the insights from prospect theory suggest that how contentious issues are framed may dramatically influence the behavior of actors. We may be able to manage conflict more effectively by managing perceptions of risk, which drives human decisionmaking. By changing actors' interpretation of their relative risks, we can change their relative utility for conflict.[46] Framing therefore influences choice.[47] Focusing attention on the costs of potential conflict, such as death tolls and economic destruction, may be a useful strategy to avoid conflict and achieve one's goals in negotiations. We have seen that unrealistic optimism leads to risky decisionmaking, and such optimism is a hallmark of all human endeavors, so focusing intensely on potential losses in the event of conflict may help prevent poor decisionmaking.

Studies show, for instance, that people interpret statistics about disease survival rates differently depending on how the information is framed. A disease that results in ten deaths per one hundred patients is interpreted much differently than a disease with a 90 percent survival rate, even though there is no functional difference between the two. When the same information is interpreted differently, people also perceive their risks to be different, which in turn may lead to different choices. Framing international decisionmaking to focus on the potential costs rather than the potential benefits of conflict may lessen its appeal as an option. Likewise, given that humans make decisions based on reference points and perceptions of relative gains and losses, alternatively framing issues around *initial* endowments or recent changes in those endowments can influence behavior.[48] In gambling, for instance, people often refer to "gambling with the house's money" when they are betting money they have recently won. While money is money, such "mental accounting" leads to differing perceptions of endowments and different behaviors.[49] It is important to note, however, that even framing itself can be a source of contention. Witness the ongoing debate about whether the reference point for Israeli-Arab territorial disputes should be based on the borders from 1948 or 1967.

Foreign policy makers should see themselves less as actors reacting to the world around them and more as "choice architects."[50] More choices create more complexity, so policymakers should focus on simplifying choices and strategies as much as possible. One way is through "aspect elimination"—by identifying the most crucial elements of choices and eliminating options that don't meet a particular threshold of those elements. Such simplification strategies can prevent mistakes and may help reduce the probability of random error. The most sophisticated poker players are the ones who can mentally reduce the number of options available to them and strategize accordingly. Interactions between international actors should be structured in a way that maximizes the amount of information available, provides mechanisms to facilitate credible commitments, and frames issues in ways that discourage unnecessary risk-taking. Although conflict can never be fully predicted or eradicated, it will be more manageable and less frequent. Actors will be more likely to reach amicable settlements that satisfy at least some part of their preferences. And this means that they will never have to play the game of war, the costliest game of all.

Interstate Wars, 1816–2007

War	Combatants	Start	End
Franco-Spanish	France, Spain	1823	1823
First Russo-Turkish	Russia, Ottoman Empire	1828	1829
Mexican-American	Mexico, United States	1846	1847
Austro-Sardinian	Tuscany, Italy, Austria, Modena	1848	1848
First Schleswig-Holstein	Prussia, Denmark	1848	1848
Roman Republic	France, Two Sicilies, Austria, Papal States	1849	1849
La Plata	Argentina, Brazil	1851	1852
Crimean	Turkey, Italy, France, United Kingdom, Russia	1853	1856
Anglo-Persian	United Kingdom, Iran	1856	1857
Italian Unification	Sardinia/Piedmont, Austria, France	1859	1859
First Spanish-Moroccan	Morocco, Spain	1859	1860
Italian-Roman	Sardinia/Piedmont, Papal States	1860	1860
Neapolitan	Two Sicilies, Sardinia/Piedmont	1860	1861
Franco-Mexican	Mexico, France	1862	1867

War	Combatants	Start	End
Ecuadorian-Colombian	Colombia, Ecuador	1863	1863
Second Schleswig-Holstein	Germany, Denmark, Austria	1864	1864
Lopez	Argentina, Paraguay, Brazil	1864	1870
Naval War	Chile, Peru, Spain	1865	1866
Seven Weeks'	Italy, Hesse Grand Duchy, Wuerttemberg, Germany, Mecklenburg-Schwerin, Hesse Electorate, Saxony, Baden, Bavaria, Austria, Hanover	1866	1866
Franco-Prussian	Wuerttemberg, Baden, Germany, Bavaria, France	1870	1871
First Central American	Guatemala, El Salvador	1876	1876
Second Russo-Turkish	Turkey, Russia	1877	1878
War of the Pacific	Chile, Peru, Bolivia	1879	1883
Conquest of Egypt	Egypt, United Kingdom	1882	1882
Sino-French	France, China	1884	1885
Second Central American	El Salvador, Guatemala	1885	1885
First Sino-Japanese	China, Japan	1894	1895
Greco-Turkish	Greece, Turkey	1897	1897
Spanish-American	Spain, United States	1898	1898
Boxer Rebellion	Russia, Japan, United States, China, United Kingdom, France	1900	1900
Sino-Russian	Russia, China	1900	1900
Russo-Japanese	Japan, Russia	1904	1905
Third Central American	Honduras, El Salvador, Guatemala	1906	1906
Fourth Central American	Nicaragua, El Salvador, Honduras	1907	1907

War	Combatants	Start	End
Second Spanish-Moroccan	Spain, Morocco	1909	1910
Italian-Turkish	Italy, Turkey	1911	1912
First Balkan	Turkey, Greece, Bulgaria, Yugoslavia	1912	1913
Second Balkan	Turkey, Yugoslavia, Greece, Bulgaria, Romania	1913	1913
World War I	Russia, Bulgaria, Yugoslavia, United Kingdom, Japan, Portugal, Turkey, Belgium, Germany, Greece, Romania, Austria-Hungary, France, Italy, United States	1914	1918
Estonian Liberation	Estonia, Finland, Russia	1918	1920
Latvian Liberation	Germany, Russia, Estonia, Latvia	1918	1920
Russo-Polish	Russia, Poland	1919	1920
Hungarian Adversaries	Czechoslovakia, Hungary, Romania	1919	1919
Second Greco-Turkish	Turkey, Greece	1919	1922
Franco-Turkish	Turkey, France	1919	1921
Lithuanian-Polish	Lithuania, Poland	1920	1920
Manchurian	Soviet Union, China	1929	1929
Second Sino-Japanese	China, Japan	1931	1933
Chaco	Paraguay, Bolivia	1932	1935
Saudi-Yemeni	Saudi Arabia, Yemen Arab Republic	1934	1934
Conquest of Ethiopia	Ethiopia, Italy	1935	1936
Third Sino-Japanese	China, Japan	1937	1941
Changkufeng	Soviet Union, Japan	1938	1938

War	Combatants	Start	End
Nomonhan	Soviet Union, Mongolia, Japan	1939	1939
World War II	Hungary, Belgium, France, Yugoslavia, Finland, Italy, Soviet Union, Norway, Canada, United States, United Kingdom, Netherlands, Romania, Bulgaria, Greece, Brazil, Italy, Australia, New Zealand, Germany, Poland, France, Japan, Mongolia, China, South Africa, Ethiopia	1939	1945
Russo-Finnish	Finland, Soviet Union	1939	1940
Franco-Thai	France, Thailand	1940	1941
First Kashmir	India, Pakistan	1947	1949
Arab-Israeli	Israel, Egypt, Syria, Lebanon, Jordan, Iraq	1948	1948
Korean	China, Belgium, Canada, Colombia, United Kingdom, Netherlands, Greece, France, Turkey, Philippines, Ethiopia, Australia, South Korea, United States, Thailand, North Korea	1950	1953
Off-shore Islands	China, Taiwan	1954	1955
Sinai	France, Israel, Egypt, United Kingdom	1956	1956
Soviet Invasion of Hungary	Hungary, Soviet Union	1956	1956
Ifni	France, Spain, Morocco	1957	1958
Taiwan Straits	People's Republic of China (PRC), Taiwan (Republic of China)	1958	1958
Assam	India, PRC	1962	1962
Vietnam, Phase 2	United States, Cambodia, South Korea, Philippines, South Vietnam, Vietnam, Thailand	1965	1975

War	Combatants	Start	End
Second Kashmir	Australia, India, Pakistan	1965	1965
Six-Day	Israel, Egypt, Syria, Jordan	1967	1967
Second Laotian, Phase 2	United States, Thailand, Laos, Vietnam	1968	1973
War of Attrition	Egypt, Israel	1969	1970
Football	Honduras, El Salvador	1969	1969
Communist Coalition	Vietnam, United States, Cambodia, South Vietnam	1970	1971
Bangladesh	India, Pakistan	1971	1971
Yom Kippur	Egypt, Saudi Arabia, Israel, Jordan, Syria, Iraq	1973	1973
Turco-Cypriot	Turkey, Cyprus	1974	1974
War over Angola	Cuba, South Africa, Democratic Republic of the Congo, Angola	1975	1976
Second Ogaden, Phase 2	Ethiopia, Cuba, Somalia	1977	1978
Vietnamese-Cambodian	Vietnam, Cambodia	1977	1979
Ugandian-Tanzanian	Uganda, Tanzania, Libya	1978	1979
Sino-Vietnamese Punitive	China, Vietnam	1979	1979
Iran-Iraq	Iraq, Iran	1980	1988
Falkland Islands	United Kingdom, Argentina	1982	1982
War over Lebanon	Israel, Syria	1982	1982
War over the Aouzou Strip	Chad, Libya	1986	1987
Sino-Vietnamese Border	Vietnam, China	1987	1987

War	Combatants	Start	End
Gulf	Kuwait, United States, Canada, United Kingdom, Morocco, Iraq, Egypt, Oman, France, United Arab Emirates, Italy, Qatar, Saudi Arabia, Syria	1990	1991
Bosnian Independence	Croatia, Bosnia, Yugoslavia	1992	1992
Azeri-Armenian	Azerbaijan, Armenia	1993	1994
Cenepa Valley	Ecuador, Peru	1995	1995
Badme Border	Eritrea, Ethiopia	1998	2000
Kosovo	Turkey, Italy, United Kingdom, United States, Netherlands, France, Yugoslavia, Germany	1999	1999
Kargil	India, Pakistan	1999	1999
Invasion of Afghanistan	Canada, France, United Kingdom, United States, Australia, Afghanistan	2001	2001
Invasion of Iraq	Australia, United Kingdom, United States, Iraq	2003	2003

Data from Meredith Reid Sarkees and Frank Whelon Wayman,
*Resort to War: A Data Guide to Inter-state, Extra-state, Intra-state,
and Non-state Wars, 1816–2007* (Washington, DC: CQ Press, 2010).

Appendix B

Casino Game Rules

TEXAS HOLD 'EM POKER

All games of poker are played with a fifty-two-card deck. The ace is the highest card, although it can be used as a low card for a straight (that is, ace, two, three, four, five). The nine poker hands that can be made are listed below in descending order.

Royal Flush	Ten, jack, king, queen, ace of same suit
Straight Flush	Five consecutive cards of same suit
Four of a Kind	Four cards of same value
Full House	Three cards of same value + two cards of same value
Flush	Five cards of same suit
Straight	Five consecutive cards of any suit
Three of a Kind	Three cards of same value
Two Pairs	Two pairs of same value
One Pair	Two cards of same value

In Texas Hold 'Em, the goal is to make the best five-card hand out of seven total cards that are dealt. Two cards are dealt directly to each player, and five cards known as "community cards" are dealt at the center of the table and can be used by all players to make their hands.

The game proceeds as follows: One player is designated as the dealer, and usually one or two players to the dealer's left are required to put up "blinds," or forced bets. Each player at the table is then dealt two cards face down known as "pocket cards" or "hole cards." All players then have the opportunity to either *see* the last blind (bet the same amount), *raise* the blind (bet more than the amount of the blind), or *fold* (exit the game without betting any money).

When the betting round has finished, the dealer turns over three cards on the table. This step, known as the "flop," is followed by another betting round in which players can check (decline to bet), call (match the most recent bet), raise (bet more than the most recent bet), or fold (exit the game). The dealer turns over another card (the "turn"), and additional betting occurs. The dealer turns over one final card (the "river"), and a final betting round occurs before players are required to show their hands in the "showdown."

BLACKJACK

All cards are valued at face value, and picture cards (jack, queen, king) are counted as tens. An ace equals either one or eleven, and its value is at the discretion of the player. So a combination of a two and an ace could either equal three or thirteen, depending on the player's preference. The objective is to beat the dealer, who represents the "house." The only way to beat the dealer is to get a combined value greater than the value of the dealer's cards without going over twenty-one. If a player draws cards valued at more than twenty-one, they "bust" and lose the hand. If the player draws cards valued the same as the dealer's cards, they "push" and nobody wins the hand. If the player draws to exactly twenty-one with their first two cards (ace plus ten, jack, queen, or king), they have blackjack, which usually pays off at 3:2 (all other wins pay even money).

Each player is dealt two cards. The dealer also draws two cards and places one face down and one face up. Once the player is dealt their cards they have the option to "hit" (draw another card) or "stand" (decline to draw additional cards). Players also have the option to "split" or "double down" on their cards. Once the player decides to stand, the dealer turns over their face-down card, the values are totaled, and the winner is declared.

ROULETTE

The roulette wheel, which lies flat on a table, comprises thirty-eight numbered grooves, including each number from zero to thirty-six, plus a "double-zero" groove (this tends to only be true of American roulette wheels; European wheels typically do not include the double-zero). In addition, the numbers are alternately colored red or black. The dealer spins the wheel, and a small ball travels around the wheel until it settles into one of the grooves. Before the wheel is spun, players can place a variety of wagers on where the ball will land. These include wagers on specific numbers, black or red, or whether the ball will fall within a range of numbers. Bets are physically placed on a table known as the "layout," which offers "inside bets" (bets on specific numbers) and "outside bets" (all other types of bets).

Notes

Introduction

1. Spencer Jones and Peter Tsouras, *Over the Top: Alternative Histories of the First World War* (London: Frontline Books, 2014).
2. John Stoessinger, *Why Nations Go to War* (Toronto: Nelson Education, 2010).
3. For example, Francis Harry Hinsley, *Power and the Pursuit of Peace: Theory and Practice in the History of Relations Between States* (Cambridge, UK: Cambridge University Press, 1963).
4. John Arquilla, "Rolling the Iron Dice: Can Kim Jong Un Use His Nukes and Get Away with It?" *Foreign Policy,* April 8, 2013, http://foreign policy.com/2013/04/08/rolling-the-iron-dice/.
5. BBC, "Has Chess Got Anything to Do with War?" May 3, 2015, http://www.bbc.com/news/magazine-32542306.
6. Steven E. Woodworth, *The Art of Command in the Civil War* (Lincoln: University of Nebraska Press, 1998), ix.
7. BBC, "Has Chess Got Anything to Do with War?"
8. Harold James Ruthven Murray, *A History of Chess: The Original 1913 Edition* (New York: Skyhorse Publishing, 2015).
9. Carl von Clausewitz, *On War* (Overland Park, KS: Digireads Publishing, 2004).
10. David Sklansky, *The Theory of Poker* (Las Vegas: Two Plus Two Publishing, 1999), 22.
11. Jennifer Ouellette, "One of the Great Frontiers for Modern Physicists: Poker," *Discover Magazine,* January 22, 2011, http://discovermagazine.com/2010/nov/22-one-great-frontier-for-modern-physicists-poker.

12. Jennifer Ouellette, "Poker Science: Math, Game Theory Can Help a Gambler's Strategy, Study Says," Huffington Post.com, August 27, 2012, http://www.huffingtonpost.com/2012/08/27/poker-science-math-gambling_n_1833404.html.

13. Dan Carlin, "Blueprint for Armageddon III," Hardcore History Podcast 52, April 24, 2014.

14. Bruce Bueno de Mesquita, *The War Trap* (New Haven: Yale University Press, 1983), 4.

15. John von Neumann and Oskar Morgenstern, *Theory of Games and Economic Behavior* (Princeton: Princeton University Press, 2007).

16. Martin J. Osborne, *An Introduction to Game Theory*, vol. 3 (New York: Oxford University Press, 2004).

17. See, for example, James D. Morrow, *Game Theory for Political Scientists* (Princeton: Princeton University Press, 1994).

18. For example, Glenn H. Snyder, "'Prisoner's Dilemma' and 'Chicken' Models in International Politics," *International Studies Quarterly* 15, no. 1 (1971): 66–103; Arthur A. Stein, *Why Nations Cooperate: Circumstance and Choice in International Relations* (Ithaca: Cornell University Press, 1990); Ethan Bueno de Mesquita, "The Quality of Terror," *American Journal of Political Science* 49, no. 3 (2005): 515–30.

19. Another popular game, bridge, offers a similar balance.

20. John McDonald, *Strategy in Poker, Business, and War* (New York: W. W. Norton, 1996).

21. Ibid., 15.

22. Ibid., 21.

23. Sean Carroll, "The World Series," Preposterousuniverse.com, May 6, 2004.

24. See James D. Fearon, "Signaling Foreign Policy Interests: Tying Hands Versus Sinking Costs," *Journal of Conflict Resolution* 41, no. 1 (1997): 68–90.

25. Sklansky, *The Theory of Poker*, 4.

26. As outlined in Ouellette, "Poker Science."

27. Sklansky, *The Theory of Poker*.

28. Carroll, "The World Series."

29. Sklansky, *The Theory of Poker*, 18.

30. Jack Levy, "An Introduction to Prospect Theory," *Political Psychology* 13, no. 2 (1994): 171–86.

31. Sklansky, *The Theory of Poker*, 172.

32. Erik Gartzke, "War Is in the Error Term," *International Organization* 53, no. 3 (1999): 567–87. This process has also been referred to as "boxes within boxes." David A. Lake and Robert Powell, eds., *Strategic Choice and International Relations* (Princeton: Princeton University Press, 1999), 17.

33. Ibid., 4.

34. The term "actors" can also refer to gamblers and poker players.

35. Lake and Powell, *Strategic Choice and International Relations*, 6–7.
36. Daniel Kahneman and Amos Tversky, "Prospect Theory: An Analysis of Decision Under Risk," *Econometrica: Journal of the Econometric Society* (1979): 263–91; Amos Tversky and Daniel Kahneman, "Advances in Prospect Theory: Cumulative Representation of Uncertainty," *Journal of Risk and Uncertainty* 5, no. 4 (1992): 297–323.
37. Nesmith C. Ankeny, *Poker Strategy: Winning with Game Theory* (New York: Perigee Books, 1982).
38. McDonald, *Strategy in Poker, Business, and War*.
39. Matthew M. Hurley, *A Worker's Way of War: The Red Army's Doctrinal Debate, 1918–1924* (Pickle Partners Publishing, 2015), 95.

Chapter 1. The Bet to End All Bets

1. James D. Fearon, "Rationalist Explanations for War," *International Organization* 49, no. 3 (1995): 379–414; Giacomo Chiozza and Hein E. Goemans, "International Conflict and the Tenure of Leaders: Is War Still Ex Post Inefficient?" *American Journal of Political Science* 48, no. 3 (2004): 604–19; Robert Powell, "War as a Commitment Problem," *International Organization* 60, no. 1 (2006): 169.
2. Many of these "surprises" also involve "unknown unknowns," often purely random events and circumstances that cannot be predicted. We address these factors in the later chapters in this book.
3. Donald Wittman, "How a War Ends: A Rational Model Approach," *Journal of Conflict Resolution* 23, no. 4 (1979): 743–63; Geoffrey Blainey, *Causes of War* (New York: Simon and Schuster, 1988).
4. John Esterbrook, "Rumsfeld: It Would Be a Short War," CBS News, November 15, 2002, http://www.cbsnews.com/news/rumsfeld-it-would -be-a-short-war/.
5. Blainey, *Causes of War*, 47.
6. It is this pervasive optimism, despite such high risks and the potential for devastating losses, that allows us to firmly classify war as a gamble.
7. Mark Fey and Kristopher W. Ramsay, in "Mutual Optimism and War," *American Journal of Political Science* 51, no. 4 (2007): 738–54, note that, contrary to popular belief, mutual optimism cannot logically lead to war. They argue that if both sides are optimistic in the lead-up to a war, they should recognize that they have either overestimated their own strength or underestimated that of their opponent. Nonetheless, optimism is often a typical characteristic of those who initiate conflicts.
8. Frank Scoblete, "The Best and Worst Bets in the Casino," Casinocenter .com, http://www.casinocenter.com/the-best-and-worst-bets-in-the -casinos/.
9. Abramo F. K. Organski and Jacek Kugler, *The War Ledger* (Chicago: University of Chicago Press, 1981).
10. Clausewitz, *On War*.

11. Ibid.
12. Gary King and Langche Zeng, "Logistic Regression in Rare Events Data," *Political Analysis* 9, no. 2 (2001): 137–63; Michael Tomz, Jason Wittenberg, and Gary King, "Clarify: Software for Interpreting and Presenting Statistical Results," 2003, http://gking.harvard.edu/.
13. Additional data on these wars are available at the Correlates of War project. Meredith Reid Sarkees and Frank Whelon Wayman, *Resort to War: A Data Guide to Inter-state, Extra-state, Intra-state, and Non-state Wars, 1816–2007* (Washington, DC: CQ Press, 2010). Wars involve sustained combat between at least two organized armed forces and must result in a minimum of one thousand battle deaths within any twelve-month period.
14. The debate over whether war is increasingly rare will be addressed in chapter five.
15. Militarized interstate disputes include any situation in which one state threatens, mobilizes, or uses military force against another state. Daniel M. Jones, Stuart A. Bremer, and J. David Singer, "Militarized Interstate Disputes, 1816–1992: Rationale, Coding Rules, and Empirical Patterns," *Conflict Management and Peace Science* 15, no. 2 (1996): 163–213.
16. Thomas C. Schelling, *The Strategy of Conflict* (Cambridge: Harvard University Press, 1960); Blainey *Causes of War*; Fearon, "Rationalist Explanations for War."
17. This is actually a common scenario, as the main issue over which conflict has been fought is territorial disputes. See John Vasquez, *The War Puzzle Revisisted* (Cambridge, UK: Cambridge University Press, 2009).
18. In chapter two, we will discuss why certain issues are more likely than others to involve all-or-nothing demands.
19. For examples of how territorial disputes may in turn involve other disputes, see Ian Bannon and Paul Collier, *Natural Resources and Violent Conflict: Options and Actions* (Washington, DC: World Bank Publications, 2003); Michael Ross, "What Do We Know About Natural Resources and Civil War?" *Journal of Peace Research* 41, no. 3 (2004): 337; Monica Duffy Toft, *The Geography of Ethnic Violence: Identity, Interests, and the Indivisibility of Territory* (Princeton: Princeton University Press, 2005); Päivi Lujala, "The Spoils of Nature: Armed Civil Conflict and Rebel Access to Natural Resources," *Journal of Peace Research* 47, no. 1 (2010): 15–28.
20. Blainey, *Causes of War.*
21. Christian Hartmann, *Operation Barbarossa: Nazi Germany's War in the East, 1941–1945* (Oxford, UK: Oxford University Press, 2013), 141.
22. Ibid.
23. The basic equation for expected utility is the probability of winning multiplied by the expected payoff from winning. This total is then added to the probability of losing multiplied by the expected payoff from losing. The expected costs are then subtracted from this sum.

24. Fearon, "Rationalist Explanations for War."

25. Ibid.

26. Sklansky, *The Theory of Poker*.

27. Ibid.

28. Ibid.

29. In *Causes of War*, Blainey cites this as one of the reasons why military alliances may be linked to higher probabilities of conflict. With more actors, the quality of decisionmaking is reduced, and the chance of miscalculations is higher.

30. Sklansky, *The Theory of Poker*, 71.

31. Bueno de Mesquita, *The War Trap*.

32. Ibid., 182.

33. Blainey, *Causes of War*.

34. Timothy M. Karcher, "The Victory Disease," *Military Review* 83, no. 4 (2003): 9.

35. Ibid. Karcher argues that personality traits such as arrogance and complacency lead to the Victory Disease, but arrogance and complacency generally thrive when actors have little information to convince them otherwise.

36. The root causes of the Franco-Prussian War were much more complicated, of course. But the issues of Spanish succession would not seem to be sufficient to start a war. Geoffrey Wawro, *The Franco-Prussian War: The German Conquest of France in 1870–1871* (Cambridge: Harvard University Press, 2005).

37. Jeffry A. Frieden, *Actors and Preferences in International Relations* (Princeton: Princeton University Press, 1999), 39–76.

38. Powell, "War as a Commitment Problem."

39. Ibid.; Jack S. Levy, "Preventive War and Democratic Politics," *International Studies Quarterly* 52, no. 1 (2008): 1–24; Dan Reiter, *How Wars End* (Princeton: Princeton University Press, 2009).

40. Stuart A. Bremer, "Dangerous Dyads: Conditions Affecting the Likelihood of Interstate War, 1816–1965," *Journal of Conflict Resolution* 36, no. 2 (1992): 309–41; Bruce Bueno De Mesquita and David Lalman, *War and Reason: Domestic and International Imperatives* (Cambridge: Harvard University Press, 1992); Charles S. Gochman, *Prisoners of War? Nation-states in the Modern Era* (Lexington, MA: Lexington Books, 1990); Douglas Lemke and Suzanne Werner, "Power Parity, Commitment to Change, and War," *International Studies Quarterly* 40, no. 2 (1996): 235–60.

41. D. Scott Bennett and Allan C. Stam, "A Universal Test of an Expected Utility Theory of War," *International Studies Quarterly* 44, no. 3 (2000): 451–80.

42. David A. Lake, "Two Cheers for Bargaining Theory: Assessing Rationalist Explanations of the Iraq War," *International Security* 35, no. 3

(2011): 7–52. It should be noted, however, that a bargaining range should still exist. That is, there will still be a range of negotiated settlements that both states prefer to war. This range, however, will be smaller in the presence of war hawks.

43. Clausewitz, *On War*; Blainey, *Causes of War.*
44. Bueno de Mesquita, *The War Trap.*
45. Gochman, *Prisoners of War?* Bueno De Mesquita and Lalman, *War and Reason*; Bremer, "Dangerous Dyads;" Lemke and Werner, "Power Parity, Commitment to Change, and War."
46. Sklansky, *The Theory of Poker.*
47. Bueno de Mesquita, *The War Trap*; Blainey, *Causes of War.*
48. Hartmann, *Operation Barbarossa.*
49. Sklansky, *The Theory of Poker*, 166.
50. Glenn Kessler, "Saddam Hussein Said WMD Talk Helped Him Look Strong to Iran," *Washington Post,* July 2, 2009, http://www.washington post.com/wp-dyn/content/article/2009/07/01/AR2009070104217.html.
51. Graham T. Allison et al., *Essence of Decision: Explaining the Cuban Missile Crisis*, 2nd ed. (New York: Longman, 1999); John Lewis Gaddis, *The Cold War: A New History* (New York: Penguin, 2005).
52. Kenneth A. Schultz, "Do Democratic Institutions Constrain or Inform? Contrasting Two Institutional Perspectives on Democracy and War," *International Organization* 53, no. 2 (1999): 233–66.
53. Ian Nish et al., *The Origins of the Russo-Japanese War* (London: Routledge, 2014).
54. Shumpei Okamoto, *The Japanese Oligarchy and the Russo-Japanese War* (New York: Columbia University Press, 1970), concludes that the emperor's advisers were not fully confident in their ability to match Russia on the battlefield. Nonetheless, they maintained quite a bit of private information about their substantial capabilities.
55. Nish et al., *The Origins of the Russo-Japanese War*, 208.
56. Eugene Poteat, "The Use and Abuse of Intelligence: An Intelligence Provider's Perspective," *Diplomacy and Statecraft* 11, no. 2 (2000): 1–16; Gaddis, *The Cold War.*
57. Paul Vorbeck Lettow, *Ronald Reagan and His Quest to Abolish Nuclear Weapons* (New York: Random House, 2006).
58. Thomas A. Heppenheimer, *The Space Shuttle Decision: NASA's Search for a Reusable Space Vehicle* (Washington, DC: Government Printing Office,1999).
59. Lettow, *Ronald Reagan and His Quest to Abolish Nuclear Weapons.*
60. Sklansky, *The Theory of Poker.* The larger the ante, incidentally, the more likely players are to bet on "marginal" hands that they otherwise wouldn't bet on. This means that in large ante situations, players are far more likely to play weaker hands and bluff.

61. Organski and Kugler, *The War Ledger*, found that in disputes between nuclear and nonnuclear states, the nuclear state was more likely to back down and concede to the nonnuclear state.

62. Blainey, *Causes of War.*

63. Michael D. Intriligator and Dagobert L. Brito, "Non-Armageddon Solutions to the Arms Race," *Contemporary Security Policy* 6, no. 1 (1985): 41–57.

64. Gaddis, *The Cold War.*

65. Ibid., 120.

66. Powell, "War as a Commitment Problem."

67. Kenneth N. Waltz, *Theory of International Politics* (Boston: McGraw-Hill, 1979); John J. Mearsheimer, *The Tragedy of Great Power Politics* (New York: W. W. Norton, 2001).

68. James Morrow, *The Strategic Setting of Choices: Signaling, Commitment, and Negotiation in International Politics* (Princeton: Princeton University Press,1999), 77–144.

69. See the following, all by James D. Fearon: "Deterrence and the Spiral Model: The Role of Costly Signals in Crisis Bargaining," presentation at annual meeting of the American Political Science Association, San Francisco, 1990; "Threats to Use Force: Costly Signals and Bargaining in International Costs," Ph.D. diss., University of California, Berkeley, 1992; "Domestic Political Audiences and the Escalation of International Disputes," *American Political Science Review* 88, no. 3 (1994): 577–92; and "Signaling Foreign Policy Interests: Tying Hands Versus Sinking Costs," *Journal of Conflict Resolution* 41, no. 1 (1997): 68–90.

70. Andrew Kydd, "Trust, Reassurance, and Cooperation," *International Organization* 54, no. 2 (2000): 325–57; Anna K. Jarstad and Desirée Nilsson, "From Words to Deeds: The Implementation of Power-sharing Pacts in Peace Accords," *Conflict Management and Peace Science* 25, no. 3 (2008): 206–23; Madhav Joshi, Erik Melander, and Jason Michael Quinn, "Sequencing the Peace: How the Order of Peace Agreement Implementation Can Reduce the Destabilizing Effects of Post-accord Elections," *Journal of Conflict Resolution* 61, no. 1 (March 2015).

71. Haseeb Qureshi, *How to Be a Poker Player: The Philosophy of Poker* (Amazon Digital Service, 2013).

72. Sklansky, *The Theory of Poker*; Qureshi, *How to Be a Poker Player.*

73. This is known as "slowplaying" a hand in poker parlance. Sklansky, *The Theory of Poker.*

74. Stephen William Van Evera, *Causes of War,* vol. 2 (Berkeley: University of California Press, 1984); Barry Nalebuff, *Brinkmanship and Nuclear Deterrence: The Neutrality of Escalation* (Princeton: Princeton University Press, 1987); Fearon, "Domestic Political Audiences and the Escalation of International Disputes."

75. Clausewitz, *On War.*

76. Ankeny, *Poker Strategy.*
77. Fearon, "Signaling Foreign Policy Interests."
78. Ibid.
79. Ibid. As Fearon notes, most military mobilizations involve both sunk costs and tying hands, and it is difficult to identify an example with *purely* sunk costs and no tying of hands.
80. David Miller, *The Cold War: A History* (London: Macmillan, 2015).
81. Fearon, "Domestic Political Audiences and the Escalation of International Disputes"; Kenneth A. Schultz, "Domestic Opposition and Signaling in International Crises," *American Political Science Review* 92, no. 4 (1998): 829–44; Alastair Smith, "International Crises and Domestic Politics," *American Political Science Review* 92, no. 3 (1998): 623–38; Bruce Bueno de Mesquita et al., "An Institutional Explanation of the Democratic Peace," *American Political Science Review* 93, no. 4 (1999): 791–807; Lisa L. Martin, *Democratic Commitments: Legislatures and International Cooperation* (Princeton: Princeton University Press, 2000); Paul K. Huth and Todd L. Allee, "Domestic Political Accountability and the Escalation and Settlement of International Disputes," *Journal of Conflict Resolution* 46, no. 6 (2002): 754–90; Bruce Bueno de Mesquita et al., *The Logic of Political Survival* (Cambridge: MIT Press, 2003).
82. Nancy Bernkopf Tucker, "China and America: 1941–1991," *Foreign Affairs* 70, no. 5 (1991): 1991–92.
83. For example, Justin Conrad, "How Democratic Alliances Solve the Power Parity Problem," *British Journal of Political Science* (2015).
84. Lake and Powell, *Strategic Choice and International Relations.*
85. The basic assumption in the game is that for each player the most preferred scenario is to defect when the other player cooperates (*D,C*), followed by the scenario where they both cooperate (*C,C*), followed by the scenario where the other player defects when they cooperate (*C,D*), followed by the scenario where they both defect (*D,D*). This is how the payoffs are derived.
86. R. Harrison Wagner, "The Theory of Games and the Problem of International Cooperation," *American Political Science Review* 77, no. 2 (1983): 330–46.
87. Glenn C. Snyder and Paul Diesing, *Conflict Among Nations: Bargaining, Decision Making, and System Structure in International Crises* (Princeton: Princeton University Press, 1977).
88. Ibid.; Robert Axelrod, *The Evolution of Cooperation* (New York: Basic Books, 1984).
89. Axelrod, *The Evolution of Cooperation.*
90. This example is adapted from Qureshi, *How to Be a Poker Player.*
91. Ibid.
92. Ibid.
93. Simon Long, "Calling Kim Jong Il's Bluff," *The Economist,* April 23, 2009, http://www.economist.com/node/13527316.

94. Schultz, "Do Democratic Institutions Constrain or Inform?"
95. Powell, "War as a Commitment Problem."

Chapter 2. How Weak Players Overcome Stronger Adversaries

1. Ankeny, *Poker Strategy*.
2. Lake, "Two Cheers for Bargaining Theory."
3. Terrorism, which is discussed in this chapter, has been referred to as a "weapon of the weak." Martha Crenshaw, "The Causes of Terrorism," *Comparative Politics* 13, no. 4 (1981): 379–99.
4. Although Sklansky argues in *The Theory of Poker* that the importance of bluffing in poker has been overestimated.
5. Thomas R. Martin, *Ancient Greece: From Prehistoric to Hellenistic Times* (New Haven: Yale University Press, 2013).
6. Akira Iriye et al., *The Origins of the Second World War in Asia and the Pacific* (New York: Routledge, 2014).
7. Max Weber, Charles Wright Mills, and Hans Heinrich Gerth, *Politics as a Vocation* (Philadelphia: Fortress Press, 1965).
8. Joseph K. Young, "The Strength of al-Shabab," PoliticalViolenceata Glance.org, 2013, http://politicalviolenceataglance.org/2013/09/26/the-strength-of-al-shabab/; Lisa De Bode, "Why Is al-Shabab Attacking Kenya?" *Al Jazeera America*, April 3, 2015, http://america.aljazeera.com/articles/2015/4/3/why-is-al-shabab-attacking-kenya.html.
9. The United States, for its part, launched raids and drone strikes against the organization in retaliation.
10. Adam Taylor, "What's Behind the Return of al-Shabab, the Terror Group that Killed at Least 147 People in Kenya?" *Washington Post*, April 3, 2015.
11. For example, Abramo F. K. Organski, *World Politics* (New York: Knopf, 1968); Waltz, *Theory of International Politics*; Organski and Kugler, *The War Ledger*; Ronald L. Tammen, "The Organski Legacy: A Fifty-Year Research Program," *International Interactions* 34, no. 4 (2008): 314–32.
12. Waltz, *Theory of International Politics*.
13. For example, Gochman, *Prisoners of War?*; Bueno De Mesquita and Lalman, *War and Reason*; Bremer, "Dangerous Dyads"; Lemke and Werner, "Power Parity, Commitment to Change, and War."
14. In many of these studies, the measurement of "power" is rather unclear. However, most quantitative studies of power distributions use a standard measure of power, which is an index including a state's total population, urban population, iron and steel production, energy consumption, military personnel, and military expenditure. J. David Singer, Stuart Bremer, and John Stuckey, *Capability Distribution, Uncertainty, and Major Power War, 1820–1965* (Beverly Hills, CA: Sage Publications, 1972), 19–48. The measure is available for most states in the international system across nearly two hundred years.

15. McDonald, *Strategy in Poker, Business, and War,* 125.

16. Qureshi, *How to Be a Poker Player.*

17. Blainey, *Causes of War.*

18. Kessler, "Saddam Hussein Said WMD Talk Helped Him Look Strong to Iran."

19. Sklansky, *The Theory of Poker.*

20. See Robert S. Litwak, *Rogue States and U.S. Foreign Policy: Containment after the Cold War* (Washington, DC: Woodrow Wilson Center Press, 2000); Robert S. Litwak, "What's in a Name? The Changing Foreign Policy Lexicon," *Journal of International Affairs* 54, no. 2 (2001): 375–94; Mary Caprioli and Peter F. Trumbore, "Rhetoric Versus Reality: Rogue States in Interstate Conflict," *Journal of Conflict Resolution* 49, no. 5 (2005): 770–91.

21. For example, Scott Sagan, Kenneth Waltz, and Richard K. Betts, "A Nuclear Iran: Promoting Stability or Courting Disaster?" *Journal of International Affairs* 60, no. 2 (2007): 135.

22. Lake, "Two Cheers for Bargaining Theory."

23. Robert H. Kupperman, Debra Van Opstal, and David Williamson, "Terror, the Strategic Tool: Response and Control," *Annals of the American Academy of Political and Social Science* 463, no. 1 (1982): 24–38; Justin Conrad, "Interstate Rivalry and Terrorism: An Unprobed Link," *Journal of Conflict Resolution* 55, no. 4 (2011): 529–55.

24. Gary Sick, "Iran: Confronting Terrorism," *Washington Quarterly* 26, no. 4 (2003): 83–98; Conrad, "Interstate Rivalry and Terrorism."

25. David E. Cunningham, Kristian Skrede Gleditsch, and Idean Salehyan, "Non-state Actors in Civil Wars: A New Dataset," *Conflict Management and Peace Science* 30, no. 5 (2013).

26. Weber, Mills, and Gerth, *Politics as a Vocation.*

27. Sklansky, *The Theory of Poker,* 55.

28. Arnold Snyder, *The Big Book of Blackjack* (New York: Cardoza Publishing, 2006).

29. William McCants, *The ISIS Apocalypse: The History, Strategy, and Doomsday Vision of the Islamic State* (New York: Macmillan, 2015).

30. This example is adapted from Sklansky, *The Theory of Poker.*

31. Ibid., 56.

32. Not surprisingly, tactics recommended to beginners or novices in games such as poker are often referred to as "guerrilla tactics" because they acknowledge the inherent disadvantage at which such players find themselves. Such tactics are specifically designed to allow beginners to compete with more sophisticated (that is, more capable) players when they otherwise might not have a chance. Frank Scoblete, *Guerrilla Gambling: How to Beat the Casinos at Their Own Games!* (Chicago: Bonus Books, 1993).

33. David A. Lake, "Rational Extremism: Understanding Terrorism in the Twenty-first Century," *Dialogue IO* 1, no. 1 (2002): 15–29.

34. This view assumes that public opinion on a given issue is distributed normally.

35. Lake, "Rational Extremism"; A. H. Kydd and B. F. Walter, "The Strategies of Terrorism," *International Security* 31, no. 1 (2006): 49–80.

36. Max Abrahms, "The Political Effectiveness of Terrorism Revisited," *Comparative Political Studies* 45, no. 3 (2012): 366–93.

37. John Talbott, "French Public Opinion and the Algerian War: A Research Note," *French Historical Studies* 9, no. 2 (1975): 354–61.

38. Louis Kriesberg, "Changing Conflict Asymmetries Constructively," *Dynamics of Asymmetric Conflict* 2, no. 1 (2009): 4–22.

39. A majority of French citizens favored negotiations with the FLN as early as 1957. Talbott, "French Public Opinion and the Algerian War."

40. Based on data compiled by Joseph K. Young and Laura Dugan, "Why Do Terrorist Groups Endure," presentation at International Studies Association meetings, New Orleans, LA, 2010.

41. *The Forever War.*

42. BBC, "Guide to the Syrian Rebels," December 13, 2013, http://www.bbc.com/news/world-middle-east-24403003.

43. Darius Rejali, *Torture and Democracy* (Princeton: Princeton University Press, 2009); Courtenay R. Conrad, Justin Conrad, and Joseph K. Young, "Tyrants and Terrorism: Why Some Autocrats Are Terrorized While Others Are Not," *International Studies Quarterly* 58, no. 3 (2014): 539–49.

44. Nils Petter Gleditsch et al., "Armed Conflict 1946–2001: A New Dataset," *Journal of Peace Research* 39, no. 5 (2002): 615–37.

45. Barbara F. Walter, "The Critical Barrier to Civil War Settlement," *International Organization* 51, no. 3 (1997): 335–64.

46. Ankeny, *Poker Strategy.*

47. Sklansky, *The Theory of Poker.*

48. Clausewitz, *On War.*

49. Ibid.

50. Cathy Otten, "Meet the Fighters Preparing to Retake Mosul from ISIL," *Al Jazeera,* March 25, 2015, http://www.aljazeera.com/news/middleeast/2015/03/meet-fighters-preparing-retake-mosul-isil-150325063226372.html.

51. Rowan Scarborough, "ISIL Shows Increasing Strength and Structure, Takes War Where al Qaeda Couldn't," *Washington Times,* July 6, 2014, http://www.washingtontimes.com/news/2014/jul/6/isil-shows-increasing-strength-structure/?page=all.

52. This analysis of decisionmaking is adapted from bluffing strategy discussions in Ankeny, *Poker Strategy*, and Sklansky, *The Theory of Poker.*

53. Abrahms, "The Political Effectiveness of Terrorism Revisited."

54. Snyder, *The Big Book of Blackjack*.
55. James T. Laney and Jason T. Shaplen, "How to Deal with North Korea," *Foreign Affairs* 82, no. 2 (2003): 16–30.
56. Lake, "Two Cheers for Bargaining Theory."
57. Colin Powell, remarks at the World Economic Forum, Davos, Switzerland, January 26, 2003.
58. James D. Fearon, "Bargaining Over Objects that Influence Future Bargaining Power," annual meeting of the American Political Science Association, Washington, DC, August 1996; Barbara F. Walter, "The Critical Barrier to Civil War Settlement," *International Organization* 51, no. 3 (1997): 335–64; Barbara F. Walter, "Designing Transitions from Civil War: Demobilization, Democratization, and Commitments to Peace," *International Security* 24, no. 1 (1999): 127–55; Barbara F. Walter, *Committing to Peace: The Successful Settlement of Civil Wars* (Princeton: Princeton University Press, 2002); Michael W. Doyle and Nicholas Sambanis, "International Peacebuilding: A Theoretical and Quantitative Analysis," *American Political Science Review* 94, no. 4 (2000): 779–801; Michael W. Doyle and Nicholas Sambanis, *Making War and Building Peace: United Nations Peace Operations* (Princeton: Princeton University Press, 2006); Virginia Page Fortna, "Scraps of Paper? Agreements and the Durability of Peace," *International Organization* 57, no. 2 (2003): 337–72; Virginia Page Fortna, *Peace Time: Cease-fire Agreements and the Durability of Peace* (Princeton: Princeton University Press, 2004).
59. Walter, "The Critical Barrier to Civil War Settlement."
60. Joakim Kreutz, "How and When Armed Conflicts End: Introducing the UCDP Conflict Termination Dataset," *Journal of Peace Research* 47, no. 2 (2010): 243–50.
61. Walter, *Committing to Peace*.
62. Joshi, Melander, and Quinn, "Sequencing the Peace."
63. We will return to these problems of resolution in the next chapter, but for now, it serves to illustrate how credibility is a significant issue in asymmetric conflicts, but particularly in intrastate conflicts.
64. Kydd and Walter, "The Strategies of Terrorism."
65. Brian Michael Jenkins, *Al Qaeda in its Third Decade* (Santa Monica, CA: RAND Corporation, 2012).
66. Bruce Riedel, "Al Qaeda Strikes Back," *Foreign Affairs* 86, no. 3 (2007): 24; Leah Farrall, "How al Qaeda Works," *Foreign Affairs* 90, no. 2 (2011): 128.
67. For instance, in October 2002 in a video statement, al-Zawahiri said the group was planning an attack against the United States that "will fill your hearts with horror." NBC News, "Timeline of al-Qaida Statements," http://www.nbcnews.com/id/4686034/ns/world_news-hunt_for _al_qaida/t/timeline-al-qaida-statements/#.WKSQPa8ixPY.

68. Arguably, al Qaeda's biggest bluff during the post-9/11 years was its pursuit of nuclear weapons. John Mueller, "Radioactive Hype," *National Interest* (September-October 2007), 59–65.

69. Such efforts all benefit from inherent cognitive biases, which are discussed in chapter four.

70. Jason Lyall, "Does Indiscriminate Violence Incite Insurgent Attacks? Evidence from Chechnya," *Journal of Conflict Resolution* 53, no. 3 (2009); Audrey Kurth Cronin, *How Terrorism Ends: Understanding the Decline and Demise of Terrorist Campaigns* (Princeton: Princeton University Press, 2009).

71. Sklansky, *The Theory of Poker,* 166.

72. Specifically, Sklansky, in *The Theory of Poker*, argues that the correct mixed strategy is to bluff "a predetermined percentage of the time, but you introduce a random element so that your opponent cannot know when you are making the play and when you are not."

73. For example, Martin W. Slann and Bernard Schechterman, *Multi-dimensional Terrorism* (Boulder, CO: Lynne Rienner, 1987); Oliver Thränert, "Preemption, Civil Defense, and Psychological Analysis: Three Necessary Tools in Responding to Irrational Terrorism," *Politics and the Life Sciences* 15, no. 2 (1996): 228–30; Max Abrahms, "Are Terrorists Really Rational? The Palestinian Example," *Orbis* 48, no. 3 (2004): 533–49.

74. Daniel Kahneman and Amos Tversky, "Subjective Probability: A Judgment of Representativeness," in *The Concept of Probability in Psychological Experiments,* ed. Carl-Axel S. Stahl von Holstein (New York: Springer, 1974), 25–48.

75. Leonard Mlodinow, *The Drunkard's Walk: How Randomness Rules our Lives* (New York: Vintage Books, 2009).

76. Richards J. Heuer, *Psychology of Intelligence Analysis* (Washington, DC: Center for the Study of Intelligence, 1999).

77. William Feller, *An Introduction to Probability Theory and Its Applications*, vol. 1 (New York: John Wiley and Sons, 1968).

78. Claude Berrebi and Darius Lakdawalla, "How Does Terrorism Risk Vary Across Space and Time? An Analysis Based on the Israeli Experience," *Defence and Peace Economics* 18, no. 2 (2007): 113–31.

79. For example,Todd Sandler and Harvey E. Lapan, "The Calculus of Dissent: An Analysis of Terrorists' Choice of Targets," *Synthese* 76, no. 2 (1988): 245–61; Walter Enders and Todd Sandler, "Causality Between Transnational Terrorism and Tourism: The Case of Spain," *Studies in Conflict and Terrorism* 14, no. 1 (1991): 49–58; G. Feichtinger et al., "Terrorism Control in the Tourism Industry," *Journal of Optimization Theory and Applications* 108, no. 2 (2001): 283–96; Ismail Onat, "An Analysis of Spatial Correlates of Terrorism Using

Risk Terrain Modeling," *Terrorism and Political Violence*, August 24, 2016, http://www.tandfonline.com/doi/full/10.1080/09546553.2016.12 15309?scroll=top&needAccess=true 0.

80. Richard A Horsley, "The Sicarii: Ancient Jewish 'Terrorists'," *Journal of Religion* 59, no. 4 (1979): 435–58.

81. McDonald, *Strategy in Poker, Business, and War*.

82. Qureshi, *How to Be a Poker Player*.

83. Sun Tzu, *The Art of War* (Boulder, CO: Shambhala Publications, 2011).

84. Max Abrahms, "What Terrorists Really Want: Terrorist Motives and Counterterrorism Strategy," *International Security* 32, no. 4 (2008): 78–105.

85. See Crenshaw, "The Causes of Terrorism"; Justin Conrad and Kevin Greene, "Competition, Differentiation, and the Severity of Terrorist Attacks," *Journal of Politics* 77, no. 2 (2015): 546–61.

86. Brunson's comments are recounted in Sklansky, *The Theory of Poker*.

87. Ibid.

Chapter 3. Game Flow and Reputation

1. In *The Theory of Poker*, Sklansky refers to these kinds of players as "suckers."

2. Some level of abstraction is necessary, however, to identify causal processes. Morris R. Cohen and Ernest Nagel, *An Introduction to Logic and Scientific Method* (New York: Harcourt Brace, 1934).

3. R. Harrison Wagner, "Bargaining and War," *American Journal of Political Science* 43, no. 4 (2000): 469–84.

4. Sklansky, *The Theory of Poker*; Qureshi, *How to Be a Poker Player*.

5. Sklansky, *The Theory of Poker*, 209.

6. Our discussion of implied odds in chapter two is just one example of how anticipation of the future can change behavior and strategy.

7. For example, James D. Morrow, "A Continuous-Outcome Expected Utility Theory of War," *Journal of Conflict Resolution* 29, no. 3 (1985): 473–502; Fearon, "Threats to Use Force"; Robert Powell, "Stability and the Distribution of Power," *World Politics* 48, no. 2 (1996): 239–67.

8. Jonathan Murphy, "Peace in our Time: Constructing Parallels Between Britain's Failure to Appease Hitler and British Policy Towards Republican Dissidents in Northern Ireland," *Eras* 12, no. 2 (2011).

9. Fearon, "Threats to Use Force"; Wagner, "Bargaining and War."

10. Clausewitz, *On War*.

11. Sklansky, in *The Theory of Poker*, argues that once bets reach a certain size, bluffing becomes a moot point.

12. Lake, "Two Cheers for Bargaining Theory."

13. For example, Jerald A. Combs, *American Diplomatic History: Two Centuries of Changing Interpretations* (Berkeley: University of California Press, 1983); Geir Lundestad, "Moralism, Presentism, Exceptionalism,

Provincialism, and Other Extravagances in American Writings on the Early Cold War Years," *Diplomatic History* 13, no. 4 (1989): 527–45; Herbert Feis, *From Trust to Terror: The Onset of the Cold War, 1945–1950* (New York: Norton, 1970).

14. For example, Thomas G. Paterson, *Meeting the Communist Threat: Truman to Reagan* (New York: Oxford University Press, 1988); Bruce Cumings, *The Origins of the Korean War*, vol. 2, *The Roaring of the Cataract, 1947–1950* (Princeton: Princeton University Press, 1999), 59; R. Craig Nation, *Black Earth, Red Star: A History of Soviet Security Policy, 1917–1991* (Ithaca: Cornell University Press, 1992).

15. Fearon, "Rationalist Explanations for War."

16. Qureshi, *How to Be a Poker Player*, 55.

17. Sklansky, *The Theory of Poker*.

18. Qureshi, *How to Be a Poker Player*.

19. Sklansky, *The Theory of Poker*.

20. Kahneman and Tversky, "Subjective Probability."

21. Qureshi, *How to Be a Poker Player*.

22. Darse Billings et al., "Approximating Game-Theoretic Optimal Strategies for Full-scale Poker," IJCAI.org, 2003, https://www.ijcai.org/Proceedings/03/Papers/097.pdf, 661–68; Doyle Brunson, "Game Theory Simplified, and Why Fixed Strategies Fail," blog post.

23. Morrow, *The Strategic Setting of Choices*.

24. Shaun Walker, "As Russia Enters War in Syria, Conflict in Ukraine Begins to Wind Down," *Guardian*, October 1, 2015, http://www.theguardian.com/world/2015/oct/01/as-russia-enters-war-in-syria-conflict-in-ukraine-begins-to-wind-down.

25. Maksymilian Czuperski et al., "Putin's Secret Warriors: Russian Soldiers Sent to Fight in Ukraine," *Newsweek*, June 6, 2015, http://www.newsweek.com/putins-secret-warriors-tales-three-russian-soldiers-sent-fight-ukraine-339665.

26. Cronin, *How Terrorism Ends*.

27. Ibid.

28. BBC, "Colombia Suspends FARC Peace Talks Over Kidnapping," BBC.com, November 17, 2014, http://www.bbc.com/news/world-latin-america-30076980.

29. The seminal analysis of spoiling is Stephen John Stedman, "Spoiler Problems in Peace Processes," *International Security* 22, no. 2 (1997): 5–53; for an important application to terrorism, see A. H. Kydd and B. Walter, "Sabotaging the Peace: The Politics of Extremist Violence," *International Organization* 56, no. 2 (2002): 263–96.

30. Stedman, "Spoiler Problems in Peace Processes," 5.

31. Kydd and Walter, "Sabotaging the Peace."

32. Justin Conrad and James I. Walsh, "International Cooperation, Spoiling, and Transnational Terrorism," *International Interactions* 40, no. 4 (2013): 453–76.

33. Molly M. Melin and Alexandru Grigorescu, "Connecting the Dots: Dispute Resolution and Escalation in a World of Entangled Territorial Claims," *Journal of Conflict Resolution* 58, no. 6 (2014): 1085–1109; Philip A. Schrodt and Alex Mintz, "The Conditional Probability Analysis of International Events Data," *American Journal of Political Science* 32, no. 1 (1988): 217–30; Mark J. C. Crescenzi, "Reputation and Interstate Conflict," *American Journal of Political Science* 51, no. 2 (2007): 382–96.

34. Melin and Grigorescu, "Connecting the Dots."

35. In *The Theory of Poker*, Sklansky notes that "the odds against a bluff's working increase almost geometrically with each extra person in a pot."

36. Ibid.

37. Clausewitz, *On War*.

38. Talbott, "French Public Opinion and the Algerian War."

39. Ankeny, *Poker Strategy*.

40. In fact, in the next chapter we examine how a losing position often leads to more risky behavior.

41. Carl H. Builder, Steven C. Bankes, and Richard Nordin, *Command Concepts* (Santa Barbara, CA: RAND Corporation, 1999).

42. David Halberstam, *The Coldest Winter: America and the Korean War* (New York: Hyperion, 2008).

43. Rotem Kowner, "Becoming an Honorary Civilized Nation: Remaking Japan's Military Image during the Russo-Japanese War, 1904–1905," *Historian* 64, no. 1 (2001): 19–38.

44. Alan C. Downs "War and Ruin: William T. Sherman and the Savannah Campaign," *Civil War History* 51, no. 3 (2005): 333–35.

45. Crenshaw, "The Causes of Terrorism"; Kydd and Walter, "The Strategies of Terrorism."

46. Olga Oliker, *Russia's Chechen Wars 1994–2000: Lessons from Urban Combat* (Santa Barbara, CA: RAND Corporation, 2001).

47. Qureshi, *How to Be a Poker Player*.

48. See the following, all by Mary Caprioli and Peter F. Trumbore: "Ethnic Discrimination and Interstate Violence: Testing the International Impact of Domestic Behavior," *Journal of Peace Research* 40, no. 1 (2003): 5–23; "Identifying Rogue States and Testing their Interstate Conflict Behavior," *European Journal of International Relations* 9, no. 3 (2003): 377–406; "Rhetoric Versus Reality"; and "Human Rights Rogues in Interstate Disputes, 1980–2001," *Journal of Peace Research* 43, no. 2 (2006): 131–48.

49. Caprioli and Trumbore, "Identifying Rogue States and Testing their Interstate Conflict Behavior"; Caprioli and Trumbore, "Rhetoric Versus Reality."

50. Caprioli and Trumbore, "Ethnic Discrimination and Interstate Violence"; Caprioli and Trumbore, "Rhetoric Versus Reality"; Caprioli and Trumbore, "Human Rights Rogues in Interstate Disputes, 1980–2001."

51. David Sobek, M. Rodwan Abouharb, and Christopher G. Ingram, "The Human Rights Peace: How the Respect for Human Rights at Home Leads to Peace Abroad," *Journal of Politics* 68, no. 3 (2006): 519–29; Timothy M. Peterson and Leah Graham, "Shared Human Rights Norms and Military Conflict," *Journal of Conflict Resolution* 55, no. 2 (2011): 248–73.

52. "Transcript: President Clinton Explains Iraq Strike," CNN.com, December 16, 1998, http://www.cnn.com/ALLPOLITICS/stories/1998/12/16/transcripts/clinton.html.

53. Powell, "War as a Commitment Problem."

54. Fearon, in "Rationalist Explanations for War," argues that "the strategic dilemma is that without some third party capable of guaranteeing agreements, state A may not be able to commit itself to future foreign policy behavior that makes B prefer not to attack at some point."

55. Robert Jervis, *Perception and Misperception in International Politics* (Princeton: Princeton University Press, 1976), 124.

56. Avery Goldstein, "First Things First: The Pressing Danger of Crisis Instability in U.S.-China Relations," *International Security* 37, no. 4 (2013): 49–89; Michael Auslin, "Could U.S. Brinksmanship in the South China Sea Mean War with Beijing?" *Newsweek*, May 13, 2015, http://www.nationalreview.com/article/418310/could-us-brinksmanship-south-china-sea-mean-war-beijing-michael-auslin.

57. Henry Kissinger, *On China* (New York: Penguin Press, 2011).

58. Ibid.; Jervis, *Perception and Misperception in International Politics*.

59. Kissinger, *On China*.

60. Clausewitz, *On War*.

61. Wagner, "Bargaining and War," 469.

62. Sklansky, *The Theory of Poker*.

63. Wagner, "Bargaining and War."

64. Reiter, *How Wars End*.

65. Kreutz, "How and When Armed Conflicts End."

66. Clausewitz, *On War*; Blainey, *Causes of War*; Reiter, *How Wars End*.

67. Blainey, *Causes of War*.

68. Fearon, "Rationalist Explanations for War."

69. Ibid.

70. Clausewitz, *On War*, 605.

71. Wagner, "Bargaining and War"; Reiter, *How Wars End*.

72. Wagner, "Bargaining and War."

73. George Daughan, *1812: The Navy's War* (New York: Basic Books, 2013).

74. Oliker, *Russia's Chechen Wars 1994–2000*.

75. Wagner, "Bargaining and War."

76. Ibid.

77. Blainey, *Causes of War*.

78. Ibid.

79. The Russo-Turkish War of 1787, for example, began with the Ottoman Empire confident that it could regain lost territories, but the war ended with the Treaty of Jassy, which formally recognized Russia's dominion over those territories.

80. J. Maynard Smith, "The Theory of Games and the Evolution of Animal Conflicts," *Journal of Theoretical Biology* 47, no. 1 (1974): 209–21; Kydd and Walter, "The Strategies of Terrorism."

81. David Herbert Donald et al., *Why the North Won the Civil War* (Baton Rouge: Louisiana State University Press, 1960).

82. Reiter, *How Wars End.*

83. Ibid.

84. Ibid.

85. Ibid.

86. Ibid.

87. Ibid.

88. Ted Hopf, "Polarity, the Offense-Defense Balance, and War," *American Political Science Review* 85, no. 2 (1991): 475–93.

89. Clausewitz, *On War.*

90. Hopf, "Polarity, the Offense-Defense Balance, and War," 476.

91. Ibid.

92. Stephen Van Evera, "Offense, Defense, and the Causes of War," *International Security* 22, no. 4 (1998): 5–43.

93. Hopf, "Polarity, the Offense-Defense Balance, and War," 477.

94. Robert Haddick, *Fire on the Water: China, America, and the Future of the Pacific* (Annapolis, MD: Naval Institute Press, 2014).

95. Jack S. Levy, "The Offensive/Defensive Balance of Military Technology: A Theoretical and Historical Analysis," *International Studies Quarterly* 28, no. 2 (1984): 219–38.

96. Though Blainey, *Causes of War*, argues against this position by noting that even after offensive technologies were introduced (chemical weapons, air strikes), the stalemate largely continued to exist. Further, the eastern front of the war did not experience the same kind of stalemate.

97. Haddick, *Fire on the Water.*

98. Karl P. Mueller et al., *Striking First: Preemptive and Preventive Attack in U.S. National Security Policy* (Santa Barbara, CA: RAND Corporation, 2006).

99. Iriye et al., *The Origins of the Second World War in Asia and the Pacific.*

100. Van Evera, "Offense, Defense, and the Causes of War."

101. Ibid.

102. Bueno de Mesquita, in *The War Trap*, notes that it is "common military wisdom" that defense is comparatively easier than offense.

103. Clausewitz, *On War.*

104. Fearon, "Signaling Foreign Policy Interests."

105. Quoted in Sklansky, *The Theory of Poker*, 11.

106. Scoblete, *Guerrilla Gambling*.
107. Clausewitz, *On War*; Blainey, *Causes of War*.
108. For example, Talbott, "French Public Opinion and the Algerian War."
109. Hopf, "Polarity, the Offense-Defense Balance, and War."
110. Powell, "War as a Commitment Problem"; Reiter, *How Wars End*.
111. For example, Margaret E. Keck and Kathryn Sikkink, "Transnational Advocacy Networks in International and Regional Politics," *International Social Science Journal* 51, no. 159 (1999): 89–101; Walter, "Designing Transitions from Civil War"; Beth A. Simmons, *Mobilizing for Human Rights: International Law in Domestic Politics* (New York: Cambridge University Press, 2009).

Chapter 4. Mistakes, Misperceptions, and Losing the Hand

1. Michael Peck, "God Save the Queen: Great Britain's Five Biggest Military Defeats," *National Interest*, November 17, 2014.
2. John H. Kagel, Raymond C. Battalio, and Leonard Green, *Economic Choice Theory: An Experimental Analysis of Animal Behavior* (Cambridge, UK: Cambridge University Press, 1995); John Alcock, *Animal Behavior: An Evolutionary Approach* (Sunderland, MA: Sinauer Associates, 1993).
3. Scoblete, *Guerrilla Gambling*, 2.
4. Economic rationality is ascribed to individuals or groups of individuals who make decisions in an effort to maximize a "well-behaved ordinal utility function." Ronald Wintrobe, "Can Suicide Bombers Be Rational?" unpublished manuscript, University of Western Ontario, 2003. In other words, rational actors make decisions in pursuit of a list of goals, with some goals more preferred than others.
5. Scoblete, *Guerrilla Gambling*, 111.
6. Ibid.
7. David J. Eicher, *The Longest Night: A Military History of the Civil War* (New York: Simon and Schuster Paperbacks, 2001).
8. Kahneman and Tversky, "Prospect Theory"; Tversky and Kahneman, "Advances in Prospect Theory."
9. Jack S. Levy, "Prospect Theory, Rational Choice, and International Relations," *International Studies Quarterly* 41, no. 1 (1997): 87–112. In many ways, however, expected utility theory and prospect theory are often considered to be mutually exclusive; see Kahneman and Tversky, "Prospect Theory"; Rose McDermott, *Risk-taking in International Politics: Prospect Theory in American Foreign Policy* (Ann Arbor: University of Michigan Press, 2001).
10. Gary S. Becker, *The Economic Approach to Human Behavior* (Chicago: University of Chicago Press, 1978).
11. Paul Anand, "The Nature of Rational Choice and the Foundations of Statistics," *Oxford Economic Papers* 43 (1991): 199–216.

12. Wintrobe, "Can Suicide Bombers Be Rational?"; Bryan Caplan, "Terrorism: The Relevance of the Rational Choice Model," *Public Choice* 128 (2006): 91–107.

13. Martha Crenshaw, "The Logic of Terrorism: Terrorist Behavior as a Product of Strategic Choice," in *Origins of Terrorism: Psychologies, Ideologies, Theologies, States of Mind*, ed. Walter Reich (Washington, DC: Woodrow Wilson Center Press, 1990), 54–56.

14. Additionally, unlike in poker, international actors often benefit from hiding their true intentions (that is, keeping their goals secret).

15. Lake and Powell, *Strategic Choice and International Relations*.

16. Anand, "The Nature of Rational Choice and the Foundations of Statistics."

17. Levy, "An Introduction to Prospect Theory," 7–22.

18. Herbert A. Simon, *Models of Man: Social and Rational* (New York: John Wiley and Sons, 1957); Herbert A. Simon, "Bounded Rationality and Organizational Learning," *Organization Science* 2, no. 1 (1991): 125–34.

19. Kahneman and Tversky, "Prospect Theory."

20. Kahneman and Tversky, "Subjective Probability."

21. Ibid. Kahneman and Tversky point out that human beings are even limited in their ability to estimate something rather objective, like their physical distance from an object.

22. McDermott, *Risk-taking in International Politics*.

23. Colin Camerer and Keith Weigelt, "Experimental Tests of a Sequential Equilibrium Reputation Model," *Econometrica: Journal of the Econometric Society* 56, no. 1 (1988): 1–36; James Andreoni and John H. Miller, "Rational Cooperation in the Finitely Repeated Prisoner's Dilemma: Experimental Evidence," *Economic Journal* 103 (1993): 570–85.

24. Of course, al Qaeda had struck the United States before, but not in the same meaningful way.

25. Daniel Bernoulli, "Exposition of a New Theory on the Measurement of Risk," *Econometrica: Journal of the Econometric Society* 22, no. 1 (1954): 23–36.

26. Fearon, "Rationalist Explanations for War."

27. Levy, "An Introduction to Prospect Theory."

28. Paul Weirich, "The St. Petersburg Gamble and Risk," *Theory and Decision* 17, no. 2 (1984): 193–202.

29. Levy, "An Introduction to Prospect Theory," 173.

30. This illustration is adapted from Daniel Kahneman, *Thinking, Fast and Slow* (New York: Macmillan, 2011).

31. Ibid.

32. Ibid., 279.

33. Ibid.

34. Sklansky, *The Theory of Poker*, 253.

35. Kahneman and Tversky, "Prospect Theory."

36. David Ortiz, *David Ortiz on Casino Gambling* (New York: Dodd, Mead, 1986); Edwin Silberstang, *The Winner's Guide to Casino Gambling* (New York: Macmillan, 2005).

37. The graph is adapted from Kahneman and Tversky, "Prospect Theory."

38. This example is adapted from Kahneman, *Thinking, Fast and Slow.*

39. Ibid.

40. Paul Rozin and Edward B. Royzman, "Negativity Bias, Negativity Dominance, and Contagion," *Personality and Social Psychology Review* 5, no. 4 (2001): 296–320.

41. Kahneman, *Thinking, Fast and Slow.*

42. Nathan Novemsky and Daniel Kahneman, "The Boundaries of Loss Aversion," *Journal of Marketing Research* 42, no. 2 (2005): 119–28.

43. Richard Thaler, "Toward a Positive Theory of Consumer Choice," *Journal of Economic Behavior and Organization* 1, no. 1 (1980): 39–60.

44. Jack L. Knetsch, "The Endowment Effect and Evidence of Nonreversible Indifference Curves," *American Economic Review* 79, no. 5 (1989): 1277–84; Daniel Kahneman, Jack L. Knetsch, and Richard H. Thaler, "Experimental Tests of the Endowment Effect and the Coase Theorem," *Journal of Political Economy* 98, no. 6 (1990): 1325–48; Daniel Kahneman, Jack L. Knetsch, and Richard H. Thaler, "Anomalies: The Endowment Effect, Loss Aversion, and Status Quo Bias," *Journal of Economic Perspectives* 5, no. 1 (1991): 193–206; Eric Van Dijk and Daan Van Knippenberg, "Buying and Selling Exchange Goods: Loss Aversion and the Endowment Effect," *Journal of Economic Psychology* 17, no. 4 (1996): 517–24.

45. Kahneman, Knetsch, and Thaler, "Anomalies."

46. Tversky and Kahneman, "Advances in Prospect Theory." Tversky and Kahneman found some evidence that the endowment effect disappears with exchange traded goods. In other words, when the transactions are more routine and expressly intended to earn money, the endowment effect does not appear to be as strong. But Van Dijk and Van Knippenberg, in their own experiments, show that the endowment effect is still present given certain conditions of uncertainty. International actors bargaining over more "mundane" issues probably demonstrate lower levels of loss aversion and endowment effects. But more salient issues, which are often correlated with higher levels of uncertainty, likely generate greater loss aversion and attachment. Van Dijk and Van Knippenberg, "Buying and Selling Exchange Goods."

47. Scott Borgerson et al., "The Emerging Arctic," Council on Foreign Relations, 2014, http://www.cfr.org/polar-regions/emerging-arctic/p32620.

48. Ibid. Even China has recently increased its activities in the region. Franz-Stefan Gady, "Russia and China in the Arctic: Is the U.S. Facing an Icebreaker Gap?" *Diplomat,* September 7, 2015, http://thediplomat.com/2015/09/russia-and-china-in-the-arctic-is-the-us-facing-an-icebreaker-gap/.

49. In addition to Israel's loss aversion in the new scenario, Fearon, in "Rationalist Explanations for War," points out that this may be viewed as a zero-sum negotiation since the loss of territory like the Golan Heights results in a strategic gain for one side at the expense of the other.

50. Qureshi, *How to Be a Poker Player*.

51. Ibid.

52. Kahneman and Tversky, "Prospect Theory."

53. Kahneman, *Thinking, Fast and Slow*.

54. Hein E. Goemans, *War and Punishment: The Causes of War Termination and the First World War* (Princeton: Princeton University Press, 2000).

55. Ibid.

56. Ibid.; Alexandre Debs and Hein E. Goemans, "Regime Type, the Fate of Leaders, and War," *American Political Science Review* 104, no. 3 (2010): 430–45.

57. Goemans, *War and Punishment*.

58. Najmeh Bozorgmehr, "Sanctions Threaten Weak Iranian Economy," *Financial Times,* June 27, 2012, http://www.ft.com/intl/cms/s/0/9506 1748-c04d-11e1–982d-00144feabdc0.html\#axzz3vutSCYIX.

59. Matt Egan, "How Cheap Oil Will Hurt Iran's Comeback," CNN.com, August 20, 2015, http://money.cnn.com/2015/08/20/investing/low-oil -prices-iran-impact-saudi-arabia/.

60. Mohammed Ghobari and Mohammed Mukhashaf, "Saudi-led Planes Bomb Sanaa Airport to Stop Iranian Plane Landing," Reuters, April 28, 2015, http://www.reuters.com/article/us-yemen-security-airport-idUSK BN0NJ24120150428; Ahmed Al Omran and Asa Fitch, "Saudi Coalition Seizes Iranian Boat Carrying Weapons to Yemen," *Wall Street Journal,* September 30, 2015, http://www.wsj.com/articles/saudi-coalition -seizes-iranian-boat-carrying-weapons-to-rebels-in-yemen-1443606304.

61. McDermott, *Risk-taking in International Politics*.

62. Ibid., 4.

63. Ibid.

64. Ibid.

65. Ibid.

66. Michael R. Beschloss, *Mayday: Eisenhower, Khrushchev, and the U-2 Affair* (New York: Harper and Row, 1986).

67. Donald Neff, *Warriors at Suez: Eisenhower Takes the United States into the Middle East* (New York: Simon and Schuster, 1981).

68. Ibid.

69. McDermott, *Risk-taking in International Politics*.

70. Ibid.

71. Ibid.

72. Philip Taubman, *Secret Empire: Eisenhower, the CIA, and the Hidden Story of America's Space Espionage* (New York: Simon and Schuster, 2003).

73. McDermott, *Risk-taking in International Politics*.

74. Ibid.
75. Ibid. McDermott also notes that Carter's popularity at home had dramatically declined over the course of the year.
76. Ibid.
77. Rose McDermott, "The Failed Rescue Mission in Iran: An Application of Prospect Theory," *Political Psychology* 13, no. 2 (1992): 237–63; McDermott, *Risk-taking in International Politics*.
78. This accords with much of the expectations of classical realist theory— for example, John J. Mearsheimer, *The Tragedy of Great Power Politics* (New York: W. W. Norton, 2001).
79. Dale C. Copeland, *The Origins of Major War* (Ithaca: Cornell University Press, 2000).
80. Ibid.
81. Ibid.
82. Kahneman, *Thinking, Fast and Slow.*
83. See Kathleen M. German, "Invoking the Glorious War: Framing the Persian Gulf Conflict Through Directive Language," *Southern Journal of Communication* 60, no. 4 (1995): 292–302, for a discussion of how Nazi Germany was invoked in an effort to justify a more recent military intervention.
84. We will return in chapter five to discuss how the probabilities of such a conflict occurring may be distorted.
85. Kahneman, *Thinking, Fast and Slow.*
86. Ibid.
87. Ibid., 327–28.
88. Amos Tversky and Daniel Kahneman, "Extensional Versus Intuitive Reasoning: The Conjunction Fallacy in Probability Judgment," *Psychological Review* 90, no. 4 (1983): 293; Kahneman, *Thinking, Fast and Slow.*
89. As an example of one of the more explicit comparisons, see Paul Johnson, "Is Vladimir Putin Another Adolf Hitler?" *Forbes,* April 16, 2014, http://www.forbes.com/sites/currentevents/2014/04/16/is-vladimir -putin-another-adolf-hitler/.
90. Stephen R. Rock, *Appeasement in International Politics* (Lexington: University Press of Kentucky, 2015); Victor Davis Hanson, "Appeasing Iran Ignores the Lessons of History," *National Review,* July 23, 2015, http://www.nationalreview.com/article/421484/appeasing-iran-ignores -lessons-history-victor-davis-hanson.
91. During the one hundredth anniversary of the start of World War I, comparisons were also frequently made between contemporary China and 1914 Germany, including by world leaders. Isabel Reynolds and Takashi Hirokawa, "Abe Comparing China Ties to Pre-war Europe Fuels Tensions," Bloomberg.com, January 23, 2014, http://www.bloomberg.com /news/articles/2014–01–23/abe-comparing-china-to-pre-world-war -one-germany-fuels-tensions.

92. The law is also known as Godwin's Law of Nazi Analogies. Mike Godwin, "Godwin's Law of Nazi Analogies (and Corollaries)," EFF.org, 1995.

93. McDermott, *Risk-taking in International Politics*.

94. Jervis, *Perception and Misperception in International Politics*.

95. See the following by Harold Hance Sprout and Margaret Sprout: *Man-milieu Relationship Hypotheses in the Context of International Politics* (Princeton: Center for International Studies, Princeton University, 1956); *The Ecological Perspective on Human Affairs* (Princeton: Princeton University Press, 1965); *An Ecological Paradigm for the Study of International Politics* (Princeton: Center of International Studies, Princeton University, 1968).

96. Jervis, *Perception and Misperception in International Politics*.

97. Ibid.

98. Ted W. Nickel, "The Attribution of Intention as a Critical Factor in the Relation Between Frustration and Aggression," *Journal of Personality* 42, no. 3 (1974): 482–92.

99. Jervis, *Perception and Misperception in International Politics*, 71.

100. Ibid.

101. For example, George F. Kennan, "The Sources of Soviet Conduct," *Foreign Affairs* 25 (1946): 566.

102. For example, John H. Herz, *International Politics in the Atomic Age* (New York: Columbia University Press, 1959).

103. Jervis, *Perception and Misperception in International Politics*.

104. For example, Kennan, "The Sources of Soviet Conduct"; John Lewis Gaddis and Paul Nitze, "NSC 68 and the Soviet Threat Reconsidered," *International Security* 4, no. 4 (1980): 164–76.

105. Jervis, *Perception and Misperception in International Politics*, 68.

106. Ibid.

107. Ibid., 252.

108. Qureshi, *How to Be a Poker Player*.

109. Ibid.

110. Sklansky, *The Theory of Poker*, 245.

111. Jervis, *Perception and Misperception in International Politics*, 55–57.

112. Ibid.

113. Ibid.

114. Ibid., 113.

115. Scott Atran, "Genesis of Suicide Terrorism," *Science* 299, no. 5612 (2003): 1534–39.

Chapter 5. Russians and Roulette

1. Blainey, *Causes of War*.

2. See Kier A. Lieber, "The New History of World War I and What It Means for International Relations Theory," *International Security* 32, no. 2 (2007): 155–91, for a discussion of the revisionist viewpoint.

3. Barbara Wertheim Tuchman, *The Guns of August* (New York: Ballantine Books, 1962).
4. Bueno de Mesquita, *The War Trap.*
5. Kahneman, *Thinking, Fast and Slow.*
6. One study, for instance, found that the average cost overrun for road construction projects around the world is 20 percent, while for rail projects it is 45 percent: Bent Flyvbjerg et al., "How Common and How Large Are Cost Overruns in Transport Infrastructure Projects?" *Transport Reviews* 23, no. 1 (2003): 71–88.
7. Sklansky, *The Theory of Poker.*
8. Qureshi, *How to Be a Poker Player.*
9. Nassim Nicholas Taleb, *Fooled by Randomness: The Hidden Role of Chance in the Markets and in Life* (London: Texere, 2001).
10. Interestingly, Richard Epstein demonstrates that a deck needs to be shuffled at least five times to generate a *true* random distribution. Richard A. Epstein, *The Theory of Gambling and Statistical Logic* (New York: Academic Press, 1967).
11. Mark Huber, "Bin Laden Raid Copters Effective, But Not New," AIN Online, May 29, 2011, http://www.ainonline.com/aviation-news/aviation-international-news/2011–05–29/bin-laden-raid-copters-effective-not-new.
12. Tony Capaccio, "Helicopter Carrying SEALs Downed by Vortex, Not Mechanical Flaw," Bloomberg, May 6, 2011, http://www.bloomberg.com/news/articles/2011–05–05/commando-black-hawk-downed-by-air-vortex-not-mechanics-in-bin-laden-raid.
13. Gartzke, "War Is in the Error Term."
14. Taleb, *Fooled by Randomness.*
15. Ibid.
16. Donald T. Campbell, *Social Attitudes and Other Acquired Behavioral Dispositions* (New York: McGraw-Hill, 1963).
17. See Theodore P. Hill, "The First Digit Phenomenon: A Century-old Observation About an Unexpected Pattern in Many Numerical Tables Applies to the Stock Market, Census Statistics, and Accounting Data," *American Scientist* 86, no. 4 (1998): 358–63, and Mark Nigrini, *Benford's Law: Applications for Forensic Accounting, Auditing, and Fraud Detection,* vol. 586 (New York: John Wiley and Sons, 2012).
18. Mlodinow, *The Drunkard's Walk.*
19. Sheila Lalwani, "How Znetix Investors Got Pulled In," *Seattle Times,* October 6, 2002.
20. Benford's Law is now a widely accepted tool in financial forensics and other analytical efforts. See Mark J. Nigrini and Linda J. Mittermaier, "The Use of Benford's Law as an Aid in Analytical Procedures," *Auditing* 16, no. 2 (1997): 52; Cindy Durtschi, William Hillison, and Carl Pacini, "The Effective Use of Benford's Law to Assist in Detecting Fraud in Accounting Data," *Journal of Forensic Accounting* 5, no. 1 (2004): 17–34.

21. Nassim Nicholas Taleb, "Black Swans and the Domains of Statistics," *American Statistician* 61, no. 3 (2007): 198–200.

22. Jervis, *Perception and Misperception in International Politics*, 321.

23. Ibid., 322.

24. Ibid.

25. Raymond James Sontag, *European Diplomatic History, 1871–1932* (New York: Century Company, 1933).

26. For example, Steve A. Yetiv, *The Absence of Grand Strategy: The United States in the Persian Gulf, 1972–2005* (Baltimore: Johns Hopkins University Press, 2008).

27. Yekaterina Kravtsova, "Observers Say Russia Had Crimea Plan for Years," *Moscow Times*, May 27, 2014, http://www.themoscowtimes .com/news/article/observers-say-russia-had-crimea-plan-for-years /496936.html. Putin himself fed this perception by claiming that the annexation was planned at least several weeks before the Crimean public referendum to join Russia.

28. Faith Karimi, "Is Russia's Annexation of Crimea Opportune or Opportunistic?" CNN, March 20, 2014, http://www.cnn.com/2014/03/19 /world/europe/crimea-points-and-counterpoints/.

29. Heuer, *Psychology of Intelligence Analysis*.

30. Tucker Reals, "Putin: Ukraine War Not Our Fault, U.S. Must Stop Meddling," CBS News, June 19, 2015, http://www.cbsnews.com/news/putin -charlie-rose-us-meddling-ukraine-rebels-russian-troops-weapons.

31. Jervis, *Perception and Misperception in International Politics*.

32. Ibid.

33. Louis Jong, *The German Fifth Column in the Second World War* (New York: Routledge, 1956).

34. See Alan Cullison, "Inside al-Qaeda's Hard Drive," *Atlantic*, September 2004, http://www.theatlantic.com/magazine/archive/2004/09/inside-al -qaeda-s-hard-drive/303428/.

35. T. S. Kittredge, "The Muddle Before Pearl Harbor," *U.S. News and World Report,* December 3, 1954.

36. Qureshi, *How to Be a Poker Player*.

37. "Is This the Unluckiest Hand in Poker History?" PokerListings.com, June 30, 2014, http://www.pokerlistings.com/is-this-the-unluckiest-hand -in-poker-history-80559.

38. Charles D. Ellis, *Winning the Loser's Game* (New York: McGraw-Hill, 2004).

39. Ibid.

40. Clausewitz, *On War.*

41. Ibid.

42. Ibid., chapter VII.

43. McDermott, *Risk-taking in International Politics*.

44. Jimmy Carter, *White House Diary* (New York: Macmillan, 2010).

45. Richard A. Radvanyi, "Operation Eagle Claw—Lessons Learned," master's thesis, Marine Corps Command and Staff College, 2002, http://www.dtic.mil/dtic/tr/fulltext/u2/a402471.pdf.
46. In the operation's most tragic mishap, one of the helicopters collided with a C-130 transport plane during the withdrawal, killing eight servicemembers.
47. Charles Perrow, *Normal Accidents: Living with High Risk Technologies* (Princeton: Princeton University Press, 2011).
48. Blainey, *Causes of War.* Notably, more military commitments also increase the probability of *nonrandom* events that lead to war.
49. Perrow, *Normal Accidents.*
50. Samuel Eliot Morison, *Strategy and Compromise* (Boston: Little, Brown, 1958).
51. Simon Ramo, *Extraordinary Tennis for the Ordinary Player* (New York: Crown Publishers, 1973).
52. Taleb, *Fooled by Randomness.*
53. Sklansky, *The Theory of Poker*, 258.
54. Taleb, *Fooled by Randomness.*
55. Taleb, "Black Swans and the Domains of Statistics."
56. Mlodinow, *The Drunkard's Walk.*
57. Avi Shlaim, "Failures in National Intelligence Estimates: The Case of the Yom Kippur War," *World Politics* 28, no. 3 (1976): 348–80; Jervis, *Perception and Misperception in International Politics*; Richard K. Betts, "Analysis, War, and Decision: Why Intelligence Failures Are Inevitable," *World Politics* 31, no. 1 (1978): 61–89.
58. Lake and Powell, *Strategic Choice and International Relations.*
59. Importantly, making this prediction also involves predicting future gross domestic product growth, which is itself problematic.
60. William H. Greene, *Econometric Analysis* (New York: Prentice Hall, 2011).
61. David F. Hendry and Mary S. Morgan, *The Foundations of Econometric Analysis* (Cambridge, UK: Cambridge University Press, 1997). A larger error term can also indicate that important variables have been omitted from the analysis.
62. Gartzke, "War Is in the Error Term."
63. Sklansky, *The Theory of Poker.*
64. Gartzke, "War Is in the Error Term."
65. Ibid.
66. Ibid.
67. Ibid., 576.
68. Ibid.
69. Ellis, *Winning the Loser's Game.*
70. This illustration is adapted from Gartzke, "War Is in the Error Term."
71. Ibid.

72. Ibid.

73. Conrad, "How Democratic Alliances Solve the Power Parity Problem."

74. My study was, in turn, based on ideas first formalized in William Reed, "Information and Economic Interdependence," *Journal of Conflict Resolution* 47, no. 1 (2003): 54–71.

75. Conrad, "How Democratic Alliances Solve the Power Parity Problem."

76. Ibid.

77. Gina Harkins, "The New Look for U.S.-Philippine Military Relations," *Marine Corps Times*, April 26, 2015, http://www.marinecorpstimes .com/story/military/2015/04/26/philippines-military-exercise-balikatan -marines/26293261/.

78. Pasquale Cirillo and Nassim Nicholas Taleb, "On the Tail Risk of Violent Conflict and its Underestimation," New York University School of Engineering Research Papers, 2015.

79. Ibid.

80. Francis Fukuyama, *The End of History and the Last Man* (New York: Simon and Schuster, 2006).

81. Joshua S. Goldstein, *Winning the War on War: The Decline of Armed Conflict Worldwide* (New York: Penguin, 2011).

82. John Mueller, "Changing Attitudes Towards War: The Impact of the First World War," *British Journal of Political Science* 21, no. 1 (1991): 1–28; Steven Pinker, *The Better Angels of our Nature: The Decline of Violence in History and Its Causes* (London: Penguin UK, 2011).

83. Nils Petter Gleditsch et al., "The Forum: The Decline of War," *International Studies Review* 15, no. 3 (2013): 396–419.

84. Ziad Obermeyer et al., "Fifty Years of Violent War Deaths from Vietnam to Bosnia: Analysis of Data from the World Health Survey Programme," *BMJ* 336, no. 7659 (2008): 1482–86.

85. Cirillo and Taleb, "On the Tail Risk of Violent Conflict and its Underestimation."

86. Ibid.

87. Ibid.

88. Ibid.

89. Ibid.

90. Ibid., 2.

91. Ibid.

92. Blainey, *Causes of War.*

93. Ibid.

94. Cirillo and Taleb, "On the Tail Risk of Violent Conflict and its Underestimation."

95. The UCDP data project lists a 2011 war between Cambodia and Thailand, for instance.

96. Gary King, Robert O. Keohane, and Sidney Verba, *Designing Social Inquiry: Scientific Inference in Qualitative Research* (Princeton: Princeton University Press, 1994).

97. Marc Mangel and Francisco J. Samaniego, "Abraham Wald's Work on Aircraft Survivability," *Journal of the American Statistical Association* 79, no. 386 (1984): 259–67.
98. Ibid.
99. Thomas J. Stanley and William D. Danko, *The Millionaire Next Door: The Surprising Secrets of America's Wealthy* (Dallas, TX: Taylor Trade Publishing, 1996).
100. Arthur Conan Doyle, "Silver Blaze," *Strand Magazine*, 1892.
101. Reed, "A Unified Statistical Model of Conflict Onset and Escalation."
102. Michael Small and Chi Kong Tse, "Predicting the Outcome of Roulette," *Chaos: An Interdisciplinary Journal of Nonlinear Science* 22, no. 3 (2012): 033150.
103. Charles Kingston, *The Romance of Monte Carlo* (London: John Lane the Bodley Head, 1996).
104. Later, in the twentieth century, a group of physicists created a small device that could be secretly worn under their clothes. The device measured the speed of the wheel and the ball and used these measures to predict where the ball would land. This suggests, once again, that even seemingly random events can often be disaggregated into causal patterns if the model specifications are correct. See Ortiz, *David Ortiz on Casino Gambling*; Thomas A. Bass, *The Eudaemonic Pie* (New York: Houghton Mifflin Harcourt, 1985).
105. Scoblete, *Guerrilla Gambling.*
106. Qureshi, *How to Be a Poker Player*, 136.
107. Sklansky, *The Theory of Poker.*
108. Qureshi, *How to Be a Poker Player*, 137.
109. Abrahms, "The Political Effectiveness of Terrorism Revisited."
110. Taleb, *Fooled by Randomness.*

Conclusion

1. Kahneman and Tversky, "Prospect Theory."
2. The details of this game are recounted in William James Florence, *The Gentlemen's Handbook on Poker* (New York: Routledge, 1892).
3. McDonald, *Strategy in Poker, Business, and War.*
4. Sklansky, *The Theory of Poker*, 2.
5. Burrhus Frederic Skinner, "'Superstition' in the Pigeon," *Journal of Experimental Psychology* 38, no. 2 (1948): 168.
6. Thomas Gilovich, Robert Vallone, and Amos Tversky, "The Hot Hand in Basketball: On the Misperception of Random Sequences," *Cognitive Psychology* 17, no. 3 (1985): 295–314.
7. Chad C. Serena, *A Revolution in Military Adaptation: The U.S. Army in the Iraq War* (Washington, DC: Georgetown University Press, 2011).
8. Of course, random outcomes can be erroneously attributed to anything, not just the ingenuity of the decisionmaker. In the first century BCE,

Cicero was disgusted by people attributing their successes to the goddess Venus. He asked in exasperation, "Are we going to be so feeble-minded then as to affirm that such a thing happened by the personal intervention of Venus rather than by pure luck?" See Florence Nightingale David, *Games, Gods, and Gambling: A History of Probability and Statistical Ideas* (Mineola, NY: Dover Publications, 1998).

9. Julian Snelder, "Hegemon: Wargaming the South China Sea," *The Interpreter*, August 18, 2015, http://www.lowyinterpreter.org/post/2015/08/18/Hegemon-Wargaming-the-South-China-Sea.aspx.

10. Sklansky, *The Theory of Poker*.

11. Scoblete, *Guerrilla Gambling*, 3.

12. Ouellette, "Poker Science."

13. Sklansky, *The Theory of Poker*.

14. Ellis, *Winning the Loser's Game*.

15. Taleb, "Fooled by Randomness."

16. McDonald, *Strategy in Poker, Business, and War*.

17. Sklansky, *The Theory of Poker*, 239.

18. See Levy, "Prospect Theory, Rational Choice, and International Relations," for a thorough discussion and application to international relations.

19. Another debate centers around the external validity of prospect theory. Some have argued that its principles do not apply to situations where the stakes are particularly high, as they are in situations of international conflict. In other words, the argument is that individuals behave more rationally when the stakes are high. The results of several experiments, however, suggest that these concerns may be overstated and that individuals still behave in accordance with prospect theory even under more high-stakes conditions—see, for example, Colin F. Camerer, "An Experimental Test of Several Generalized Utility Theories," *Journal of Risk and Uncertainty* 2, no. 1 (1989): 61–104; Steven J. Kachelmeier and Mohamed Shehata, "Examining Risk Preferences under High Monetary Incentives: Experimental Evidence from the People's Republic of China," *American Economic Review* (1992), 1120–41.

20. Levy, "Prospect Theory, Rational Choice, and International Relations."

21. David E. Bell, "Disappointment in Decision Making under Uncertainty," *Operations Research* 33, no. 1 (1985): 1–27; Graham Loomes and Robert Sugden, "Regret Theory: An Alternative Theory of Rational Choice under Uncertainty," *Economic Journal* 92, no. 368 (1982): 805–24.

22. Colin Camerer, *Behavioral Game Theory: Experiments in Strategic Interaction* (Princeton: Princeton University Press, 2003).

23. McDermott, *Risk-taking in International Politics*.

24. Sklansky, *The Theory of Poker*.

25. Edward O. Thorp, *Beat the Dealer: A Winning Strategy for the Game of Twenty-one* (New York: Vintage, 1966); Ortiz, *David Ortiz on Casino Gambling.*

26. Powell, "War as a Commitment Problem"; Reiter, *How Wars End.*

27. Powell, "War as a Commitment Problem."

28. See Douglass North and Barry Weingast, "Constitutions and Commitment: The Evolution of Institutions Governing Public Choice in 17th Century England," *Journal of Economic History* 49, no. 4 (1989): 803–32.

29. For example, Brett Ashley Leeds, "Domestic Political Institutions, Credible Commitments, and International Cooperation," *American Journal of Political Science* 43, no. 4 (1999): 979–1002; Brett Ashley Leeds, "Alliance Reliability in Times of War: Explaining State Decisions to Violate Treaties," *International Organization* 57, no. 4 (2003): 801–27; Conrad, "How Democratic Alliances Solve the Power Parity Problem."

30. Peter F. Cowhey, "Domestic Institutions and the Credibility of International Commitment: Japan and the United States," *International Organization* 47, no. 2 (1993): 299–326.

31. Ibid., 302.

32. Bruce M. Russett, *Grasping the Democratic Peace: Principles for a Post–Cold War World* (Princeton: Princeton University Press, 1993); Zeev Maoz and Bruce M. Russett, "Normative and Structural Causes of Democratic Peace, 1946–1986," *American Political Science Review* 87, no. 3 (1993): 624–38; William J. Dixon, "Democracy and the Peaceful Settlement of International Conflict," *American Political Science Review* (1994), 14–32.

33. Kurt T. Gaubatz, "Democratic States and Commitment in International Relations," *International Organization* 50, no. 1 (1996): 109–39; Leeds, "Domestic Political Institutions, Credible Commitments, and International Cooperation."

34. Ajin Choi, "The Power of Democratic Cooperation," *International Security* 28, no. 1 (2003): 142–53.

35. Fearon, "Threats to Use Force"; Fearon, "Domestic Political Audiences and the Escalation of International Disputes"; Fearon, "Rationalist Explanations for War."

36. Jessica L. Weeks, "Autocratic Audience Costs: Regime Type and Signaling Resolve," *International Organization* 62, no. 1 (2008): 35–64.

37. Beth A. Simmons, "International Law and State Behavior: Commitment and Compliance in International Monetary Affairs," *American Political Science Review* (2000), 819–35.

38. Robert O. Keohane and Lisa L. Martin, "The Promise of Institutionalist Theory," *International Security* 20, no. 1 (1995): 39–51.

39. Emilie M. Hafner-Burton, "Sticks and Stones: Naming and Shaming and the Human Rights Enforcement Problem," *International Organization* 62, no. 4 (2008): 689–716.

40. Beth A. Simmons and Allison Danner, "Credible Commitments and the International Criminal Court," *International Organization* 64, no. 2 (2010): 225–56.

41. George W. Downs and David M. Rocke, "Conflict, Agency, and Gambling for Resurrection: The Principal-Agent Problem Goes to War," *American Journal of Political Science* 38, no. 2 (1994): 362–80.

42. Clausewitz, *On War.*

43. William Reed, "Information and Economic Interdependence," *Journal of Conflict Resolution* 47, no. 1 (2003): 54–71; Conrad, "How Democratic Alliances Solve the Power Parity Problem."

44. Ellis, *Winning the Loser's Game.*

45. Snyder, *The Big Book of Blackjack.*

46. McDermott, *Risk-taking in International Politics.*

47. Amos Tversky and Daniel Kahneman, "The Framing of Decisions and the Psychology of Choice," *Science* 211, no. 4481 (1981): 453–58.

48. Levy, "An Introduction to Prospect Theory," 7–22.

49. Richard Thaler and Cass Sunstein, *Nudge: The Gentle Power of Choice Architecture* (New Haven: Yale University Press, 2008).

50. Ibid.

Index

About the Author

Justin Conrad, PhD, is associate professor of political science at the University of North Carolina at Charlotte. Dr. Conrad has published studies on international conflict and terrorism in leading academic journals. He is also an officer in the U.S. Navy Reserve and a terrible poker player.

The Naval Institute Press is the book-publishing arm of the U.S. Naval Institute, a private, nonprofit, membership society for sea service professionals and others who share an interest in naval and maritime affairs. Established in 1873 at the U.S. Naval Academy in Annapolis, Maryland, where its offices remain today, the Naval Institute has members worldwide.

Members of the Naval Institute support the education programs of the society and receive the influential monthly magazine *Proceedings* or the colorful bimonthly magazine *Naval History* and discounts on fine nautical prints and on ship and aircraft photos. They also have access to the transcripts of the Institute's Oral History Program and get discounted admission to any of the Institute-sponsored seminars offered around the country.

The Naval Institute's book-publishing program, begun in 1898 with basic guides to naval practices, has broadened its scope to include books of more general interest. Now the Naval Institute Press publishes about seventy titles each year, ranging from how-to books on boating and navigation to battle histories, biographies, ship and aircraft guides, and novels. Institute members receive significant discounts on the Press' more than eight hundred books in print.

Full-time students are eligible for special half-price membership rates. Life memberships are also available.

For a free catalog describing Naval Institute Press books currently available, and for further information about joining the U.S. Naval Institute, please write to:

Member Services
U.S. NAVAL INSTITUTE
291 Wood Road
Annapolis, MD 21402-5034
Telephone: (800) 233-8764
Fax: (410) 571-1703
Web address: www.usni.org